THE TIMES

Guide to the European Parliament 1979

Written and edited by
David Wood
European Political Editor, The Times
Alan Wood
Head of Parliamentary Staff, The Times

Times Books

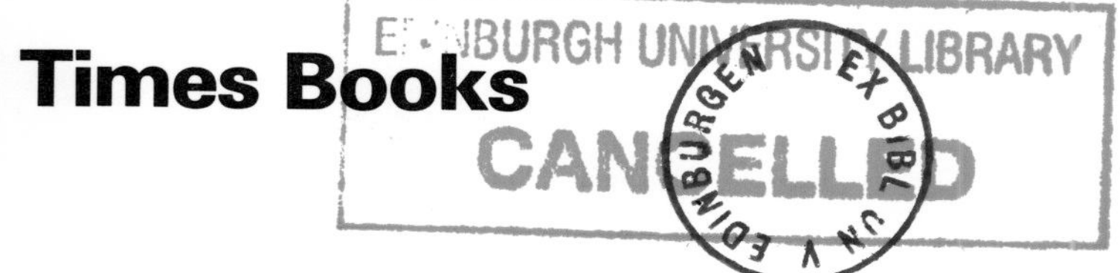

Published by Times Books Limited, 18 Ogle Street, London W1P 7LG

British Library Cataloguing in Publication Data

Wood, David
The 'Times' guide to the European Parliament.
1. European Parliament
I. Title II. Wood, Alan
328'.3'094 JN36

ISBN 0-7230-0231-2

Acknowledgement
In compiling this guide, the authors, *The Times* and Times Books wish to acknowledge their indebtedness for the assistance and cooperation given by the Directorate General of Information and Public Relations of the European Parliament based in Luxembourg, the staffs of the offices of the Parliament in the member states, the Secretariats of all the Political Groups of the Parliament, and Conservative Central Office and Labour Party Headquarters in the United Kingdom.

GDW
AHW

Printed in Great Britain by Tonbridge Printers Limited

Contents

First direct elections in European Community

The first direct elections in the nine states of the European Community to send 410 members to the European Parliament were held between June 7 and June 10, 1979. The inaugural meeting of the new Parliament, increased from 198 seats, took place in the Palais de l'Europe in Strasbourg on July 17, 1979, when the oldest member, Mme Louise Weiss, aged 86, occupied the chair for the election of the President. There was a contest for the presidency and two ballots were necessary before Mme Simone Veil, aged 52, a former Minister in the administration of President Giscard d'Estaing, received an absolute majority of votes over Sgr Mario Zagari, the nominee of the Socialist Group.

Between the elections and the Parliament's inauguration some members elected on the continental list system had withdrawn and had been replaced, and the election of Miss Shelagh Roberts, one of the 60 Conservatives returned in the 78 English, Scottish, and Welsh constituencies, had been declared invalid because at the time she sat on a Government body regarded as an office of profit under the Crown.

Some of the Giscardian candidates, including Mme Veil, joined the Liberal and Democrat Group, as did Mr Thomas Maher, who had been returned as an Independent in the Republic of Ireland; and Mrs Winifred Ewing, the Scottish National Party's only representative, decided against sitting as an Independent and joined the DEP group of Gaullists and members of Fianna Fail. The anti-Community representative from Greenland joined the Socialist Group.

Two of the numerically strongest groups in the Parliament also changed their names in between the direct elections and the forming of the Parliament. The Christian Democrats restyled themselves the European People's Party; and the British Conservatives, reinforced by Danes and one official Ulster Unionist to a total strength of 63, adopted the name of European Democrats.

After these changes the composition of the Parliament's main political groups on July 17 was as follows:

Socialists	112
European People's Party	108
European Democrats	63
Communists	44
Liberals and Democrats	40
Progressive Democrats	22
Non-aligned	20

In the defunct nominated Parliament, which held its final plenary session in May, 1979, the composition of the political groups was as follows:

Socialists	66
Christian Democrats	53
Liberals and Democrats	23
Conservatives	18
Communists	18
Progressive Democrats	17
Independents	3

Group leaders were appointed as follows: Socialist – Mr Ernest Glinne (Belgium); European People's Party – Herr Egon Klepsch (Germany); European Democratic Group – Mr James Scott-Hopkins (Britain); Liberals and Democrats – Herr Martin Bangemann (Germany); European Democrats for Progress – M. Christian de la Malène (France); Communist – Sgr Giorgio Amendola (Italy).

Of about 180m eligible electors in the European Community, nearly 111m voted on June 7 or June 10, or 62·8 per cent. There were 3,692 candidates to choose from, and at the time the results were announced 77 of the new MEPs had served in the old Parliament and 125 MEPs sat on the dual mandate – that is, they also sat in their national parliaments. Of the 410 MEPs 344 were men and 66 women, with the proviso that Miss Roberts by United Kingdom law was disallowed from taking her seat (See pages 66 and 72).

Taking the nine countries of the Community as a whole, the Group percentages in the elections were as follows: Socialist, 26·6 per cent. (29,506,704 votes); Christian Democrats, 29·5 per cent. (32,783,553); Conservative (including Denmark), 6·2 per cent.

(6,861,580); Communist, 13·5 per cent. (14,943,458); Liberal, 10·6 per cent. (11,761,510); Progressive Democrats, 3·5 per cent. (3,867,132); Others, 5·5 per cent. (6,174,043). The Socialist Group alone had candidates in all the Nine countries of the Community, and the Christian Democrats had candidates in all countries except the United Kingdom.

The lowest turn-out for direct elections occurred in Britain, where fewer than a third of voters on the electoral register bothered to go to the polls; the highest turn-outs were in Luxembourg, where a simultaneous general election helped to bring out 88·9 per cent. of the register; in Belgium, where compulsory voting produced a 91·4 per cent. poll; and in Italy, where a convention of hallowing the suffrage, produced 85·5 per cent.

In England, Scotland, and Wales the Conservatives won 60 seats with 48·4 per cent. of the poll, Labour 17 seats with 32·6 per cent., and the Liberals won no seat at all with 12·6 per cent. With under 2 per cent. of the British poll, the Scottish National Party took one seat.

Distribution of seats

Distribution of seats among the political groups of the European Parliament after direct elections in June, 1979 and at the first session of the Parliament in July, 1979.

Country	Soc	EPP	ED	Comm	LD	DEP	TCDG	Others	Totals
Belgium	7	10	—	—	4	—	1	2	24
Denmark	4	—	3	1	3	1	4	—	16
France	21	9	—	19	17	15	—	—	81
Germany	35	42	—	—	4	—	—	—	81
Italy	13	30	—	24	5	—	5	4	81
Luxembourg	1	3	—	—	2	—	—	—	6
Netherlands	9	10	—	—	4	—	—	2	25
Republic of Ireland	4	4	—	—	1	5	1	—	15
United Kingdom	18	—	60*	—	—	1	—	1	80*
Totals	112	108	63	44	40	22	11	9	409

*The election of one UK member (Miss Shelagh Roberts) was ruled invalid because at the time she stood she was a member of the Occupational Pensions Board. A by-election was held in September, 1979 (See pages 66 and 72) which she won. With Miss Roberts, there are 66 women members.

Distribution of seats among the political groups of the European Parliament before direct elections

Country	Soc	C-D	L	C	Comm	DEP	Others	Total
Belgium	5	7	2	—	—	—	—	14
Denmark	4	—	1	2	1	2	—	10
France	10	3	9	—	5	9	—	36
Germany	15	18	3	—	—	—	—	36
Italy	5	15	2	—	12	—	2	36
Luxembourg	2	2	2	—	—	—	—	6
Netherlands	6	5	3	—	—	—	—	14
Republic of Ireland	1	3	—	—	—	6	—	10
United Kingdom	18	—	1	16	—	—	1	36
Total	66	53	23	18	18	17	3	198

There were 12 women members.

The President and Vice Presidents

Mme Simone Veil, of France, who was elected President of the European Parliament in July, 1979.

The 12 Vice Presidents are:

Mr Marcel Vandewiele

Sgr Guido Gonella

Herr Johann Katzer

M Pierre Pflimlin

Herr Bruno Friedrich

M Gérard Jaquet

Mr Anne Vondeling

Mr Basil de Ferranti

Sgr Mario Zagari

Mr Pøul Møller

Mr Allan Rogers

Mme Danielle Demarch

Mr Vondeling was killed in a road accident on November 21, 1979.

The Leaders of the Political Groups

Mr Ernest Glinne
Belgium
Socialist

p.7 Herr Egon Klepsch
Germany
European People's Party

Mr James Scott-Hopkins
United Kingdom
European Democratic

p.7 Herr Bangemann
Germany
Liberal and Democratic

M Christian de la Malène
France
European Progressive Democratic

Sgr Giorgio Amendola
Italy
Communist and Allies

Members elected to the European Parliament

In this list of members elected to the European Parliament in the first direct elections of the European Economic Community held on June 7–10, 1979, a * denotes those who were members of the outgoing nominated Parliament.

The abbreviations used to designate the political groups of the Parliament are: Comm — Communist and allies; DEP — European Progressive Democrats; ED — European Democratic (formerly European Conservative group); EPP — European People's Party (former Christian-Democratic group); LD — Liberal and Democratic; Ind — Independent or non-aligned; Soc — Socialist; TCDG — Group for the Technical Coordination and Defence of Independent Groups and Members.

Abbreviations of the political parties of the MEPs in the member states of the EEC are set out at the end of the list.

Name	Member state	Political group	Party
	A		
Abens, Victor	Luxembourg	Soc	POSL
Adam, Gordon	United Kingdom	Soc	Lab
Adonnino, Pietro	Italy	EPP	DC
Agnelli, Signora Susanna	Italy	LD	PRI
*Aigner, Heinrich	Germany	EPP	CSU
*Alber, Siegbert	Germany	EPP	CDU
*Albers, Willem	Netherlands	Soc	PvdA
Almirante, Giorgio	Italy	Ind	MSI-DN
*Amendola, Giorgio	Italy	Comm	PCI
*Ansart, Gustave	France	Comm	PCF
*Ansquer, Vincent	France	DEP	DIFE
Antoniozzi, Dario	Italy	EPP	DC
Arfe', Gaetano	Italy	Soc	PSI
Arndt, Rudi	Germany	Soc	SPD
	B		
Baduel Glorioso, Signora Maria	Italy	Comm	PCI
Baillot, Louis	France	Comm	PCF
Balfe, Richard	United Kingdom	Soc	Lab
Balfour, Neil	United Kingdom	ED	C
*Bangemann, Martin	Germany	LD	FDP
Barbagli, Giovanni	Italy	EPP	DC
Barbarella, Signora Carla	Italy	Comm	PCI
Barbi, Paolo	Italy	EPP	DC
Battersby, Robert	United Kingdom	ED	C
Baudis, Pierre	France	LD	UFE
Beazley, Peter	United Kingdom	ED	C
*Berkhouwer, Cornelis	Netherlands	LD	VVD
Berlinguer, Enrico	Italy	Comm	PCI
*Bersani, Giovanni	Italy	EPP	DC
*Bethell, Lord	United Kingdom	ED	C
*Bettiza, Vincenzo	Italy	LD	PLI
Beumer, Bouke	Netherlands	EPP	CDA
Blaney, Neil	Ireland	TCDG	Ind
*Blumenfeld, Erik	Germany	EPP	CDU
Bocklet, Reinhold	Germany	EPP	CSU
Bøgh, Rev Jørgen	Denmark	TCDG	Folkebevaegelsen

Name	Member state	Political group	Party
Bonaccini, Aldo	Italy	Comm	PCI
Bonde, Jens-Peter	Denmark	TCDG	Folkebe-vaegelsen
Bonino, Signora Emma	Italy	TCDG	PR
Boot, Mrs Elise	Netherlands	EPP	CDA
Boserup, Ms Bodil	Denmark	Comm	SF
Boyes, Roland	United Kingdom	Soc	Lab
Brandt, Willy	Germany	Soc	SPD
Brookes, Miss Beata	United Kingdom	ED	C
Buchan, Mrs Janey	United Kingdom	Soc	Lab
Buchou, Hubert	France	DEP	DIFE
Buttafuoco, Antonio	Italy	Ind	MSI-DN
	C		
Caborn, Richard	United Kingdom	Soc	Lab
*Caillavet, Henri	France	LD	UFE
Calvez, Corentin	France	LD	UFE
Capanna, Mario	Italy	TCDG	DP
Cardia, Umberto	Italy	Comm	PCI
Cariglia, Antonio	Italy	Soc	PSDI
Carossino, Angelo	Italy	Comm	PCI
*Cassanmagnago Cerretti, Signora Maria Luisa	Italy	EPP	DC
Castellina, Signora Luciana	Italy	TCDG	PDUP
Castle, Mrs Barbara	United Kingdom	Soc	Lab
Catherwood, Sir Frederick	United Kingdom	ED	C
Cecovini, Manlio	Italy	LD	PLI
Ceravolo, Domenico	Italy	Comm	PCI
Chambeiron, Robert	France	Comm	PCF
Charzat, Mme Gisèle	France	Soc	PS
Chirac, Jacques	France	DEP	DIFE
Chouraqui, Mme Nicole	France	DEP	DIFE
Cinciari Rodano, Signora Maria	Italy	Comm	PCI
Clinton, Mark	Ireland	EPP	F-Gael
Cohen, Robert	Netherlands	Soc	PvdA
Colla, Marcel	Belgium	Soc	BSP
Colleselli, Arnaldo	Italy	EPP	DC
Collins, Kenneth	United Kingdom	Soc	Lab
Collomb, Francisque	France	EPP	UFE
*Colombo, Emilio	Italy	EPP	DC
Combe, Francis	France	LD	UFE
Coppieters, Mauritz	Belgium	TCDG	VU
Costanzo, Roberto	Italy	EPP	DC
Cottrell, Richard	United Kingdom	ED	C
Craxi, Bettino	Italy	Soc	PSI
Cresson, Mme Edith	France	Soc	PS
Cronin, Jeremiah	Ireland	DEP	F-Fáil
Croux, Lambert	Belgium	EPP	CVP-EVP
Curry, David	United Kingdom	ED	C
	D		
Dalsass, Joachim	Italy	EPP	SVP
Dalziel, Ian	United Kingdom	ED	C
Damette, Felix	France	Comm	PCF
*Damseaux, André	Belgium	LD	PRL
D'Angelosante, Francescopaolo	Italy	Comm	PCI
*Dankert, Pieter	Netherlands	Soc	PvdA
Davern, Noel Michael	Ireland	DEP	F-Fáil
Debatisse, Michel	France	EPP	UFE
Debré, Michel	France	DEP	DIFE

Name	Member state	Political group	Party
de Clercq, Willy	Belgium	LD	PVV-ELD
de Courcy Ling, John	United Kingdom	ED	C
de Ferranti, Basil	United Kingdom	ED	C
de Goede, Arie	Netherlands	Ind	D'66
*de Keersmaeker, Paul	Belgium	EPP	CVP-EVP
Dekker, Mrs Suzanne	Netherlands	Ind	D'66
*de la Malène, Christian	France	DEP	DIFE
Delatte, Charles	France	LD	UFE
Deleau, Gustave	France	DEP	DIFE
*Delmotte, Fernand	Belgium	Soc	PSB
Delorozoy, Robert	France	LD	UFE
Delors, Jacques	France	Soc	PS
Demarch, Mme Danielle	France	Comm	PCF
Denis, Jacques	France	Comm	PCF
de Pasquale, Pancrazio	Italy	Comm	PCI
Desmond, Mrs Eileen	Ireland	Soc	Lab
de Valera, Miss Sile	Ireland	DEP	F-Fáil
Diana, Alfredo	Italy	EPP	DC
Dido', Mario	Italy	Soc	PSI
Dienesch, Mme Marie-Madeleine	France	DEP	DIFE
Diligent, André	France	EPP	UFE
Donnez, Georges	France	LD	UFE
d'Ormesson, Olivier	France	EPP	UFE
Douro, the Marquess of	United Kingdom	ED	C
Druon, Maurice	France	DEP	DIFE
Dunn, William Newton	United Kingdom	ED	C
	E		
Elles, Lady	United Kingdom	ED	C
Enright, Derek	United Kingdom	Soc	Lab
Estgin, Nicolas	Luxembourg	EPP	CSV
Estier, Claude	France	Soc	PS
*Ewing, Mrs Winifred	United Kingdom	DEP	Scot Nat
	F		
Fanti, Guido	Italy	Comm	PCI
Faure, Edgar	France	LD	UFE
*Faure, Maurice	France	Soc	PS
*Fellermaier, Ludwig	Germany	Soc	SPD
Fergusson, Adam	United Kingdom	ED	C
Fernandez, Guy	France	Comm	PCF
Ferrero, Bruno	Italy	Comm	PCI
Ferri, Mauro	Italy	Soc	PSDI
Filippi, Renzo	Italy	EPP	DC
Fischbach, Marc	Luxembourg	EPP	CSV
Flanagan, Sean	Ireland	DEP	F-Fáil
*Flesch, Mrs Colette	Luxembourg	LD	DP
Focke, Frau Katharina	Germany	Soc	SPD
Forster, Miss Norvella	United Kingdom	ED	C
Forth, Eric	United Kingdom	ED	C
Friedrich, Bruno	Germany	Soc	SPD
Friedrich, Ingo	Germany	EPP	CSU
Frischmann, Georges	France	Comm	PCF
*Früh, Isidor	Germany	EPP	CDU
*Fuchs, Karl	Germany	EPP	CSU
Fuillet, Mme Yvette	France	Soc	PS
	G		
Gabert, Volkmar	Germany	Soc	SPD
Gaiotti de Biase, Signora Paola	Italy	EPP	DC

Name	Member state	Political group	Party
Gallagher, Michael	United Kingdom	Soc	Lab
Galland, Yves	France	LD	UFE
*Galluzzi, Carlo Alberto	Italy	Comm	PCI
Gaspard, Mme Françoise	France	Soc	PS
Gatto, Vincenzo	Italy	Soc	PSI
Gendebien, Paul-Henry	Belgium	Ind	FDF-RW
*Geurtsen, Aart	Netherlands	LD	VVD
Ghergo, Alberto	Italy	EPP	DC
Giavazzi, Giovanni	Italy	EPP	DC
Gillot, Alain	France	DEP	DIFE
Giummarra, Vincenzo	Italy	EPP	DC
*Glinne, Ernest	Belgium	Soc	PSB
Gonella, Guido	Italy	EPP	DC
Goppel, Alfons	Germany	EPP	CSU
Gouthier, Anselmo	Italy	Comm	PCI
Gredal, Ms Eva	Denmark	Soc	S
Gremetz, Maxime	France	Comm	PCF
Griffiths, Winston	United Kingdom	Soc	Lab
Groes, Mrs Mette	Denmark	Soc	S
	H		
Haagerup, Niels	Denmark	LD	V
Habsburg, Otto	Germany	EPP	CSU
*Hahn, Wilhelm	Germany	EPP	CDU
Hamilius, Jean	Luxembourg	LD	DP
Hammerich, Ms Else	Denmark	TCDG	Folkebe-vaegelsen
Hänsch, Klaus	Germany	Soc	SPD
Harmar-Nicholls, Lord	United Kingdom	ED	C
Harris, David	United Kingdom	ED	C
Hauenschild, Karl	Germany	Soc	SPD
Helms, Wilhelm	Germany	EPP	CDU
Henckens, Jaak	Belgium	EPP	CVP
Herklotz, Frau Luise	Germany	Soc	SPD
Herman, Fernand	Belgium	EPP	PSC
Hoff, Frau Magdalene	Germany	Soc	SPD
Hoffman, Mme Jacqueline	France	Comm	PCF
Hoffman, Karl-Heinz	Germany	EPP	CDU
Hooper, Miss Gloria	United Kingdom	ED	C
Hopper, William	United Kingdom	ED	C
Hord, Brian	United Kingdom	ED	C
Howell, Paul	United Kingdom	ED	C
Hume, John	United Kingdom	Soc	SDLP
Hutton, Alisdair	United Kingdom	ED	C
	I		
Ippolito, Felice	Italy	Comm	PCI
Irmer, Ulrich	Germany	LD	FDP
	J		
Jackson, Christopher	United Kingdom	ED	C
Jackson, Robert	United Kingdom	ED	C
*Jakobsen, Erhard	Denmark	ED	CD
Janssen van Raay, James	Netherlands	EPP	CDA
Jaquet, Gérard	France	Soc	PS
Johnson, Stanley	United Kingdom	ED	C
Jonker, Sjouke	Netherlands	EPP	CDA
Josselin, Charles	France	Soc	PS
Jürgens, Heinrich	Germany	LD	FDP

Name	Member state	Political group	Party
	K		
Katzer, Johann	Germany	EPP	CDU
*Kavanagh, Liam	Ireland	Soc	Lab
Kellett-Bowman, Edward	United Kingdom	ED	C
*Kellett-Bowman, Mrs Elaine	United Kingdom	ED	C
Key, Brian	United Kingdom	Soc	Lab and Co-op
Kirk, Kent	Denmark	ED	KF
*Klepsch, Egon Alfred	Germany	EPP	CDU
Klinkenborg, Jan	Germany	Soc	SPD
Köhler, Herbert	Germany	EPP	CDU
*Krouwel-Vlam, Mrs Johanna	Netherlands	Soc	PvdA
Kühn, Heinz	Germany	Soc	SPD
	L		
Labbe, Claude	France	DEP	DIFE
Lalor, Patrick	Ireland	DEP	F-Fáil
*Lange, Erwin	Germany	Soc	SPD
Langes, Horst	Germany	EPP	CDU
Lecanuet, Jean	France	EPP	UFE
Lega, Silvio	Italy	EPP	DC
Lemmer, Gerd Ludwig	Germany	EPP	CDU
Lenz, Frau Marlene	Germany	EPP	CDU
*Leonardi, Silvio	Italy	Comm	PCI
Leroux, Mme Sylvie	France	Comm	PCF
*Lezzi, Pietro	Italy	Soc	PSI
*Ligios, Giosuè	Italy	EPP	DC
Lima, Salvatore	Italy	EPP	DC
Linde, Erdmann	Germany	Soc	SPD
Linkohr, Rolf	Germany	Soc	SPD
Lizin-Vanderspeeten, Mrs Anne-Marie	Belgium	Soc	PSB
Loderer, Eugen	Germany	Soc	SPD
Lomas, Alfred	United Kingdom	Soc	Lab
Loo, Charles-Emile	France	Soc	PS
Louwes, Hendrik	Netherlands	LD	VVD
*Lücker, Hans August	Germany	EPP	CSU
*Luster, Rudolf	Germany	EPP	CDU
Lynge, Finn	Denmark	Soc	Siumut
	M		
Macario, Luigi	Italy	EPP	DC
Maffre-Bauge, Emmanuel	France	Comm	PCF
Maher, Thomas	Ireland	Ind	Ind
Maij-Weggen, Mrs Johanna	Netherlands	EPP	CDA
Majonica, Ernst	Germany	EPP	CDU
Malangré, Kurt	Germany	EPP	CDU
Marchais, Georges	France	Comm	PCF
Marshall, John	United Kingdom	ED	C
Martin, Maurice	France	Comm	PCF
Martin, Mme Simone	France	LD	UFE
Martinet, Gilles	France	Soc	PS
Mauroy, Pierre	France	Soc	PS
McCartin, John	Ireland	EPP	F-Gael
Megahy, Thomas	United Kingdom	Soc	Lab
Mertens, Meinolf	Germany	EPP	CDU
Messmer, Pierre	France	DEP	DIFE
Michel, Victor	Belgium	EPP	PSC
Modiano, Marcello	Italy	EPP	DC
Møller, Pøul	Denmark	ED	KF
Moorhouse, James	United Kingdom	ED	C

Name	Member state	Political group	Party
Moreau, Jacques	France	Soc	PS
Moreau, Mme Louise	France	EPP	UFE
Moreland, Robert	United Kingdom	ED	C
Motchane, Didier	France	Soc	PS
*Müller-Hermann, Ernst	Germany	EPP	CDU
Muntingh, Hemmo	Netherlands	Soc	PvdA
	N		
Narducci, Angelo	Italy	EPP	DC
Nicholson, Sir David	United Kingdom	ED	C
*Nielsen, Jørgen	Denmark	LD	V
Nielsen, Mrs Tove	Denmark	LD	V
Nord, Hans R.	Netherlands	LD	VVD
Nordlohne, Franz-Josef	Germany	EPP	CDU
*Normanton, Tom	United Kingdom	ED	C
*Notenboom, Harry	Netherlands	EPP	CDA
Nothomb, Charles-Ferdinand	Belgium	EPP	PSC
*Nyborg, Kai	Denmark	DEP	FRP
	O		
O'Connell, Dr John F.	Ireland	Soc	Lab
O'Donnell, Thomas	Ireland	EPP	F-Gael
Oehler, Jean	France	Soc	PS
*O'Hagan, Lord	United Kingdom	ED	C
O'Leary, Michael	Ireland	Soc	Lab
Olesen, Kjeld	Denmark	Soc	S
Orlandi, Flavio	Italy	Soc	PSDI
	P		
Paisley, the Rev Ian	United Kingdom	Ind	Dem U
Pajetta, Giancarlo	Italy	Comm	PCI
Pannella, Marco	Italy	TCDG	PR
Papapietro, Giovanni	Italy	Comm	PCI
Patterson, Ben	United Kingdom	ED	C
Pearce, Andrew	United Kingdom	ED	C
*Pedini, Mario	Italy	EPP	DC
Pelikan, Jiri	Italy	Soc	PSI
Penders, Johannes	Netherlands	EPP	CDA
Percheron, Daniel	France	Soc	PS
Peters, Johannes Wilhelm	Germany	Soc	SPD
Petronio, Francesco	Italy	Ind	MSI-DN
Pfennig, Gero	Germany	EPP	CDU
Pflimlin, Pierre	France	EPP	UFE
Piccoli, Flaminio	Italy	EPP	DC
Pininfarina, Sergio	Italy	LD	PLI
*Pintat, Jean-Francois	France	LD	UFE
Piquet, René	France	Comm	PCF
Plumb, Sir Henry	United Kingdom	ED	C
Poirier, Mme Henriette	France	Comm	PCF
Poncelet, Christian	France	DEP	DIFE
Poniatowski, Michel	France	LD	UFE
Pöttering, Hans-Gert	Germany	EPP	CDU
Prag, Derek	United Kingdom	ED	C
Pranchere, Pierre	France	Comm	PCF
Price, Peter	United Kingdom	ED	C
Prout, Christopher	United Kingdom	ED	C
Provan, James	United Kingdom	ED	C
Pruvot, Mme Marie-Jane	France	LD	UFE
Puletti, Ruggero	Italy	Soc	PSDI
Pürsten, Albert	Germany	EPP	CDU

Name	Member state	Political group	Party
Purvis, John	United Kingdom	ED	C
	Q		
Quin, Miss Joyce	United Kingdom	Soc	Lab
	R		
Rabbethge, Frau Renate-Charlotte	Germany	EPP	CDU
*Radoux, Lucien	Belgium	Soc	PSB
Remilly, Eugène	France	DEP	DIFE
Rey, Jean	Belgium	LD	PRL
*Rhys Williams, Sir Brandon	United Kingdom	ED	C
Rinsche, Günter	Germany	EPP	CDU
Ripa di Meana, Carlo	Italy	Soc	PSI
Roberts, Mrs Ann Clwyd	United Kingdom	Soc	Lab
Roberts, Miss Shelagh	United Kingdom	ED	C
Rogers, Allan	United Kingdom	Soc	Lab
Romagnoli Carettoni, Signora Tullia	Italy	Comm	PCI
*Romualdi, Pino	Italy	Ind	MSI-DN
*Rossi, André	France	LD	UFE
Roudy, Mme Yvette	France	Soc	PS
Ruffolo, Giorgio	Italy	Soc	PSI
Rumor, Mariano	Italy	EPP	DC
*Ryan, Richie	Ireland	EPP	F-Gael
	S		
Sablé, Victor	France	LD	UFE
Salisch, Frau Heinke	Germany	Soc	SPD
Sälzer, Bernhard	Germany	EPP	CDU
Sarre, Georges	France	Soc	PS
Sassano, Mario	Italy	EPP	DC
Schall, Wolfgang	Germany	EPP	CDU
Schieler, Rudolf	Germany	Soc	SPD
Schinzel, Dieter	Germany	Soc	SPD
Schleicher, Frau Ursula	Germany	EPP	CSU
Schmid, Gerhard	Germany	Soc	SPD
Schmitt, Heinz	Germany	Soc	SPD
Schnitker, Paul	Germany	EPP	CDU
Schön, Karl	Germany	Soc	SPD
Schön, Konrad	Germany	EPP	CDU
Schwartzenberg, Roger-Gérard	France	Soc	PS
Schwencke, Olaf	Germany	Soc	SPD
†Sciascia, Leonardo	Italy	TCDG	PR
*Scott-Hopkins, James	United Kingdom	ED	C
Scrivener, Mme Christiane	France	LD	UFE
Seal, Barry	United Kingdom	Soc	Lab
*Seefeld, Horst	Germany	Soc	SPD
Seeler, Hans-Joachim	Germany	Soc	SPD
Segre, Sergio	Italy	Comm	PCI
Seibel-Emmerling, Frau Lieselotte	Germany	Soc	SPD
Seitlinger, Jean	France	EPP	UFE
Seligman, Madron	United Kingdom	ED	C
Sherlock, Dr Alexander	United Kingdom	ED	C
*Sieglerschmidt, Hellmut	Germany	Soc	SPD
Simmonds, Richard	United Kingdom	ED	C
Simonnet, Maurice-René	France	EPP	UFE
Simpson, Anthony	United Kingdom	ED	C
Skovmand, Sven	Denmark	TCDG	Folkebevaegelsen
Spaak, Mrs Antoinette	Belgium	Ind	FDF-RW
Spautz, Jean	Luxembourg	EPP	CSV
Spencer, Tom	United Kingdom	ED	C

†Resigned in September, 1979.

Name	Member state	Political group	Party
*Spicer, James	United Kingdom	ED	C
*Spinelli, Altiero	Italy	Comm	Ind Sin
*Squarcialupi, Signora Vera	Italy	Comm	PCI
Stewart-Clark, Sir John	United Kingdom	ED	C
Sutra de Germa, Georges	France	Soc	PS
	T		
Taylor, John David	United Kingdom	ED	Off UU
Taylor, John Mark	United Kingdom	ED	C
Tindemans, Leo	Belgium	EPP	CVP
*Tolman, Teun	Netherlands	EPP	CDA
Travaglini, Giovanni	Italy	EPP	DC
Tuckman, Frederick	United Kingdom	ED	C
Turner, Amédée	United Kingdom	ED	C
Tyrrell, Alan	United Kingdom	ED	C
	V		
*van Aerssen, Jochen	Germany	EPP	CDU
van den Heuvel-Blank, Mrs Ien	Netherlands	Soc	PvdA
*van der Gun, Frans	Netherlands	EPP	CDA
Vanderpoorten, Herman	Belgium	LD	PVV-ELD
*Vandewiele, Marcel	Belgium	EPP	CVP-EVP
van Miert, Karel	Belgium	Soc	BSP
van Minnen, Johan	Netherlands	Soc	PvdA
Vanneck, Sir Peter	United Kingdom	ED	C
Vayssade, Mme Marie-Claude	France	Soc	PS
Veil, Mme Simone	France	LD	UFE
*Vergeer, Willem	Netherlands	EPP	CDA
Verges, Paul	France	Comm	PCF
*Verhaegan, Joris	Belgium	EPP	CVP-EVP
Vernimmen, Willy	Belgium	Soc	BSP
Veronesi, Protogene	Italy	Comm	PCI
Verroken, Joannes	Belgium	EPP	CVP-EVP
Vetter, Heinz Oskar	Germany	Soc	SPD
Visentini, Bruno	Italy	LD	PRI
von Alemann, Frau Mechthild	Germany	LD	FDP
*von Bismarck, Philipp	Germany	EPP	CDU
Vondeling, Anne	Netherlands	Soc	PvdA
von der Vring, Thomas	Germany	Soc	SPD
von Hassel, Kai-Uwe	Germany	EPP	CDU
von Wogau, Karl	Germany	EPP	CDU
	W		
Wagner, Manfred	Germany	Soc	SPD
Walter, Gerd	Germany	Soc	SPD
*Walz, Frau Hanna	Germany	EPP	CDU
Warner, Sir Frederick	United Kingdom	ED	C
*Wawrzik, Kurt	Germany	EPP	CDU
Weber, Frau Beate	Germany	Soc	SPD
Weiss, Mme Louise	France	DEP	DIFE
Welsh, Michael	United Kingdom	ED	C
Wettig, Klaus	Germany	Soc	SPD
Wieczorek-Zeul, Frau Heidemarie	Germany	Soc	SPD
Woltjer, Eisso	Netherlands	Soc	PvdA
Wurtz, Francis	France	Comm	PCF
	Z		
Zaccagnini, Benigno	Italy	EPP	DC
*Zagari, Mario	Italy	Soc	PSI
Zecchino, Ortensio	Italy	EPP	DC
zu Sayn Wittgenstein Bealeburg, Prince Casimir	Germany	EPP	CDU

Member state political parties of European MPs

Belgium

BSP	Belgische Socialistische Partij
PSB	Parti socialiste belge
CVP-EVP	Christelijke Volkspartij (Europese Volkspartij)
PSC-PPE	Parti social-chrétien (Parti Populaire Européen)
FDF-RW	Front démocratique des Francophones (Rassemblement Wallon)
PRL	Parti des reformes et de la liberté
PVV-ELD	Partij voor vrijheid en vooruitgang (Europese Liberalen en Demokraten)
VU	Volksunie

Denmark

CD	Centrum-Demokraterne
FRP	Fremskridtspartiet
KF	Det konservative folkeparti
S	Socialdemokratiet
SF	Socialistisk folkeparti
V	Venstre, Danmarks liberale parti
Siumut	Greenland party

West Germany

CDU	Christlich-Demokratische Union
CSU	Christlich-Soziale Union
FDP	Freie Demokratische Partei
SPD	Sozialdemokratische Partei Deutschlands

France

DIFE	Défense des intérêts de la France en Europe
PCF	Parti communiste français
PS	Parti socialiste
UFE	Union pour la France en Europe

Republic of Ireland (Eire)

F-Fáil	Fianna Fail Party
F-Gael..............	Fine Gael Party
Lab	Labour Party
Ind	Independent

Italy

DC	Democrazia cristiana
DP	Democrazia proletaria
Ind Sin	Indipendente di Sinistra
MSI-DN	Movimento sociale italiano – Destra nazionale
PCI	Partito comunista italiano
PDUP	Partito democratico di unità proletaria
PLI	Partito liberale italiano
PR	Partito radicale
PRI	Partito repubblicano italiano
PSDI	Partito socialista democratico italiano
PSI	Partito socialista italiano
SVP	Südtiroler Volkspartei (Partito popolare sudtirolese)

Luxembourg

PCS . . . . Parti chrétien social
PD . . . . Parti démocratique
POSL . . . . Parti ouvrier socialiste luxembourgeois

Netherlands

CDA . . . . Christen Democratisch Appèl
D'66 . . . . Demokraten '66
PvdA . . . . Partij van de Arbeid
VVD . . . . Volkspartij voor Vrijheid en Democratie

United Kingdom

C . . . . Conservative Party
Dem U . . . . Democratic Unionist Party
Lab . . . . Labour Party
Off UU . . . . Official Ulster Unionist Party
SDLP . . . . Social Democratic and Labour Party
Scot Nat . . . . Scottish National Party

Groups in the European Parliament

Socialist Group

Country	Party	Members
Belgium	Parti Socialiste	4
	Belgische Socialistische Partij	3
Denmark	Socialdemokrater	3
	Siumut	1
Germany	Sozialdemokratische Partei Deutschlands	35
France	Parti Socialiste et Mouvement des Radicaux de Gauche	21
Ireland	Labour	4
Italy	Partito Socialista Italiano	9
	Partito Socialista Democratico Italiano	4
Luxembourg	Letzeburger Sozialistesch Arbechter-Partei	1
Netherlands	Partij van de Arbeid	9
United Kingdom	Labour	17
	Social Democratic and Labour Party	1
9	13	112

European People's Party Group (formerly Christian-Democrat)

Country	Party	Members
Belgium	Christelijke Volkspartij	7
	Parti Social-Chrétien	3
West Germany	CDU	34
	CSU	8
France	Union pour la France en Europe (UFE)	9
Ireland	Fine Gael	4
Italy	Democrazia Cristiana	29
	Südtiroler Volkspartei	1
Luxembourg	Chreschlech-Sozial Volskpartei	3
Netherlands	Christen-democratisch Appél	10
7	10	108

European Democratic Group (formerly European Conservative)

Country	Party	Members
Denmark	Konservative Folkeparti	2
	Centrum Demokraterne	1
United Kingdom	Conservative Party	60
	Official Ulster Unionist	1
2	4	64

Communist & Allies Group

Country	Party	Members
Denmark	Socialistisk Folkeparti	1
France	Parti Communiste	19
Italy	Partito Comunista Italiano	24
3	3	44

Liberal and Democratic Group

Country	Party	Members
Belgium	Partij voor Vrijheld en Vooruitgang	2
	Parti des Réformes et de la Liberté	2
West Germany	Freie Demokratische Partei	4
Denmark	Venstre	3
France	Union pour la France en Europe (UFE)	17
Italy	Partito Liberale Italiano	3
	Partito Repubblicano Italiano	2
Luxembourg	Demokratesch Partei	2
Netherland	Volkspartij voor Vrijheid en Democratie	4
Ireland	Independent	1
8	10	40

European Democrats for Progress

Country	Party	Members
Denmark	Fremskridtspartiet	1
France	Défense des Intérêts de la France en Europe (DIFE)	15
Ireland	Fianna Fáil	5
United Kingdom	Scottish National Party	1
4	4	22

Non-aligned*

Country	Party	Members
Belgium	Front der Frankophonen und wallonische Sammlungsbewegung	2
	Volksunie	1
Denmark	Folkebevaegelsen (Volksbewegung gegen die EG)	4
Ireland	Independent	1
Italy	Movimento Sociale Italiano	4
	Partito Radicale	3
	Partito Democratico di Unita Proletaria	1
	Democrazia Proletaria	1
Netherlands	Demokraten '66	2
United Kingdom	Democratic Unionist Party	1
6	10	20

*includes new Independent Group (TCDG) as follows:

Folkebevaegelsen — Denmark	4
Partito Radicale (PR) — Italy	3
Independent — Ireland	1
Democrazia Proletaria — Italy	1
Partito Democratico di Unità Proletaria — Italy	1
Volksunie — Belgium	1
Total	11

Membership of the 15 committees

The directly-elected European Parliament decided in July 1979 to increase the number of its committees from 12 to 15. The membership, which was not finally agreed until the September, 1979, session of the Parliament in Strasbourg, is as follows:

Political Affairs Committee (41 members):

Amendola
Ansart
Antoniozzi
Berkhouwer
Berlinguer
Bethell
Bettiza
Blumenfeld
Brandt
Cariglia
Colombo
Debré
Diligent
Elles
Faure, Maurice
Fergusson
Friedrich, Bruno
Haagerup
Habsburg
Hansch
Hammerich
Jackson, Christopher
Klepsch
Lalor
Lomas
Marchais
Mauroy
Møller
Nothomb
Olesen
Penders
Rey
Romualdi
Rumor
Schieler
Scott-Hopkins
Seitlinger
van den Heuvel
van Miert
von Hassel
Zagari

The chairman is Sgr Emilio Columbo (Italy, EPP) and the vice-chairmen are M Pierre Mauroy (France, Soc), Lord Bethell (United Kingdom, ED) and Mr Jean Rey (Belgium, LD).

Committee on Agriculture (39 members):

Barbarella
Battersby
Bocklet
Buchou
Caillavet
Castle
Clinton
Colleselli
Cresson
Curry
Dalsass
Davern
Debatisse
Delatte
Diana
Früh
Gatto
Hauenschild
Helms
Herklotz
Howell
Jurgens
Kirk
Ligios
Lynge
Maffre-Bauge
Maher
Nielsen
Papapietro
Plumb
Pranchere
Provan
Quin
Skovmand
Sutra
Tolman
Vernimmen
Wettig
Woltjer

The chairman is Sir Henry Plumb (United Kingdom, ED) and the vice-chairmen are M Michel Debatisse (France, EPP), M Henri Caillavet (France, LD) and Sgr Giosué Ligios (Italy, EPP).

Committee on Budgets (37 members):

Adonnino
Aigner
Ansquer
Arndt
Baillot
Balfe
Barbi
Bonde
Boserup
Colla
Dankert
Flanagan
Forth
Gaspard
Gouthier
Gredal
Hoff
Hord
Jackson, Robert
Lange
Langes
Lega
Motchane
Nord
Notenboom
O'Hagan
O'Leary
Orlandi
Pfennig
Rossi
Ryan
Schön, Konrad
Scrivener
Simonnet
Spinelli
Taylor, J. M.
Tuckman

The chairman is Herr Erwin Lange (Germany, Soc) and the vice-chairmen are Mr Harry Notemboom (Netherlands, EPP), Sgr Altiero Spinelli (Italy, Comm) and M André Rossi (France, LD).

Committee on Economic and Monetary Affairs (37 members):

Balfour
Beumer
Bonaccini
Caborn
Collomb
Damseaux
de Goede
de Ferranti
Deleau
Delorozoy
Delors
Fernandez
Forster
Friedrich, Ingo
Giavazzi
Hopper
Leonardi
Macario
Moreau, Jacques
Nicolson
Nyborg
Petronio
Piquet
Rhys Williams
Rogers
Ruffolo
Schinzel
Schnitker
Schwartzenberg
Tindemans
Visentini
Vondeling
Wagner
Walter
von Bismarck
von Wogau
zu Sayn-Wittgenstein-Berleburg

The chairman is M Jacques Delors (France, Soc) and the vice-chairmen are Mr Basil de Ferranti (United Kingdom, ED), Sgr Luigi Macario (Italy, EPP) and M Gustave Deleau (France, DEP).

Committee on Energy and Research (34 members):

Adam	Fuchs	Muller-Hermann	Sassano
Beazley	Gallagher	Normanton	Schmid
Bonino	Galland	Paisley	Seligman
Capanna	Groes	Percheron	Vanneck
Charzat	Herman	Pintat	Veronesi
Croux	Ippolito	Poncelet	von Alemann
de la Malène	Linde	Purvis	Walz
d'Ormesson	Linkohr	Rinsche	
Douro	Lizin-Vanderspeeten	Salzer	

The chairman is Frau Hanna Walz (Germany, EPP) and the vice-chairmen are Mr Michael Gallagher (United Kingdom, Soc), Sgr Felice Ippolito (Italy, Comm) and Mr Tom Normanton (United Kingdom, ED).

Committee on External Economic Relations (36 members):

Agnelli	Fellermaier	Louwes	Schmitt
Almirante	Filippi	Majonica	Seal
Antoniozzi	Galluzzi	Martinet	Seeler
Bøgh	Giummarra	Moreau, Louise	Segre
Catherwood	Gremetz	Pannella	Stewart-Clark
Chouraqui	Jonker	Poirier	van Aerssen
de Courcy Ling	Kellett-Bowman, Edward	Poniatowski	Vandewiele
de Clercq	Lemmer	Radoux	Welsh
Dienesch	Lenz	Ripa di Meana	Wieczorek-Zeul

The chairman is Sir Frederick Catherwood (United Kingdom, ED), and the vice-chairmen are Frau Heidemarie Wieczorek-Zeul (Germany, Soc), Herr Jochen van Aerssen (Germany, EPP) and Mr Barry Seal (United Kingdom, Soc).

Legal Affairs Committee (25 members):

Chambeiron	Geurtsen	Megahy	Vanderpoorten
Cinciari Rodano	Gillot	Modiano	Vayssade
Dalziel	Gonella	Pelikan	Vetter
d'Angelosante	Goppel	Prout	A N Other
Donnez	Janssen van Raay	Sieglerschmidt	
Ferri	Luster	Turner	
Fischbach	Melangré	Tyrrell	

The chairman is Sgr Mauro Ferri (Italy, Soc) and the vice-chairmen are Herr Rudolf Luster (Germany, EPP), Mr Amédée Turner (United Kingdom, ED) and M Robert Chambeiron (France, Comm).

Committee on Social Affairs and Employment (27 members):

Baduel Glorioso	Clwyd Roberts	Nordlohne	Spautz
Barbagli	Dekker	Oehler	Spencer
Boyes	de Valera	Peters	Spicer
Brookes	Dido	Pininfarina	van der Gun
Calvez	Frischmann	Prag	van Minnen
Carettoni Romagnoli	McCartin	Salisch	Verhaegen
Cassanmagnago Cerretti	Nielsen, Tove	Sarre	

The chairman is Mr Frans van der Gun (Netherlands, EPP) and the vice-chairmen are Sgr Mario Dido (Italy, Soc), Herr Johannes Peters (Germany, Soc) and M Georges Frischmann (France, Comm).

Committee on Regional Policy and Regional Planning (29 members):

Blaney	Desmond	Josselin	Schön, Karl
Boot	Ewing	Kellett-Bowman, Elaine	Taylor, J David
Cecovini	Fanti	Lima	Travaglini
Costanzo	Faure, Edgar	Martin, Simone	von der Vring
Cronin	Griffiths	O'Donnell	Zecchino
Damette	Harris	Pottering	
Delmotte	Hume	Pürsten	
de Pasquale	Hutton	Puletti	

The chairman is Sgr Pancrazio de Pasquale (Italy, Comm) and the vice-chairmen are Mrs Eileen Desmond (Ireland, Soc), Sgr Roberto Costanzo (Italy, EPP) and M Edgar Faure (France, LD).

COMMITTEES

Committee on Transport (25 members):

Albers, Baudis, Buttafuoco, Cardia, Carossino, Chirac, Cottrell, Crazi, de Keersmaeker, Gabert, Gendebien, Harmar-Nicholls, Hoffman, Karl-Heinz, Jakobsen, Key, Klinkenborg, Labbé, Loo, Martin, Maurice, Moorhouse, Moreland, Pflimlin, Schnitker, Seefeld, Zaccagnini

The chairman is Herr Horst Seefeld (Germany, Soc) and the vice-chairmen are Mr Erhard Jakobsen (Denmark, ED), Mr Paul de Keersmaeker (Belgium, EPP) and Sgr Angelo Carossino (Italy, Comm).

Committee on the Environment, Public Health and Consumer Protection (27 members):

Alber, Ceravolo, Collins, Combe, Fuillet, Ghergo, Hamilius, Hooper, Johnson, Krouwel-Vlam, Maij-Weggen, Mertens, Muntingh, Newton Dunn, O'Connell, Remilly, Roudy, Schleicher, Scrivener, Seibel-Emmerling, Spaak, Squarcialupi, Verroken, Weber, Wurtz, Zaccagnini

The chairman is Mr Kenneth Collins (United Kingdom, Soc) and the vice-chairmen are Herr Siegbert Alber (Germany, EPP), Mr Stanley Johnson (United Kingdom, ED) and Frau Beate Weber (Germany, Soc).

Committee on Youth, Culture, Education, Information and Sport (25 members):

Abens, Arfe, Buchan, Coppieters, Demarch, Druon, Estier, Galotti de Biase, Hahn, Henckens, Hoffman, Jacqueline, Irmer, Kavanagh, Leroux, Loderer, Patterson, Pedini, Piccoli, Price, Pruvot, Roberts, Miss S., Schall, Schwencke, Simpson, Weiss

The chairman is Sgr Mario Pedini (Italy, EPP) and the vice-chairmen are Mr Liam Kavanagh (Ireland, Soc), Herr Wilhelm Hahn (Germany, EPP) and Mme Sylvie Leroux (France, Comm).

Committee on Development and Cooperation (27 members):

Bersani, Castellina, Cohen, Denis, Enright, Ferrero, Focke, Glinne, Jaquet, Kuhn, Lecanuet, Lezzi, Lücker, Marshall, Messmer, Michel, Narducci, Pajetta, Pearce, Poniatowski, Rabbethge, Sable, Simmonds, Vergeer, Verges, Warner, Wawrzik

The chairman is M Michel Poniatowski (France, LD) and the vice-chairmen are Sgr Giovanni Bersani (Italy, EPP), M Jacques Denis (France, Comm) and Herr Heinz Kühn (Germany, Soc).

Committee on Budgetary Control (27 members):

Aigner, Alber, Antoniozzi, Bangemann, Battersby, Boserup, Colla, Dankert, Filippi, Fuillet, Gabert, Gouthier, Irmer, Kellet-Bowman, Edward, Key, Nielsen, Brøndlund, Notenboom, O'Leary, Orlandi, Pflimlin, Poncelet, Price, Ryan, Simonnet, Taylor, J Mark, Wettig, A. N. Other

The chairman is Herr Heinrich Aigner (Germany, EPP) and the vice-chairmen are Mr Pieter Dankert (Netherlands, Soc), Ms Bodil Boserup (Denmark, Comm) and Mr Peter Price (United Kingdom, ED).

Committee on the Rules of Procedure and Petitions (27 members):

Adonnino, Bonino, Boot, Chambeiron, d'Angelosante, Druon, Elles, Ferrero, Fischbach, Flanagan, Friedrich, Bruno, Galland, Gaiotti de Biase, Hansch, Jaquet, Luster, Malangré, Nord, Patterson, Rogers, Sieglerschmidt, Turner, Tyrrell, Vanderpoorten, Vayssade, Verroken, Vondeling

The chairman is Mr Kai Nyborg (Denmark, DEP) and the vice-chairmen are Mme Marie-Claude Vayssade (France, Soc), Mr March Fischbach (Luxembourg, EPP) and Herr Kurt Malangré (Germany, EPP).

First direct elections mark long-heralded date with history

by David Wood
European Political Editor of *The Times*

On June 7 and 10, 1979, 180 million electors in nine west European countries had a long-heralded appointment with history. They had the opportunity to vote in the world's first election to bring into being a multinational Parliament that will give, and be seen to give, the European Community the blessings of democracy. Some 110.9 million of them did so. Instead of a Parliament of 198 members nominated or delegated from the nine national Parliaments within the EEC, there would be 410 members directly elected in accordance with differing national practice, here on a national or regional list system, there on the transferable vote system, or in Britain on a simple majority system.

Whatever the system, the new members of the European Parliament would have a constituency to which they would be answerable, and, because they were not nominees or delegates from one Parliament to another, they might be expected to have more democratic legitimacy and, perhaps, become more of a match for the EEC Council of Ministers and the Commission, the two Community bodies with power to propose and dispose.

It was an event that the bygone generation of West European statesmen who faced the rebuilding of a continent left derelict by war had dreamt of; an event on which some of their successors had expended much rhetoric. Yet when it came there was scant general sense of history in the making, or of more than a timid step towards multinational democracy. Everywhere in the Nine, at almost all times, the first direct elections to the European Parliament were fought out, as they were presented by journalists, in terms of national politics, and the results were analysed usually for their national political significance.

Now and then some party leaders crossed national frontiers to campaign, and the main party groups attempted cross-frontier manifestos, but the emphasis was on nine countries with distinctive interests and party balance rather than on the Community of Nine. That gave point to the exhortation in the British *Guardian* that the task for the new European Parliament would not be to serve as an enfeebled outpost of national parliaments: "It is, simply, to raise several sorts of democratic hell. Thus, slowly but inescapably, the parliament will begin to ask the central question about its own identity and about the future development of Europe. The big question at the back of the book is when the politicians who say so fervently that the EEC must and can become a third or fourth world power . . . are ready to make the sacrifices of national sovereignty which this implies". Yet it was *Le Monde*, not *The Guardian*, that made the effort to try to cross frontiers and report the results of the first direct European elections as a whole, rather than stop short at Dover or Calais.

To be fair to the politicians and the party managers, there were often excuses for a national approach to a European campaign. In the United Kingdom, there had been a general election on May 3, overlapping the start of the European exercise, and, therefore, the European Parliament became secondary to Westminster, alike in terms of organisational effort and financial demands. And so it happened that the European campaign proved to be limited to a fortnight, after the Whitsun break, with little-known candidates attempting to cover constituencies of about 500,000 electors who had never been allied politically before.

In Italy there was a national election on June 3, seven days before polling for the European Parliament, so that the European campaign ran effectually only for a week. In Luxembourg a general election coincided on June 10 with the European election, and the question was the survival of Mr Gaston Thorn's government.

In France, the followers of President Giscard d'Estaing and M Jacques Chirac conducted a trial of strength by way of rehearsal for the presidential election in 1981, and the parties of the Left tried to settle their internal and private rivalries. In Denmark a well-organised coalition of anti-Community politicians revived the argument over Community membership that the pre-entry referendum had never completely ended.

In the Republic of Ireland, in spite of the surge of prosperity that Community membership has brought, the European election carried to the bar of public opinion a Government that had forfeited popularity by long-running domestic industrial troubles and petrol scarcity; and over the border, in the six counties of Northern Ireland (an integral part of the United Kingdom), the parties, the party leaders, and the voters continued their sectarian struggle and played out another chapter of their troubled history.

In Greenland, where the Danish Government allowed one member to be chosen by the first-past-the-post system, the issue was as much eventual independence from Copenhagen as membership of the European Parliament. And in West Germany, Holland and Belgium, disregarding regional or linguistic self expression, there is so little dispute about Community membership that the European election could arouse interest among voters only to the extent that it turned into a partisan contest, a test of the top names on party lists.

Of the 180 million electors in the Nine rather more than 60 per cent. voted, an average that covers a range from the deplorable 32 per cent. poll in Britain to nearly 90 per cent. in Luxembourg, where a simultaneous general election helped in motivation. Generally, the swing was towards the Centre and Right parties, most pronounced of course in England, Scotland and Wales, where the first-past-the-post system based on amalgamated urban and rural constituencies brought into the new European Parliament 60 Conservatives and only 17 Labour members.

It was settled by the European Council, the strategic body of Heads of Government and Prime Ministers that has no recognition in the Treaty of Rome, that for the first direct elections to the European Parliament each country should do what came naturally, or follow its electoral tradition. Consequently, countries used to voting on a Thursday could choose June 7, and countries used to voting on a Sunday could choose June 10. More important, each country could follow or improvise its own election law and procedures.

The list system, unfamiliar in the United Kingdom at general elections but generally worked on the mainland Continent, needs some brief account. There are variations in the list system. In West Germany, for example, parties may choose to present to the electorate a national or Lander list of centrally chosen candidates; in France, the main parties chose a national list. In any event, a big national party may head its list with candidates of considerable political stature.

In West Germany the former Chancellor, Willy Brandt, stood at the head of the SPD list as first choice, a name to be reckoned with not only in his own country but on the international stage. In France, the Giscard list had Simone Veil, the popular Minister of Health, and Jean Lecanuet at the top; François Mitterand led the list of Socialists and Radicals of the Left; George Marchais led the French Communists; and Jacques Chirac, with his presidential ambitions, led the Gaullists of Defence of the Interests of France in Europe.

Outside Britain, there was no party ruling like Labour's against the dual mandate, and no tacit discouragement of the dual mandate as in the Conservative leadership and party management. Indeed, in the French lists were names of well-established and substantial politicians who not merely serve in Parliament but are also Mayors in their native towns: a French politician is at hand for all political purposes. Though the list system may thereby have cast the personae of the European election campaigns for a familiar party and national role, it is also undeniable that, compared with the British practice, it provided the electoral interest of big names, of an important question to settle, and ensured that the financial and other logistic needs of the campaign would not be meagre.

In Britain Mrs Barbara Castle was the only former Cabinet Minister to offer herself for European election; she is now the leader of the British Labour group in the European Parliament. Inadequate financial and organisational support was a fairly general complaint of Labour candidates in the United Kingdom, whether moderate or Left, pro-Community or anti-Community. Conservative candidates, without central financial support, also had their difficulties and limitations in the new huge constituencies.

And now to events in each of the member states:

France

President Giscard d'Estaing of France won another round in his personal fight to contain the aspirations of M Chirac; and M Chirac found himself coming under fire for tactical errors or vanities from his fellow Gaullists, much as M Mitterand came under fire from disappointed Socialists. With Simone Veil as standard bearer, the Giscardians led with nearly 28 per cent of the national poll, and M Chirac's RPR (Rassemblement pour la Republique) was beaten into last place, in PR terms, by the Socialists 23.4 per cent. and M Marchais' Communists at 20.4 per cent.

Some of M Chirac's leading colleagues had difficulty in following the logic of supporting the Giscard Government while opposing the President at every opportunity, and the energy and vivacity of M Chirac's European campaign did nothing to damp down criticism before or after the votes had been cast. M Chirac, after the election post mortem, stood firmly planted as RPR's leader, yet with his judgment under question for giving further proof of the President's strength.

M Mitterand had no sooner been elected to the European Parliament than he had occasion, or found occasion, to resign. The initial count gave Giscard's Union for France in Europe 25 seats and the Socialists 22. On a recount by the authorities, the Giscardians were given one more seat and the Socialists lost a seat. M Mitterand, already a disappointed politician, spoke of "fraud", and his vehement protests served as a distraction from the party storm that had begun to break over his head on the faults of his campaign. He united the Socialist executive bureau in a declaration that the second count of dubious votes was inadmissible; and by his resignation from the European Parliament he made sure that he will not be absent from the bureau if any of his critics attempt a coup. No French Socialist seemed to note that M Mitterand had in part fallen victim to an ebb-tide for Socialism in western Europe.

In the old nominated Parliament most of the 17 Communists were Italian. Direct elections have brought in reinforcements of 19 French Communists who follow George Marchais' line of French interests first and last to join 24 Italian Communists, who so far have shown a more marked Community spirit. The Communists now fill more than a tenth of the seats at Strasbourg, and compare in strength with the Liberal Party. They will sit on the extreme left of the chamber as viewed by the President of the Parliament.

French parties of the extreme right found themselves forced to withdraw from the contest for want of money. Two former presidential candidates, M Jean-Louis Tixier-Vignancour and M Jean-Marie le Pen, were prominent members of the "Eurodroite" alliance, but they found the cost of a national campaign beyond their means.

West Germany

The main parties in contention in West Germany certainly had no complaints about their financial resources, thanks to the electoral practice of allowing 3.50 DM. for every party vote. Consequently, it was reckoned that collectively the parties had at call about £20 million for campaigning, and there was an outburst of electoral festival and ballyhoo, on top of rallies and conferences, that made Europeanism fun as well as politically attractive. But among the party managers there seemed to be little doubt about the outcome; the national and regional lists could be ticked off for winners days before the votes were cast. There could not be the occasional surprise that occurred in Britain on the first-past-the-post system.

German politicians felt disappointed by a turn-out of about 66 per cent., compared with more than 90 per cent. in the general election, but it must be reckoned a respectable muster in a country where the major parties have none of the disputes about the Community and its strategic aims that are to be found in France and Britain. The Christian Democrats, with their allies the CSU in Bavaria, lead the European federalist cause, with German Liberals assenting.

Herr Willy Brandt, for the SPD, argued during his campaign that political union was decades away and it would be silly for the new Parliament to try to force the pace of integration. Nevertheless, Herr Brandt's credentials as a Europeanist are as good as anybody's, and if politics, like the theatre, needs conflict of ideas to arouse and hold interest, then the German parties were wise to call in the brass bands and the dancing girls.

Compared with the 1976 election, both SPD and their coalition allies lost ground on the lower poll. CDU (49 per cent.) and CSU (65 per cent. in Bavaria) made gains, and would probably have done even better if they were not bedevilled by an internal leadership dispute. Although the victorious Christian Democrats campaigned on European unity and integration, wry observers noted that the main point of discussion was the portent for next year's national election; there was free speculation about a Christian Democrat landslide that had to be moderated by reminders that the European poll could scarcely be reckoned high enough to be a reliable test of party strengths, especially after the SPD's relatively low key campaign, and that 15 months is a long time in politics.

The European election did nothing to help in the reconciliation between Herr Helmut Kohl's CDU and Herr Franz-Josef Strauss's CSU. Herr Kohl complained that the alliance would have enjoyed a larger success if there had been no dispute over choosing a joint candidate for Chancellor, and Herr Strauss retorted that if there had been two separate national lists of candidates, instead of Lander lists, the alliance would have been even more successful.

In general, the West German elections have produced the strongest and most experienced national team for the new European Parliament. Outside West Germany, as well as within, the appearance of Willy Brandt's name at the head of the SPD list gave particular pleasure. Insofar as he chooses to concentrate on parliamentary duties and involve himself in the work of the Parliament, he will draw attention to a chamber that for the present contains no other statesman of the first class and too few politicians whose voices will reach from Strasbourg to a European audience.

For its part, the CSU has brought into the chamber a Habsburg, a member of the family that ruled the Austrian Empire: Dr Otto von Habsburg, a son of the last Austro-Hungarian Emperor. A historian and journalist, he is not strictly a member of the CSU, although his speeches showed that he shares its federalist, Christian, and anti-socialist commitment, and also symbolises the distinctive Bavarian sense of history. No less, as a political freelance, he is thus able to be a candid friend of CD leaders and thereby prosper Herr Strauss's ambitions for the Chancellorship candidature.

Italy

Italians, not least Italian politicians, may use a rehetoric that makes the United Kingdom an exemplar of democracy at work, but the levels of polling in the European election scarcely justified it. If Britain's 32 per cent. turn-out was to be explained by the fact that there had been a general election more than a month before, leaving the parties and the voters apathetic or convalescent, how account for a turnout of 86 per cent. in Italy only seven days after a poll of nearly 90 per cent. in a general election that, as usual, had created almost as many problems as it had solved?

If Sicily, Sardinia, and the other islands had voted up to average, Italy's turnout would have been extraordinarily good; and it is not very relevant to say that in Italy voting is regarded not only as a right but a civic duty. True, failure to vote is recorded and theoretically bears on the issue of passports or the appointment to some jobs. In practice, nobody seems to suffer.

The European election repeated the general election in a shift away from the Christian Democrats and the Communists towards the smaller centre parties. CD fell from 38.3 per cent. on June 3 to 36.5 per cent. on June 10, and the Communists from 30.4 per cent. to 29.6 per cent. Nevertheless, in terms of European seats, the two main parties kept their dominance with 29 and 24 MPs respectively. The Socialists rose in a week from 9.8 per cent. to 11 per cent. of the poll; the Social Democrats rose to 4.3 per cent.; and the Liberals almost doubled their figure to 3.6 per cent.

For the first time, incidentally, the European election allowed votes cast for parties representing Italy's abundant ethnic and cultural minorities to be added together for PR purposes in the five electoral districts that covered the country. Representatives of 11 parties will represent Italy in the European Parliament.

As a political event, the European election in Italy became a secondary factor after the general election in the evolution of a new national coalition government; as such it played a part in the shifting alignments within the main parties and between them. The self-examination within the Italian Communist Party proved to be particularly searching, because the double electoral setback opened a flank to hard-line critics of the "soft" approach to cooperation with the Christian Democrats. It remains to be seen, at the time of writing, whether a reconstruction of the leadership hierarchy will precipitate drastic policy changes, or stiffer terms for Communist cooperation in keeping a Government in being. At least, Sgr Enrico Berlinguer was immediately confirmed as the Communist Party's secretary general after the two elections, and his influence is expected to be undiminished when the dust settles.

There is no question that the Italian national election virtually extinguished European campaigning until the last three or four days before polling, and several of the best known politicians kept their names off the European lists.

Denmark

There was much less apathy in Denmark about the European election, if only because a coalition of anti-membership parties was formed to conduct what was in effect a new referendum on being out or within the Community. In the 1972 referendum there was a vote of 57 per cent. for entry and 33 per cent. against, almost the same as the United Kingdom referendum vote of 2–1 on entry.

On June 7 the anti-membership coalition, called the Popular Movement against the EEC, won 21 per cent. of the votes and four seats, and the allied Socialist People's Party won one seat. Left Socialists and the Single-tax Party, who are also anti-Market, failed to get a seat, but the first-past-the-post election in Greenland sent to Strasbourg Mr Finn Lynge, of the Siumut Party, which has committed itself to withdrawal from the Community after a referendum in 1981 or 1982.

Six of the 16 Danish MPs in Europe are anti-membership, not a large enough number to have the financial and other benefits of forming an independent group on their own, although they said they have no intention of associating with any other group. The Danish critics of the Community will nevertheless have some fellow feeling for 11 of Britain's 17 Labour members who are in varying degrees sympathetic to withdrawal unless there are radical changes to stop the erosion of British parliamentary sovereignty and to reform the common agricultural policy.

The success of the anti-membership coalition was the more surprising to non-Danes because Denmark has been one of the principal economic beneficiaries of Community policies. In practical political terms, the Danish pro-EEC parties won the moral victory, and that no doubt explained why the Social Democrat Prime Minister, Mr Anker Joergensen, and the Liberal Foreign Minister, Mr Henning Christopherson, promptly commented that the European election result would have no impact on the Danish Government's Europeanist commitment and policies. Mr. Jørgen Bøgh, however celebrated his return as an anti-Market MP by predicting that "we could have Denmark out of the Community in five years'time". Three of the Danish MPs, incidentally, will join the British group of 60 Conservatives, led by Mr James Scott-Hopkins, along with Mr John Taylor, the Official Ulster Unionist returned for Northern Ireland.

Nevertheless, anti-membership feelings find a footing in nearly all the Danish political parties in one form or another, sometimes in opposition to political integration, sometimes on Communist or left-wing grounds that Danes should keep independent, except as a trading partner, from an anti-Eastern political block. The Prime Minister's own party, the Social Democrats, are probably as much divided as Mr Callaghan's Labour Party in Britain, even though they lack the Labour argument that Britain, a relatively poor member of the Community, is financing richer members.

Republic of Ireland

For electors in the Republic of Ireland, the European elections provided a mid-term opportunity to pass a judgment on Mr Jack Lynch, the Prime Minister, and his Fianna Fail administration, rather than to adjudge the undoubted national advantages that have accrued from Community membership. Domestic troubles made sure that Fianna Fail would not win a majority of the 15 seats on offer: a postal strike of 17 weeks' duration, a crippled system of telephone communications, a garbagemen's strike in Dublin, and for a time, a scarcity of petrol.

Mr Lynch's men came out ahead of Dr Garret FitzGerald's Fine Gael, though by little more than 20,000 votes, and took five seats instead of the eight that the last general election might have indicated. The Government's share of national first preferences, under the elaborate PR system, was, at 34.7 per cent., lower than at any time since the party's formation in 1926 and contrasted with 50.6 per cent. in the 1977 general election.

On a turn-out of 63 per cent., Fine Gael went up to 33.1 per cent. of the poll and Labour to 14.5 per cent., and both parties won four seats, for Labour a markedly better result than expected. In Dublin, the opposition parties pushed Fianna Fail into third place, with Miss Sile de Valera winning a seat on the ninth count.

Fianna Fail fared poorly in its rural heartlands, where the farmers showed a loss of faith in the Government, though not in Community membership and the common agricultural policy. The most remarkable feature of the election was the success of two Independents. Mr Thomas Maher, former president of the Irish Farmers' Association, headed the poll in the southern constituency of Munster, where politicians had expected him to be obliterated; and Mr Neil Blaney surprisingly led the poll in Connacht Ulster on the first count.

Mr Blaney was sacked as a Cabinet Minister by Mr Lynch and left Fianna Fail, but his strongly republican campaign prospered and he won the second highest first-preference vote in the country. The Maher-Blaney vote was Fianna Fail's loss.

Netherlands

Sceptics about the Community are hard, if not impossible, to find among the substantial and reckonable politicians of the Benelux countries, and critical voices make themselves heard usually to complain that progress towards multinational unity is too slow, or even that the big four countries of the Nine sin against mutinationalism by consistently sinning in the asserting of national interest. In the Netherlands, therefore, Community membership and a directly-elected Parliament were taken without serious question as a good thing, particularly for the Dutch, and the parties had an unexciting election on their hands. A turnout of 58 per cent., pretty low by Netherlands standards, reflected the popular sense that there was no argument in principle to be decided.

The moderate Christian Democrats took 10 of the 25 seats in return for 35.6 per cent., of the vote, compared with Labour's nine seats for 30.4 per cent. The Left-inclined Democrats 66 Party surpassed expectation by taking 9 per cent. of the poll and thereby captured two seats, a much stronger performance than in the 1977 national election. Labour candidates appeared to suffer from apathy in the main urban areas, not least among younger voters.

The Liberals, who share power with the Christian Democrats in the national Government, are Right-wing by international Liberal reckoning, and on 16.1 per cent. of poll, they took four seats. The first name on the Liberal list was that of Mr Cornelis Berkhouwer, a former president of the European Parliament and a long-standing friend of Britain, and the second name that of Mr Hans Nord, who left the general secretaryship of the Parliament to stand as a candidate. It is worth noting that nine of the 25 MEPs from the Netherlands, apart from Mr Nord, were members of the defunct nominated Parliament.

Belgium

No summary may hope to do justice to the niceties of Belgian elections and the interplay of political forces, simply because of the multiplicity of parties created on top of party ideological differences by the linguistic division of the country. The PR system adopted on June 10, for example, allowed for 13 seats out of 24 to Dutch-speaking Flanders, 11 seats for the Francophones, with Brussels electors free to vote either Fleming or Walloon.

The most significant outcome was the personal success of Mr Leo Tindemans, the Prime Minister until he resigned in November, 1978, who led the list of the Christian People's Party, which gained 48 per cent. of the Flanders vote and was rewarded with seven of the 13 Flemish seats. Mr Tindemans tried to discourage commentators and analysts from translating his notable victory into an ominous domestic political event.

In general, the Fleming vote moved to the Social Christians, but in Wallonia the Social Christians collected only three seats out of 11.

In Belgium, where non-voting in an election is a punishable offence, the turn-out was rather better than 91 per cent., although there was a high incidence of spoilt papers.

Luxembourg

In Luxembourg a simultaneous national election ensured a high turnout of nearly 89 per cent. for the European election to fill six seats, and there was a decisive swing to the Right that led Mr Gaston Thorn, the Liberal Prime Minister in coalition with Socialists, to concede governmental defeat before the count had been completed. His supporters held on to their 14 places in the 59-seat Luxembourg Assembly, but Socialist losses altered the balance of power in the chamber, so that Mr Thorn began to consider a future as a candidate for the presidency of the new European Parliament.

Mr Pierre Werner's Christian Socialist People's Party gained six seats in the domestic election to bring its total to 24, and Mr Werner, Prime Minister of the Duchy from 1959 to 1974, also won a place (with two party colleagues) in the European Parliament but he subsequently resigned.

The United Kingdom campaign is analysed in the next article of this guide.

Venue dilemma

After he had resigned as Prime Minister to the Grand Duke, Mr Thorn still had the duty to attend the Strasbourg summit of the leaders of the Nine, and apparently he angrily opposed an indiscreet remark in the draft communique that Strasbourg was and would continue to be the natural meeting place of the European Parliament. The incident emphasises a dilemma that the new Parliament will want to escape from, although it may not soon succeed.

No Parliament has ever had imposed upon it from outside logistics that must either diminish its efficiency or place upon its members unnecessary burdens of travel and wasted time, quite apart from an indefensible increase in the Parliament's administrative costs. The Council of Ministers has laid down that the plenary sessions of the Parliament should be held more or less alternately in Luxembourg, which is the administrative headquarters, and in Strasbourg, where M Pflimlin, the Mayor and French elder statesman, skilfully keeps France one step ahead with buildings, facilities, and unmatched hospitality. (M Pflimlin is also a Gisgardian MEP.) Consequently, for every meeting in Strasbourg all the senior officials, their staffs, and their documents as well as interpreters and translators, must be expensively transported down the autoroute from Luxembourg.

Meanwhile, the Parliament's committee meetings are commonly held in Brussels, where the Commission has its headquarters in the Berlaymont complex, and the Parliament keeps a cadre at No. 3 Boulevard de l'Empereur. The arrangement may satisfy the French need for prestige and Luxembourg's sense of amour propre, but there will not be many European politicians who will not regard it as shortlived, especially if air communications to Luxembourg and Strasbourg alike remain inadequate. Yet officially Brussels, the obviously convenient Community centre, purports not to want any further international and diplomatic congestion, although parliamentarians have had no difficulty in locating suitable sites.

Pay and allowances

There is another question that the new Parliament may be expected to take a view on: the ludicrously wide gap, in absolute and relative terms, between the salaries paid to members of the European Parliament. The British Labour Government prescribed that no United Kingdom MP could draw two parliamentary salaries, and Mrs Thatcher's Conservative Government has merely modified that rule. Mainly because of British envy about continental salary levels, the European Council in December 1978 laid down that MEPs be payable out of the national budget and not the Community budget and therefore be kept under the control of national legislatures.

At the time of the European elections in June the disparities in pay proposed for the new MEPs were as follows:

	National salaries converted £	Relative purchasing power £
Belgium	22,500	15,614
Denmark	12,300	11,353
France	23,000	20,542
Germany	24,000	13,041
Netherlands	20,600	13,181
Ireland	6,775	6,427
Italy	10,500	10,697
Luxembourg	4,763	3,305
United Kingdom	6,897	6,897

There were also allowances in the European Parliament: £59 a parliamentary day; travel allowance of 21p a kilometre up to 400km and then 8p a kilometre; secretarial allowance of £375 a month paid direct by the European Parliament to a named secretary, or £93 monthly if no secretary was named.

It follows that inequity is built into the European Parliament's salary structure, and it would be unusual if any democratically elected body for long tolerated first, second, and third class conditions of membership. The effect is that British and Irish MEPs will be worse paid than many fairly humble employees of the Parliament.

The new Parliament adopted the following scale of expense allowances: 1,800 European units of account a month for staff, paid to named individuals, and 900 EUAs a month for general administrative costs (office, typewriters, telephones, etc.) of which 500 shall be reimbursed against specific expenses. On July 31 EUAs were multiplied by three-fifths for conversion into sterling. Rounded in sterling, the allowances for a year worked out at £13,000 for staff, and £6,500 a year for administrative costs. A sum of £3,600 will be paid against specific bills. The old Parliament's final figure for subsistence expenses of £59 a day on parliamentary business has also been continued. (In Britain, the Inland Revenue is fighting the case to tax the subsistence allowance except on proof of expenditure, with retrospective effect on former members of the nominated Parliament.)

The new Parliament has not yet determined what travel allowances should be paid on a mileage basis. The nominated Parliament paid for journeys on the assumption that they began at the national parliament, and that practice may continue for six months, although the point of departure for directly-elected MEPs (especially all British members, except four MEPs on a dual mandate) must now be reckoned to be either their constituencies or their homes.

There is another aspect of European Parliament support for its members that aroused controversy before and after the election. The British Labour Party's national executive committee claimed that the Parliament's allotment to groups for researchers, or rather the share of the Socialist Group's allotment for the 17 British members, should be directly payable to the British party headquarters and come under the control of the NEC. Critics, including some of the newly-elected Labour MEPs, resented the proposal as a device for increasing central party funds. Members and officials of the Socialist Group may well outflank the NEC by tying research expenditure to named researchers, as named secretaries are already treated.

Meanwhile, moves were made to transfer the London headquarters of the European Parliament and Commission from 20 Kensington Palace Gardens to new premises close to the Westminster Houses of Parliament in SW1. At the time of writing the building of the former Junior Carlton Club, in Pall Mall clubland, seemed to be the most probable choice; and there, or in a similar building, Britain's MEPs will have office space and such non-partisan facilities as the Parliament may properly provide.

New appointments

An innovation for the Parliament was the creation, in September, 1979, of the new post of Quæstors – five in number – who will sit with the Bureau (the managerial committee of the European Parliament), which hitherto has consisted of the President and the 12 Vice-Presidents. The five elected in September, 1979, were Herr Ludwig Fellermaier (Germany, Soc), Mrs Colette Flesch (Luxembourg, LD), Mr Patrick Lalor (Ireland, DEP), Mr Ritchie Ryan (Ireland, EPP) and Mr Anthony Simpson (United Kingdom, ED). They will have a non-voting advisory role. The "enlarged" Bureau of the Parliament consists of the members of the Bureau with the political group leaders added. It is contended by many European parliamentarians that the creation of Quæstors is necessary to ensure that backbench opinion and independent or non-aligned members' opinions are represented in both the Bureau and the enlarged Bureau, which arrange the agenda of the Parliament and deal with procedural and administrative matters.

United Kingdom campaign

A European landslide for the Conservatives

No British politician, party manager, or political observer expected the first direct elections in England, Scotland, and Wales for the European Parliament to have much more buoyancy than a lead balloon. Few, however, would have confidently predicted that the turn-out to the polls for 78 of the United Kingdom's allotment of 81 seats would sink so low as 32 per cent., or under one in three of every voter on an electoral register freshly in use since mid-February. That is what happened.

The first multi-national democratic election that the world has known, which many ardent Europeanists on both sides of British politics had acclaimed as a landmark that would be much noted and long remembered, produced a no stronger motivation among electors to vote than an election to fill a council seat in a local government district where politics languish and where the democratic drive is weak.

Some of Britain's leading politicians, in domestic contexts, have found phrases to fit the event. As Mr William Whitelaw, deputy Conservative leader, said on one occasion: there had been stirring up of apathy. Or as Mr Roy Hattersley, a rising star on the Labour side, once described his opponents: they were "profoundly superficial".

Some of the reasons for the low British turnout at the polls, easily the lowest in the Nine, must be discussed below. For the present, it is needful to record that the beneficiaries were the Conservative candidates, simply because the Conservative Party under the Prime Ministership of Mr Edward Heath took the United Kingdom into the European Community and the party under new leadership has consistently reaffirmed its Europeanist commitment. A deeply divided Labour Party could not offer any challenge, but merely spread confusion. In a landslide, 60 Conservatives were elected for the new democratic European Parliament, 17 Labour, and one member of the Scottish National Party.

Of the 78 members of the European Parliament elected for England, Scotland, and Wales, only one has ever attained Cabinet rank in Westminster politics: Mrs Barbara Castle, wife of Lord Castle, who was a member of the outgoing nominated Parliament, and a vehement critic of United Kingdom membership of the Community as its affairs are now conducted. Mrs Castle could stand for election because she retired from Westminster before the last domestic election on May 3; other Labour politicians who retired and hoped to stand, or even Labour peers who had European experience, were not selected by the groups of management committee delegates that had hurriedly to choose their standard bearers between January and March, 1979. The refusal to consider Labour peers sprang from the Labour Party's commitment to abolish the House of Lords, a non-elected half of Parliament at Westminster that is partly hereditary and partly nominated by Prime Ministers and party machines.

Throughout the life of the Wilson and Callaghan Labour Governments, March, 1974, to the general election of May 3, 1979, the seams of party unity split under the pressure of dissension over Community membership and direct elections. Sir Harold Wilson had devised the EEC referendum of 1975 to end the argument, but that apparently conclusive affirmation of the popular will did not deter Labour's annual conference from opposing the principle of direct elections to the European Parliament – within a month of a Labour Foreign Secretary's signing a commitment to hold them in the spring of 1978. Nevertheless, the referendum had tactical uses when Mr Callaghan, his majority in the Commons eroded, found sanctuary in a Lib-Lab pact with Mr David Steel, the new Liberal leader.

The Labour Government's difficulties continued. The prospectus for the 1976–77 parliamentary session promised a European Assembly Elections Bill, though it was delayed for second reading until July 7, too late to be carried to Royal Assent until the next session. For the second reading vote, Mr Callaghan, the Prime Minister, formally had to announce that the constitutional doctrine of collective Cabinet responsibility would be abandoned. Six Cabinet Ministers and 26 other Ministers voted against the Government's own legislation.

The Bill was reintroduced in the 1977–78 session, with time running out for any direct elections in the spring of 1978. With heavy Conservative and Liberal support, it carried on second reading, although more than half the Parliamentary Labour Party thumbed their noses at a two-line whip and voted "No" and seven Cabinet Ministers abstained. Liberals, under their pact with Mr Callaghan, made a regional list system for direct elections a condition of support for the Government, but there was no majority in the Commons for the proposal.

The Government noted its preference for PR in the European election, but allowed a free vote to its rank and file. The House of Commons carried an amendment to keep to the first-past-the-post system by 319 votes to 222. The House also insisted on a new clause in the Bill making any increase in the powers of the directly elected European Parliament conditional upon Westminster legislation.

In January, 1978, Dr David Owen, the Foreign Secretary, had to tell the Council of Ministers that the United Kingdom would not be ready for direct elections until 1979, in spite of what had been called the Government's "best endeavours".

The story of Labour disunity and half-heartedness about Europe continued after the European Assembly Elections Bill had become an Act until Mr Tony Benn, the hard-line critic of membership, became chairman of the Labour NEC's European liaison committee and the publication of a European manifesto that a large section of the Parliamentary Labour Party considered to be at odds with established Labour Party policy in government.

The Conservative delegation to the new European Parliament, 60 strong, does slightly benefit from the party's avoidance of any rule against what is called the "dual mandate": that is, a member's sitting in both the House of Commons at Westminster and also in the European Parliament. Mrs Thatcher and her party managers, before the domestic general election on May 3 had fully assured them of a working majority in the Commons, had discouraged the dual mandate but had not issued a diktat against it. MPs and candidates who wanted to take on a double role in Westminster and European politics were left to find constituency associations that accepted their willingness to be in two places at once.

Four Conservative MPs had no difficulty in persuading Westminster and European selection committees that they had proved their capability of working in two Parliaments already, and were duly elected. Mr James Scott-Hopkins, deputy Conservative leader of the European Conservative Group and a Vice-President of the European Parliament, resigned his candidature for the Westminster Parliament on being designated group leader by Mrs Thatcher, and he, too, was elected – so becoming the leader of the largest national party delegation in the hemicycle that formed in the Palais de l'Europe, Strasbourg, on July 17, 1979.

There are two points worth noting. First, England provides the only man and wife members of the European Parliament in Mr and Mrs Kellett-Bowman (Mrs Kellett-Bowman was a member of the nominated Parliament and a specialist in regional policy). Secondly, Britain sent to Strasbourg a total of 11 women members out of 78, a much higher ratio than Westminster has ever known since women were admitted to membership of the House of Commons in 1918.

Among the women is Mrs Winifred Ewing, who lost her Westminster seat in Moray and Nairn in the general election on May 3 but succeeded in defeating both Mr Russell Johnston, Liberal leader in Scotland, and also a strong Conservative farmers' candidate, to win the European constituency of the Scottish Highlands and Islands – an area larger than the whole of Belgium. Mrs Ewing was the only representative from Britain (England, Scotland, and Wales) who did not belong to the Government party or the alternative government party.

That fact itself will be reckoned here and there in Britain, and widely on the mainland of western Europe, to be an adverse comment on the decision of the United Kingdom Parliament, more particularly the House of Commons, to adopt for the first direct elections to the European Parliament the first-past-the-post system; that is, as Winston Churchill once put it, a majority of one vote is enough. Everywhere else throughout the Nine, except for 25,000 voters in Greenland and the three members who will represent West Berlin, some system of proportional representation was in use, often combined with the list system whereby parties produce lists and candidates are then selected in numerical order on the basis of the total party vote.

In the time of the Lib-Lab pact, 1977–78, with Mr Callaghan as a minority Prime Minister, the Labour Government yielded to the Liberals a proposal for a regional list system in Britain, to complement a one-constituency transferable vote system for Northern Ireland. The House of Commons would not accept that, although Northern

Ireland, with surprising and perhaps educative consequences, by general consent was left with PR and a single constituency in Westminster's hope that a population divided by religion, history and politics would produce three genuinely representative members of the European Parliament.

In Northern Ireland, as events turned out, the three members chosen by transferable vote were an extreme Protestant; the *second* nominee of the dominant Official Unionist Party, instead of its leader; and the deputy leader of the mainly Catholic Social and Democratic Labour Party, which at Westminster aligns with the Labour Party.

It is not easy to assert what the consequences would have been in England, Scotland and Wales if there had been some form of PR that the Westminster Parliament did not determine. But advocates of PR in all the three main British parties argued after the event that instead of 60 MEPs the Conservatives would have had about 40, instead of 17 Labour would have had 26, instead of one the Scottish National Party would have had two, and instead of no member the Liberal Party would have had 10.

Even some zealous Conservatives, tempering their joy at Mrs Thatcher's completion of her 1979 Westminster and European double, conceded that questions are raised by a British voting system, at any rate for the European Parliament, that on a poll of under a third of the electorate obliterates all but the dominant party of the day and seriously distorts the European picture of the balance of political party strength in Britain. For example, Labour dominates in Scotland and largely relies on that for its Westminster majorities when in government: it won only two Scottish European seats. There are times when it dominates in London: it won only two seats.

Except for those politicians and political commentators who for party or historic reasons have dedicated themselves to the first-past-the-post system for elections, questions have to be asked whether the overwhelming numerical strength of the Conservative delegation to Strasbourg does not weaken its democratic authority, simply because it makes less sense in Europe than at Westminster.

There is another question no less important or urgent to be asked by Conservative Europeanists – what will be the reaction of the Labour side of British politics where, now virtually leaderless after the departure of Mr Roy Jenkins to become President of the Commission, the Europeanists are under pressure and on the retreat?

Seven members of the Wilson-Callaghan Cabinets between March, 1974 and May, 1979, were anti-Community membership. Three of the most likely successors to Mr Callaghan as Labour Leader were among them; and there is no easier or more facile way to make a Labour Party reputation nowadays than to set up as critic of the Community and its failings. The voice of the pro-Europeanists becomes muted; and it may sink into silence as the British Labour Party sees that the 78 British constituencies of half-a-million or more voters, mixing Conservative rural areas with Labour urban areas, are weighted heavily under the first-past-the-post system in favour of the Conservative Group in Europe. It will need a brave as well as a zealous Europeanist Labour politician to defend a European Parliament that is disliked, if not feared, by the Labour Party national executive committee and the Labour Party conference.

The overwhelming Conservative success in the first direct elections may work powerfully to consolidate anti-Europeanism inside the Labour Party. Six out of the 17 Labour MEPs may be described broadly as pro-Community and pro-Parliament, but the electoral system itself has helped to complete the Labour Party campaign to downgrade the importance or the usefulness of the European Parliament. The danger is that the European Parliament will be seen increasingly by Labour as a forum for anti-Europeanism.

It may also be asked how Mr Scott-Hopkins and his strong band of British Conservatives will carry their role of speaking for Britain in the European Parliament. They are a strong force in Luxembourg and Strasbourg, and in the membership of committees. For a time, however, they will lack political experience and European authority; and they begin with the knowledge that they raise no sense of affinity in the hearts and minds of politicians from mainland Europe.

They will be closest in spirit, in strategy, and in tactics to the Christian Democrats, though for ideological as well as practical group financial reasons they will not be ready to subsume themselves in all the implications of a merger. They will want to keep their identity, which for European purposes, apart from a Dane or two, has the disadvantage in a multi-national parliament of being a national identity.

It merits notice, therefore, that within a day or two of the European election, hints were being dropped by one of two European Conservatives that it would be tactful, if not tactical, to jettison the word "Conservative", which carries unacceptable undertones even for the Gaullists in Europe. The alert *Guardian* correspondent in Brussels reported that talk could be heard that the European Conservative Group should be renamed the European Democratic Group, at least for the sake of appearances. Yet how would that be received by the Conservative Party managers, constituency magnates, and voters still glorying in a great victory?

Another problem has to be reckoned with, as a consequence of the Conservative Party's apparently disproportionate European landslide. Much thought has been given, at least by Lord Greenwood's European Committee in the House of Lords, to the links between Westminster and the European Parliament, and questions remain for decision whether European MPs should have right of access to Westminster as well as the necessary right of contact with party headquarters. If the party delegations to the European Parliament had been broadly undistorted, there might have been a soluble problem; in the present circumstances, Labour MPs may well be reluctant to give MEPs any status at all.

Yet Westminster deals with European legislation, and, as the Greenwood committee's report showed, it would be absurd to have the two Parliament's working as though the other did not exist, without links, without exchanging information and ideas, without a common objective. Here, again, there is a positive invitation to the Labour Party critics of United Kingdom membership of the Community to fight, or rather refight, their Powellite campaign for the supreme sovereignty of Westminster, in spite of the implications of Mr Heath's Treaty of Accession.

Whatever opinions may be held about the rightness of the first-past-the-post system in Britain for the initial direct elections to the European Parliament, it is necessary to weigh the consequences and attempt to form a judgment about what attitude the two main British parties should take to the next round of European elections, which will come in 1984, at the end of a fixed term of five years. The general reading of Article 138 of the Treaty of Rome is that the 1984 election shall require "a uniform procedure in all Member States", with the condition that "the Council (of Ministers), acting by means of a unanimous vote, shall determine the provisions which it shall recommend to Member States for adoption in accordance with their respective constitutional rules". The condition is likely to prove important, for the Council of Ministers has not hesitated to bend the Treaty to its convenience.

Significantly, both Mrs Thatcher, the Prime Minister, and Mr James Callaghan, the Opposition Leader, launching their parties' European manifestos, put it beyond doubt that for them the hallowed British system of "first-past-the-post" was and would remain their choice. The portent of a United Kingdom veto, whichever party may be in power at the time, was there to be heard.

Yet those leaders' statements came before the British European poll results could be known. After the event, Mr Angus Maude, formerly a party policymaker and now Paymaster General in Mrs Thatcher's Cabinet, took a different line. Replying to a question from Mr Robin Day on BBC television, as the results of the Conservative landslide came in, he said he was sure that there would be Proportional Representation for the next direct elections in five years' time.

In the same programme, Mr Roy Jenkins, President of the Commission, spoke of "an unbalanced result" in Britain, although M Claude Cheysson, another Commissioner, put it more bluntly when he commented that "the Labour Party has made a ridiculously low effort that is going to reduce the Socialist Group in the European Parliament".

Britain's abysmally low poll on the first-past-the-post system confirmed the Eight's doubts on the depth and extent of the national commitment to a European destiny, although criticism in West Germany, France, and the Netherlands suffered the constraint of relatively low polls of their own. The fact is that the Nine had different histories, including electoral histories; and if some of the Eight question first-past-the-post, so there are British poltiicians and party managers who look askance at the continental list system as a profoundly dubious mixture of democracy and party management.

But one problem remains for British politicians to justify, explain away, or solve: the Liberal Party attracted about one vote in eight throughout Britain and got no seat in Europe at all; the Scottish National Party drew under two per cent. of the total British poll and got one seat, out of the eight in Scotland.

The poor consolation prize for the British Liberals is that the Liberal confederation, no doubt hoping for a conversion to PR by 1984, have invited Mr Russell Johnston, who had been a member of the European Parliament since United Kingdom entry in January, 1973, to attend its group meetings and continue to have limited facilities in Strasbourg, Luxembourg, and Brussels.

There may be no excuse for a British poll in which only one out of every three electors on the national register voted, but there is no dearth of reasoning to explain it. To begin a long rationale, the ordinary British voter has at no time shown any serious understanding of the political and economic arguments, favourable or not, for United Kingdom membership of a Community that moves in a mysterious way – and usually moves (if British reports from Brussels provide the criterion) against the consumer or taxpayer interest or on the apparent trivialities of harmonisation. Only an intense commitment to or against Europeanism by the three main parties (Conservative, Labour, and Liberal) could have supplied the political education about the Community that would have motivated voters.

For example, when Mr Harold Wilson brought a divided Labour Party back into power in March, 1974, a year after the United Kingdom's entry, he began with a renegotiation of the Heath terms of membership, and then outflanked his party critics by introducing the constitutional innovation of a national referendum to say "Yes" or "No" to continued membership. On June 5, 1975, there was a national vote in that referendum of about twice the 32 per cent. on June 7, 1979, and the "Yes" vote exceeded the "No" vote by two to one. But at that time the leaders of all the three main parties were on the hustings together campaigning for the "Yes" cause. Even the most zealous critics and sceptics for a time regarded the referendum verdict as conclusive, a confirmation of the judgment of every United Kingdom Government since 1960 that the country's destiny, politically and economically, must lie with membership of the European Community.

Unfortunately, the United Kingdom's entry in 1973, after delays imposed by France, roughly coincided with a world trade recession and the soaring of oil prices. The miracle of the Six's growth had ended, and forecasts of any economic advantages deriving from membership had to be revised until, during the direct elections campaign, it could be shown that the United Kingdom Government, although running one of the weakest economies in the Nine, would soon become the largest contributor to Community funds.

Scarcely any news out of the Brussels Commission reported by Fleet Street could be reckoned favourable by Europeanist candidates and publicists; and perhaps it was fortunate that most of it took a technical turn that made it incomprehensible, at least to everybody except politicians and qualified economists. In such circumstances, all the three main parties, even the most Europeanist, were thrown on to the defensive. They began to say that the task of good Europeans, men and women imbued with a community spirit, must be to assert the United Kingdom interest by yet another negotiation of the terms of membership, including a radical reform of the rubric of the common agricultural policy. It made for a half-hearted campaign.

Significantly, once they had launched their European manifestos, neither Mrs Thatcher, the Prime Minister, nor Mr Callaghan, Opposition Leader, made more than a token contribution to their European campaign. What mattered far more to them, and their rank and file, was the Westminster election that took place on May 3, a date that overlapped the opening of the European campaign.

The pro-membership campaign principally relied on Mr Edward Heath for the Conservatives, now a backbencher in the House of Commons, and the anti-membership campaign on Mr Tony Benn, a former Cabinet Minister in the outgoing Labour Government who has chosen to move to the back benches for the sake of freedom from front-bench collective responsibility: a calculated act of dissociation from Labour Cabinet policy and of alliance with the mass party outside Westminster for the future.

Almost certainly the British poll in the European direct election would have been markedly higher if it had preceded the Westminster election of May 3. The two main parties would have regarded direct elections for the European Parliament as a rehearsal for the domestic election that they regard as immensely more important in terms of national power, and the leaders would have been obliged to play a more prominent part, much as the newspapers and broadcasting would have brought to bear a greater concentration of interest.

Incidentally, the European Commission and the European Parliament offices in London, Cardiff, and Edinburgh would have been freer to spend resources on educative advertising and conferences if election law had not imposed constraints, along with an inter-party agreement that European money should be "non-politically" oriented.

In the event, Conservative and Labour local constituencies, which had been grouped to comprise about 500,000 electors so late as November, 1978, were left to finance their own European campaigns because party central funds had been preempted for the national general election on May 3. The new groups of European constituencies, having been hastily mapped, had hastily to choose their candidates, although the Conservative Party ran well ahead of Labour in its selection procedures.

Most of the rural European constituencies brought into association a number of domestic constituencies that had no common ties, interests, or attitude, with areas (outside the cities) so large that no candidate could cover them in the available time. Indeed, that time was limited in two ways: first, candidates had to wait for the electors to get over the fever of the national election and its consequences; secondly, the incidence of the Whitsun holiday virtually cut the European campaign down to a fortnight. Scarcely a handful of European candidates would claim to have run a reasonably thorough campaign in the circumstances, so compounding the electorate's ignorance or apathy about all things European; and no candidate had enough resources to make lavish use of the media.

At least the Conservative candidates, chosen from a list carefully sifted at Central Office by Mr Marcus Fox, a vice-chairman, and colleagues, had the advantage that they were associated clearly with Europeanism and that they were sometimes publicly recognisable figures, if not politicians. Labour candidates not only came late on the scene; they were also handicapped by the Labour Party's ambivalence about Community membership.

Theoretically, all Labour's European candidates were required to endorse the party's European manifesto, published in January, which ended with an implied threat of withdrawal from the EEC if British socialist interests were not conceded. That did not prevent some groups of constituency Labour parties, even with an anti-membership tendency, adopting pro-membership candidates. But there remained the handicap that the European liaison committee of Labour's national executive committee had an anti-membership majority and had Mr Benn, the leading critic of United Kingdom membership, as its chairman. In a sense, therefore, Labour activists were asked to work to send a member to a European Parliament in which the party had no faith and little respect: circumstances that must have damped down enthusiasm and helped to concede the battle to the Conservatives by default.

The formal launching of Labour's European manifesto had to be delayed until May 24, a week after Mrs Thatcher's launching of the Conservative manifesto, because Mr Callaghan, the party leader, told his colleagues, in effect, that he was not prepared to be exploited by the anti-membership majority of the national executive committee as (to use his phrase) "a wheel horse". In the end, Mr Ron Hayward, the anti-membership general secretary of the party, agreed to preside over the manifesto's launching; Mr Callaghan led the advocacy in terms of realpolitik; and Mr Benn, rather on guard, spoke with restraint. But Mr Callaghan did dismiss the manifesto threat of possible withdrawal on the pragmatic argument that for the next five years there would be a Conservative Government and therefore (he almost audibly sighed with relief) Mr Benn and his friends could do nothing about it.

Labour's launching of its European manifesto had a touch of pathos, if not farce. It was announced to take place at 10.30 a.m. in Transport House, the party headquarters. At the last moment it was realised that the hall would not be free, and the press and broadcasting conference took place a quarter-mile off and at 10 a.m. Many journalists arrived in time to see Mr Callaghan and Mr Benn leaving. It seemed an apt if cynical footnote to Labour's handling of Europeanism, much in line with its Birmingham conference for European candidates, at which most candidates seemed to complain that party headquarters had done and intended to do so very little to help them.

At least Mr Callaghan went to Paris to join all other Socialist Party leaders in a European demonstration of solidarity and common cause: a solidarity that the British Labour Party had not shown when the international committee of the NEC refused to underwrite the Socialist Group manifesto for all the countries of the Nine during direct elections.

In the circumstances, the European elections stood no chance of commanding much attention in the newspapers or on television and radio. In Fleet Street, the *Daily Telegraph*, the *Financial Times*, and the *Guardian* carried a few columns each day of special reports, mostly about Britain though not ignoring the Eight; television, having drenched viewers with politics during the national election during April and early May, did little about European elections, except for Lord Grade's Eurogala, a costly Sabbath entertainment involving European stars; and BBC radio's main contribution was the customary "phone-in" conducted by the admirable Robin Day. Mr Heath and Mr Benn, with Mr Enoch Powell intervening, made a few headlines.

But, at the end of the day, the British media concluded apparently that the British electors were fatigued with electioneering, or else more preoccupied with what their new Conservative Government was doing. Notably, not one Fleet Street paper thought sufficiently European to publish the full 410 names of the new European Parliament, in spite of leading articles that emphasized the historic and democratic significance of the event. As politicians in all parties, and on both sides of the Community argument, commented: it would have been a different story if *The Times* had still been printing.

Dons, commentators, and politicians are free from now on to make what they will of

Britain's low poll on June 7. Some anti-membership advocates argue that a non-vote must be reckoned a vote against the existence of the European Parliament, or against its importance or British membership of it, although it has to be remembered that some of them argued after the devolution referendums on March 1 that large-scale abstention meant a vote against change, against devolution of power to Edinburgh from Westminster. Certainly nobody may easily argue that the two-thirds of the British electorate that did not turn out to vote on June 7 had very passionate feelings one way or the other about the European Community or the European Parliament.

The truth may be that Britain showed in the first direct elections that Europeanism is not even skin deep, that the only politics intelligible to the mass vote are national politics; and those who look around the rest of the countries in the Nine with knowledge may add that the British elector is not alone.

It remains for the members of the new European Parliament to prove its worth, to complete the political education of the European electorate either for or against the Community, and to be content to let the European Parliament grow slowly from what it now is to what the founding fathers thought it eventually may become. The best hope for it is that the Parliament will be less nationalistic than the Council of Ministers and more democratic and less bureaucratic than the Commission. The worst fate for it is that the new Parliament will come into being, attract no public attention, and end up forgotten until the next direct elections come round in 1984.

PR in Northern Ireland

There was never serious question at Westminster over the United Kingdom Government's proposal of a system of Proportional Representation for the six counties of Northern Ireland, with its electorate of about a million voters divided by 300 years of history and religion. Through the 1970s there had been a bipartisan Westminster and Whitehall policy of reconciling the differences between the dominant Protestants and the minority Catholics, and between the Unionists of various brands who relied on the British connection and politicians who looked to union with the Republic of Ireland.

Westminster legislation provided for the "province" to be treated as one constituency, with three seats. That meant the over-representation of Northern Ireland in the European Parliament, compared with British seats of about 500,000 electors, whereas at Westminster Northern Ireland has 12 seats and is under-represented on the test of national electoral quotas.

All candidates appeared on the single list, and voters had to number them in order of preference. Surplus votes of a candidate or candidates who won outright were then transferred to other candidates. By that electoral device, it was assumed that the Catholic part of the population who are in a minority of two to one to Protestants, would have a reasonable chance of returning one MEP of the three. At Westminster it was widely assumed that the leading Protestant standard bearers would take the other two seats.

Most calculations of the results of Northern Ireland PR, however, proved wrong, though not the calculation that religious and political differences would assure far less apathy among the voters than in the rest of the United Kingdom.

The only outright winner on the first count, before votes were transferred, was the Rev. Ian Paisley, the formidable leader of the Democratic Unionist Party and already established as a Member of Parliament at Westminster, with two more MPs under his leadership since the general election of May 3 this year. Mr Paisley, a fundamentalist orator as preacher or politician in a style more familiar in the United States, opposes United Kingdom membership of the Community, opposes any move towards union between Northern Ireland and the Republic of Ireland, and opposes Catholicism wherever he catches a whiff of incense. He swept to personal victory on a popular vote, although political commentators thought his anti-Community platform had been attractive to Northern Ireland farmers.

On a 56.9 per cent. total poll (respectable by Britain's standards on the same day), Mr Paisley left the strongly entrenched Official Unionist candidates, led by Mr Harry West, at the post. He had 170,688 votes, with a surplus for redistribution on the second count of 27,628 votes.

Then came the next surprise: Mr John Hume, deputy leader of the Social Democratic and Labour Party, the largest Catholic Party in Northern Ireland (a party that holds only one seat at Westminster), won the second seat, and Mr John Taylor, the Official Ulster Unionist Party's second choice candidate, took the third place. Mr Hume's success may have owed something to the nationalist undertones in his campaign, but it brings to the European Parliament a politician with Community experience as an adviser to Dublin's Commissioner, Mr Richard Burke. He may be said to have been groomed for his new role, even before direct elections were in prospect.

Only Irishmen, North and South, could confidently interpret what PR in Northern Ireland has proved, and most of them could be relied upon to bring sectarian prejudices and preconceptions to bear on their analysis. For most British politicians and party managers, the Northern Ireland results will not be reckoned acceptable evidence that PR as a system strengthens the moderate centre, as some advocates of PR claim it would or should; and those who share the preference of Mrs Thatcher and Mr Callaghan for the first-past-the-post system, along with the disappointed Official Unionist Party, may question whether the European results are an undistorted mirror of the realities of Northern Ireland political strength. The two most successful candidates, Mr Paisley and Mr Hume, stand at the sectarian and political extremes, and the Alliance Party, which embraces both Protestants and Catholics, failed to appeal to the mass vote.

Yet one thing is certain: none of the opponents of PR in British politics may now plausibly argue that a transferable vote system of PR is difficult to comprehend by the ordinary elector or cumbersome to handle by returning officers and their staffs. The count upon count in Belfast City Hall went smoothly and quickly, and the evidence was that voters knew exactly what they wanted and how to use the numerals on the ballot papers.

Results of voting in the first direct elections to the European Parliament

BELGIUM

Polling day: June 10 Electorate: 6,800,584

Valid votes cast: 5,442,867 Invalid votes: 789,616 Turnout: 91·6%

Seats: 24

Party	Valid votes	% of valid votes	Seats
Christian People's Party	1,607,927	29·5	7
Belgian Socialist Party	698,892	12·8	3
Socialist Party	575,886	10·6	4
Party for Freedom and Progress	512,355	9·4	2
Social Christian Party	445,940	8·2	3
Democratic Front of French-speaking Belgians	414,412	7·6	2
Reform and Freedom Party	372,857	6·9	2
People's Union	324,569	6·0	1
Communist Party	145,804	2·7	—
Ecologists	185,821	3·4	—
Others	158,404	2·9	—
Totals	5,442,867	—	24

Voting system: Regional list, PR. One Flemish constituency of 13 seats and one Wallon constituency of 11 seats (Brussels electors could opt to vote in either seat).

The following were elected:

Christian Peoples' Party (7 seats):
Leo Tindemans
Marcel Vandewiele
Paul De Keersmaeker
Jaak Henckens
Lambert Croux
Joannes Verroken
Joris Verhaegen

Belgian Socialist Party (3 seats):
Karel Van Miert
Marcel Colla
Willy Vernimmen

Socialist Party (4 seats):
Ernest Glinne
Anne-Marie Lizin-Vanderspeeten
Lucien Radoux
Fernand Delmotte

Party for Freedom and Progress (2 seats):
Willy De Clercq
Herman Vanderpoorten

Social Christian Party (3 seats):
Charles-Ferdinand Nothomb
Victor Michel
Fernand Herman

Democratic Front of French-speaking Belgians (2 seats):
Antoinette Spaak
Paul-Henry Gendebien

Reform and Freedom Party (2 seats):
Jean Rey
André Damseaux

Peoples' Union (1 seat):
Mauritz Coppieters

FRANCE

Polling date: June 10 Electorate: 35,180,531
Votes cast: 20,331,440 Turnout: 60·7%
Seats: 81

Party	Votes	% of turnout	Seats
Union for France in Europe	5,666,984	27·9	26
Socialists and Radicals of the Left	4,763,026	23·4	21
Communist Party	4,153,710	20·4	19
Defence of the interests of France in Europe	3,301,980	16·2	15
Ecologists	891,683	4·4	—
Regionalists	623,663	3·1	—
Others	930,394	4·6	—
Totals	20,331,440	—	81

Voting system: National list with whole country as one constituency, PR. Minimum 5 per cent. of vote needed to qualify.

The following were elected:

Union for France in Europe (26 seats):
Simone Veil
Jean Lecanuet
Edgar Faure
Christiane Scrivener
Pierre Pflimlin
Francisque Collomb
Pierre Baudis
Michel Debatisse
Francis Combe
Robert Delorozoy
Corentin Calvez
Michel Poniatowski
André Rossi
André Diligent
Louise Moreau
Henri Caillavet
Victor Sablé
Charles Delatte
Yves Galland
Jean Seitlinger
Georges Donnez
Marie-Jane Pruvot
Maurice-René Simonnet
Jean-François Pintat
Simone Martin
Olivier d'Ormesson

Socialists and Radicals of the Left (21 seats):
*Francois Mitterand
Pierre Mauroy
Edith Cresson
Gilles Martinet
Didier Motchane
Maurice Faure
Gérard Jaquet
Georges Sutra de Germa
Marie-Claude Vayssade
Françoise Gaspard
Georges Sarre
Charles-Emile Loo
Jean Oehler
Charles Josselin
Daniel Persheron
Gisèle Charzat
Claude Estier
Yvette Roudy
Jacques Moreau
Roger-Gérard Schwartzenberg
Jacques Delors

Yvette Fuillet

*Resigned: Replacement named at end of list

French Communist Party (19 seats):
Georges Marchais
Jacqueline Hoffman
Gustave Ansart
Paul Verges
Emmanuel Maffre-Bauge
René Piquet
Pierre Pranchere
Félix Damette
Danielle Demarch
Maxime Gremetz
Georges Frischmann
Robert Chambeiron
Sylvie Leroux
Maurice Martin
Francis Wurtz
Louis Baillot
Henriette Poirier
Guy Fernandez
Jacques Denis

Defence of the Interests of France in Europe (15 seats):

Jacques Chirac
Michel Debre
Pierre Messmer
Claude Labbe
Louise Weiss
Gustave Deleau
Marie-Madeleine Dienesch
Maurice Druon
Hubert Buchou
Nicole Chouraqui
Christian de la Malene
Christian Poncelet
Alain Gillot
Eugène Remilly
Vincent Ansquer

DENMARK

Polling days: June 7 in Denmark and June 8 in Greenland

Electorate: 3,725,235

Votes cast: 1,754,850 Turnout: 47·1%

Seats: 16

Party	Votes	% of turnout	Seats
Social Democracy	382,487	21·8	3
Popular Movement against EEC	365,760	20·8	4
Liberals	252,767	14·4	3
Conservative People's Party	245,309	14·0	2
Centre Democracy	107,790	6·1	1
Progress Party	100,702	5·7	1
Socialist People's Party	81,991	4·7	1
Siumut (Greenland)	5,118	0·3	1
Left Socialists	60,964	3·5	—
Retsforbundet (Single tax party)	59,379	3·4	—
Social Liberals	56,944	3·2	—
Christian People's Party	30,985	1·8	—
Others (including Atassut, Greenland)	4,654	0·3	—
Totals	1,754,850	—	16

Voting system: National list, with all Denmark a 15-seat constituency. PR. In Greenland the simple majority, or first past the post, system.

The following were elected:

Social Democracy (3 seats):

Kjeld Olesen
Ms Mette Groes
Ms Eva Gredal

Popular Movement against EEC (4 seats):

Ms Else Hammerich
Rev Jørgen Bøgh
Sven Skovmand
Jens Peter Bonde

Liberals (3 seats):

Ms Tove Nielson
Niels Jørgen Haagerup
Jørgen Brøndlund Nielsen

Conservative Peoples' Party (2 seats):

Pøul Møller
Kent Kirk

Centre Democracy (1 seat):

Erhard Jakobsen

Progress Party (1 seat):

Kai Nyborg

Socialist Peoples' Party (1 seat):

Ms Bodil Boserup

Siumut (1 seat) Greenland:

Finn Lynge

GERMANY

Polling day: June 10 Electorate: 42,751,940
Votes cast: 27,847,109 Turnout: 65·1%
Seats: 81

Party	Votes	% of turnout	Seats
Social Democrats (SDP)	11,370,045	40·8	35
Christian Democratic Union (CDU)	10,883,085	39·1	34
Christian Social Union (CSU)	2,817,120	10·1	8
Liberals (FDP)	1,662,621	6·0	4
Communists (DKP)	112,055	0·4	—
Die Grünen (Ecologists)	893,683	3·2	—
Others	108,500	0·4	—
Totals	27,847,109	—	81

Voting system: PR on the national or Länder list system. There are three MEPs for Berlin.

The following were elected:

Social Democrats (35 seats):
Willy Brandt
Heinz Oskar Vetter
Bruno Friedrich
Beate Weber
Heinz Kühn
Eugen Loderer
Katharina Focke
Karl Hauenschild
Gerd Walter
Volkmar Gabert
Hans-Joachim Seeler
Rudi Arndt
Karl Schön
Manfred Wagner
Thomas von der Vring
Rudolf Schieler
Klaus Wettig
Johannes Wilhelm Peters
Gerhard Schmid
Klaus Hänsch
Horst Seefeld
Dieter Schinzel
Jan Klinkenborg
Ludwig Fellermaier
Erdmann Linde
Erwin Lange
Rolf Linkohr
Heidemarie Wieczorek-Zeul
Olaf Schwencke
Luise Herklotz
Lieselotte Seibel-Emmerling
Magdalene Hoff
Heinz Schmitt
Heinke Salisch
Hellmut Sieglerschmidt (Berlin)

Christian Democrats (34 seats):
Kai-Uwe von Hassel
Erik Blumenfeld
Hans Edgar Jahn
Philipp von Bismarck
Franz-Josef Nordlohne
Hans-Gert Pöttering
Renate-Charlotte Rabbethge
Johann Katzer
Paul Schnitker
Jochen van Aerssen
Albert Pürsten
Herbert W Köhler
Karl-Heinz Hoffmann
Marlene Lenz
Günter Rinsche
Ernst Gottfried Majonica
Kurt Malangré
Meinolf Mertens
Gerd Ludwig Lemmer
Hanna Walz
Prince Casimir zu Sayn
Konrad Schön
Bernhard Sälzer
Egon Alfred Klepsch
Horst Langes
Ernst Müller-Hermann
Siegbert Alber
Wilhelm Hahn
Karl von Wogau
Isidor Früh
Wolfgang Schall
Kurt Wawrzik
Rudolf Luster (Berlin)
Gero Pfennig (Berlin)

Christian Social Union (8 seats):
Alfons Goppel
Ursula Schleicher
Otto Habsburg-Lothringen
Ingo Friedrich
Heinrich Aigner
Hans August Lücker
Reinhold Bocklet
Karl Fuchs

Liberals (4 seats):
Martin Bangemann
Mechthild von Alemann
Heinrich Jürgens
Ulrich Irmer

IRELAND

Polling date: June 10 Electorate: 2,188,798

Valid votes cast: 1,339,072 Spoiled votes: 53,213 Turnout: 63·6%

Seats: 15

Party	Votes	% of valid votes	Seats
Fianna Fáil	464,450	34·7	5
Fine Gael	443,652	31·1	4
Labour	193,898	14·5	4
Independent	189,499	14·2	2
Sinn Fein	43,943	3·3	—
Others	3,630	0·3	—
Totals	1,339,072		15

Voting system: Regional list, country divided into four constituencies and seats allotted on PR.

The following were elected:

Fianna Fáil (5 seats):
Jeremiah Cronin
Michael Davern
Miss Sile de Valera
Sean Flanagan
Patrick Lalor

Fine Gael (4 seats):
Mark Clinton
John McCartin
Richie Ryan
Thomas O'Donnell

Labour (4 seats):
Mrs Eileen Desmond
Liam Kavanagh
John O'Connell
Michael O'Leary

Independent (2 seats):
Neil Blaney
Thomas Maher

Vote Analysis (Elected Members):

	Votes	*Quota*
Maher	86,208	71,766
Blaney	81,522	76,542
Clinton	78,762	76,725
Ryan	48,411	59,084
Lalor	62,094	76,725
O'Connell	44,832	59,084
Desmond	53,614	71,766
De Valera	41,357	59,084
O'Donnell	46,820	71,766
McCartin	47,519	76,542
Cronin	43,439	71,766
O'Leary	34,511	59,084
Davern	37,647	71,766
Kavanagh	40,072	76,725
Flanagan	38,232	76,542

Voting details in Ireland's four constituencies

DUBLIN

Electorate	618,454	
Total Poll	304,068	49·16%
Spoiled votes	8,653	2·84%
Total valid poll	295,415	47·77%
Seats	4	
Quota	59,084	
Candidates	13	

First Preferences	Number	Percentage	Seats
Fianna Fáil	84,008	28·44	1
Fine Gael	89,658	30·35	1
Labour	87,150	29·50	2
Sinn Fein	11,915	4·03	—
Community Democrats of Ireland	915	0·31	—
Independent	21,769	7·37	—

Elected:

O'Connell	(Lab)	8th count
Ryan	(FG)	8th count
De Valera	(FF)	9th count
O'Leary	(Lab)	10th count

LEINSTER

Electorate	486,248	
Total Poll	322,312	66·28%
Spoiled votes	15,416	4·78%
Total valid poll	306,896	63·11%
Seats	3	
Quota	76,725	
Candidates	9	

First preferences	Number	Percentage	Seats
Fianna Fáil	127,327	41·48	1
Fine Gael	125,021	40·73	1
Labour	40,072	13·06	1
Sinn Fein	14,476	4·72	—

Elected:

Clinton	(FG)	1st count
Lalor	(FF)	4th count
Kavanagh	(Lab)	5th count

MUNSTER

Electorate	641,625		
Total poll	445,192	69·39%	
Spoiled votes:	14,597	3·28%	
Total valid poll	430,595	67·11%	
Seats	5		
Quota	71,766		
Candidates	13		

First preference	Number	Percentage	Seats
Fianna Fáil	161,370	37·47	2
Fine Gael	115,609	26·84	1
Labour	53,614	12·45	1
Sinn Fein	11,526	2·68	—
Community Democrats of Ireland	2,268	0·51	—
Independent	86,208	20·02	1

Elected:

Maher	(Ind)	1st count
O'Donnell	(FG)	7th count
Desmond	(Lab)	7th count
Cronin	(FF)	9th count
Davern	(FF)	9th count

CONNACHT/ULSTER

Electorate	442,471		
Total poll	320,713	72·48%	
Spoiled votes	14,547	4·53%	
Total valid poll	306,166	69·19%	
Seats	3		
Quota	76,542		
Candidates	11		

First preferences	Number	Percentage	Seats
Fianna Fáil	91,746	29·96	1
Fine Gael	113,364	37·02	1
Labour	13,062	4·26	—
Sinn Fein	6,025	1·96	—
Community Democrats of Ireland	447	0·15	—
Independent	81,522	26·62	1

Elected:

Blaney	(Ind)	1st count
Flanagan	(FF)	7th count
McCartin	(FG)	7th count

Details of the 10 counts in Dublin

NAME	PARTY	1st Count	2nd Count		3rd Count		4th Count		5th Count	
		Votes	Transfer of Clear's Votes	Result	Transfer of Dillon-Byrne's Votes	Result	Transfer of Fox's Votes	Result	Transfer of MacGiolla's Votes	Result
Brugha, Ruairi	FF	21,758	+ 40	21,798	+ 78	21,876	+1,190	23,066	+ 260	23,326
Clear, Kevin	CDI	915	−915	—	—	—	—	—	—	—
de Valera, Sile	FF	41,357	+ 82	41,439	+ 264	41,703	+3,349	45,052	+ 586	45,638
Dillon-Byrne, Jane	Lab	7,807	+161	7,968	−7,968	—	—	—	—	—
Dublin Bay-Rockall Loftus, Sean	Ind	21,769	+225	21,994	+ 650	22,644	+ 226	22,870	+ 1,785	24,655
Fennell, Nuala	FG	26,951	+ 81	27,032	+1,020	28,052	+ 177	28,229	+ 450	28,679
Fox, Joe	FF	8,178	+ 21	8,199	+ 166	8,365	−8,365	—	—	—
Mc Giolla, Tomas	SFWP	11,915	+ 71	11,986	+ 458	12,444	+ 119	12,563	−12,563	—
Manning, Maurice	FG	14,296	+ 30	14,326	+ 249	14,575	+ 189	14,764	+ 378	15,142
O'Connell, John	Lab	44,832	+ 64	44,896	+3,132	48,028	+ 400	48,428	+ 4,452	52,880
O'Leary, Michael	Lab	34,511	+ 37	34,548	+1,433	35,981	+ 325	36,306	+ 2,047	38,353
Ryan, Richie	FG	48,411	+ 23	48,434	+ 157	48,591	+ 316	48,907	+ 372	49,279
Yeats, Michael	FF	12,715	+ 14	12,729	+ 50	12,779	+1,623	14,402	+ 141	14,543
	Non-transferable:		+ 66	66	+ 311	377	+ 451	828	+ 2,092	2,920

Dublin (Continued)

	6th Count		7th Count		8th Count		9th Count		10th Count	
	Transfer of Yeat's Votes	Result	Transfer of Manning's Votes	Result	Transfer of Loftus's Votes	Result	Transfer of Brugha's Votes	Result	Transfer of De Valera's Surplus	Result
Brugha, Ruairi	+ 5,077	28,403	+ 152	28,555	+ 1,544	30,099	−30,099	—	—	—
Clear, Kevin	—	—	—	—	—	—	—	—	—	—
De Valera, Sile	+ 6,061	51,699	+ 552	52,251	+ 2,587	54,838	+24,334	*79,172*	−20,088	*59,084*
Dillon-Byrne, Jane	—	—	—	—	—	—	—	—	—	—
Dublin Bay-Rockall Loftus, Sean	+ 509	25,164	+ 827	25,991	−25,991	—	—	—	—	—
Fennell, Nuala	+ 368	29,047	+ 5,017	34,064	+ 4,916	38,980	+ 994	39,974	+ 2,850	42,824
Fox, Joe	—	—	—	—	—	—	—	—	—	—
Mac Giolla, Tomas	—	—	—	—	—	—	—	—	—	—
Manning, Maurice	+ 322	15,464	−15,464	—	—	—	—	—	—	—
O'Connell, John	+ 519	53,399	+ 1,358	54,757	+ 6,098	*60,855*	—	*60,855*	—	*60,855*
O'Leary, Michael	+ 407	38,760	+ 1,186	39,946	+ 3,652	43,598	+ 1,089	44,687	+ 2,398	*47,085*
Ryan, Richie	+ 690	49,969	+ 5,849	55,818	+ 3,824	*59,642*	—	*59,642*	—	*59,642*
Yeats, Michael	−14,543	—	—	—	—	—	—	—	—	—
Non-Transferable:	+ 590	3,510	+ 523	4,033	+ 3,370	7,403	+ 3,682	11,085	+14,840	25,925

Details of the five counts in Leinster

NAME	PARTY	1st Count	2nd Count		3rd Count		4th Count		5th Count	
		Votes	Transfer of McRaghnaill & Walsh's Votes	Result	Transfer of Barnes' Votes	Result	Transfer of Power's Votes	Result	Transfer of McDonald's Votes	Result
Barnes, Monica	FG	21,384	+1,077	22,461	−22,461	—	—	—	—	—
Clinton, Mark	FG	*78,762*	—	*78,762*	—	*78,762*	—	*78,762*	—	*78,762*
Kavanagh, Liam	Lab	40,072	+3,632	43,704	+ 4,097	47,801	+ 1,386	49,187	+ 9,389	*58,576*
Lalor, Paddy	FF	62,094	+1,444	63,538	+ 1,729	65,267	+12,523	*77,790*	—	*77,790*
McDonald, Charlie	FG	24,875	+ 762	25,637	+12,204	37,841	+ 953	38,794	−38,794	—
McRaghnaill, Donnchadha	SFWP	8,414	−8,414	—	—	—	—	—	—	—
Nolan, Tom	FF	34,210	+1,292	35,502	+ 546	36,048	+12,327	48,375	+ 2,968	51,343
Power, Paddy	FF	31,023	+1,096	32,119	+ 549	32,668	−32,668	—	—	—
Walsh, Sean	SFWP	6,062	−6,062	—	—	—	—	—	—	—
	Non-transferable:		5,173	5,173	+ 3,336	8,509	+ 5,479	13,988	+26,437	40,425

Details of 9 counts in Munster

NAME	PARTY	1st Count Votes	2nd Count Transfer of Maher's Surplus	2nd Count Result	3rd Count Transfer of Crowe's and Dunphy's Votes	3rd Count Result	4th Count Transfer of French's Votes	4th Count Result	5th Count Transfer of Blair's Votes	5th Count Result
Blair, John	FG	21,615	+ 602	22,217	+ 478	22,695	+ 524	23,219	–23,219	—
Cronin, Jerry	FF	43,439	+ 985	44,424	+ 699	45,123	+ 5,942	51,065	+ 1,686	52,751
Crowe, Michael	CDI	2,268	+ 80	2,348	– 2,348	—	—	—	—	—
Davern, Noel	FF	37,647	+ 1,496	39,143	+ 963	40,106	+ 2,599	42,705	+ 657	43,362
Desmond, Eileen	Lab	53,614	+ 916	54,530	+ 3,292	57,822	+ 889	58,711	+ 4,230	62,941
Dukes, Alan	FG	21,510	+ 3,156	24,666	+ 859	25,525	+ 131	25,656	+ 7,516	33,172
Dunphy, Michael	SFWP	11,526	+ 175	11,701	–11,701	—	—	—	—	—
French, Sean	FF	16,655	+ 296	16,951	+ 376	17,327	–17,327	—	—	—
Herbert, Michael	FF	34,034	+ 1,179	35,213	+ 517	35,730	+ 2,915	38,645	+ 207	38,852
Maher, Thomas J.	Ind	*86,208*	–14,442	*71,766*	—	*71,766*	—	*71,766*	—	*71,766*
O'Connor, Timothy	FF	29,595	+ 929	30,524	+ 486	31,010	+ 1,905	32,915	+ 286	33,201
O'Donnell, Tom	FG	46,820	+ 3,089	49,909	+ 928	50,837	+ 157	50,994	+ 3,588	54,582
O'Keeffe, Jim	FG	25,664	+ 1,539	27,203	+ 280	27,483	+ 184	27,667	+ 2,306	29,973
	Non-transferable:				5,171	5,171	+ 2,081	7,252	+ 2,743	9,995

(Continued on p. 50)

Munster (Continued)

	6th Count		7th Count		8th Count		9th Count	
	Transfer of O'Keeffe's Votes	Result	Transfer of O'Connor's Votes	Result	Transfer of Duke's Votes	Result	Transfer of O'Donnell's Surplus	Result
Blair, John	—	—	—	—	—	—	—	—
Cronin, Jerry	+ 873	53,624	+ 7,025	60,649	+ 773	61,422	+ 890	*62,312*
Crowe, Michael	—	—	—	—	—	—	—	—
Davern, Noel	+ 437	43,799	+ 4,533	48,332	+ 1,133	49,465	+ 727	*50,192*
Desmond, Eileen	+ 4,250	67,191	+ 1,864	69,055	+ 3,545	*72,600*	—	*72,600*
Dukes, Alan	+ 6,347	39,519	+ 566	40,085	–40,085	—	—	—
Dunphy, Michael	—	—	—	—	—	—	—	—
French, Sean	—	—	—	—	—	—	—	—
Herbert, Michael	+ 332	39,184	+ 7,127	46,311	+ 689	47,000	+ 754	47,754
Maher, Thomas J.	—	*71,766*	—	*71,766*	—	*71,766*	—	*71,766*
O'Connor, Timothy	+ 665	33,856	–33,856	—	—	—	—	—
O'Donnell, Tom	+10,946	65,528	+ 1,476	67,004	+25,471	*92,475*	–20,709	*71,766*
O'Keeffe, Jim	–29,973	—	—	—	—	—	—	—
Non-transferable:	+ 6,133	16,128	+11,265	27,393	+ 8,474	35,867	+18,338	54,205

Details of seven counts in Connacht/Ulster

NAME	PARTY	1st Count	2nd Count		3rd Count		4th Count		5th Count	
		Votes	Transfer of Coffey's, Rodger's and Morris's Votes	Result	Transfer of Higgins's Votes	Result	Transfer of Blaney's Surplus	Result	Transfer of McEniff's Votes	Result
Blaney, Neil	Ind	*81,522*	—	—	—	—	−4,980	*76,542*	—	*76,542*
Coffey, Tony	SFWP	3,329	−3,329	—	—	—	—	—	—	—
Cooney, Patrick	FG	33,360	+ 782	34,142	+ 2,454	36,596	+ 685	37,281	+ 725	38,006
Doolan, Jim	FF	27,739	+ 524	28,263	+ 1,518	29,781	+ 825	30,606	+ 7,175	37,781
Flanagan, Sean	FF	38,233	+ 420	38,653	+ 825	39,478	+1,254	40,732	+11,677	52,405
Higgins, Michael D.	Lab	13,062	+ 951	14,013	−14,013	—	—	—	—	—
McCartin, Joe	FG	47,519	+ 470	47,989	+ 1,708	49,697	+ 777	50,474	+ 1,222	51,696
McEniff, Sean	FF	25,774	+ 493	26,267	+ 515	26,782	+1,036	27,818	−27,818	—
Morris, Christopher	CDI	447	− 447	—	—	—	—	—	—	—
Rodgers, Seamus	SFWP	2,696	−2,696	—	—	—	—	—	—	—
Staunton, Myles	FG	32,485	+ 288	32,773	+ 2,570	35,343	+ 403	35,746	+ 443	36,189
	Non-transferable:		2,544	2,544	+ 4,423	6,967	—	6,967	+ 6,576	13,543

(continued on p. 52)

Connacht/Ulster (Continued)

	6th Count		7th Count	
	Transfer of Staunton's Votes	Result	Transfer of Doolan's Votes	Result
Blaney, Neil	—	*76,542*	—	*76,542*
Coffey, Tony	—	—	—	—
Cooney, Patrick	+12,019	50,025	+ 1,242	51,267
Doolan, Jim	+ 795	38,576	−38,576	—
Flanagan, Sean	+ 2,417	54,826	+27,383	*82,209*
Higgins, Michael D.	—	—	—	—
McCartin, Joe	+13,775	65,471	+ 1,430	*66,901*
McEniff, Sean	—	—	—	—
Morris, Christopher	—	—	—	—
Rodgers, Seamus	—	—	—	—
Staunton, Myles	−36,189	—	—	—
Non-transferable:	+ 7,183	20,726	+ 8,521	29,247

ITALY

Polling date: June 10 Electorate: 42,193,369
Votes cast: 34,981,852 Turnout: 85·5%
Seats: 81

Party	Votes	% of turnout	Seats
Christian Democrats (DC)	12,753,350	36·5	29
Communist Party (PCI)	10,343,991	29·6	24
Socialist Party (PSI)	3,857,670	11·0	9
Social Movement (MSI)	1,907,505	5·4	4
Social Democratic (PSDI)	1,511,562	4·3	4
Radical Party (PR)	1,282,841	3·7	3
Liberal Party (PLI)	1,269,612	3·6	3
Republican Party (PRI)	896,526	2·6	2
Proletarian Party (PDUP)	404,989	1·1	1
Proletarian Democracy (DP)	250,577	0·7	1
S. Tyrol People's Party (SVP)	196,199	0·6	1
Aosta Valley Union (UV)	165,285	0·5	—
National Democratic (DN)	141,745	0·4	—
Totals	34,981,852	—	81

Voting system: Regional list with five constituencies. PR.

The following were elected (†since resigned: replacement named at end of party list):

Christian Democrats (29 seats)

	Preference
Colombo, Emilio	860,147
Zaccagnini, Benigno	737,499
†Selva, Gustavo	398,401
Antoniozzi, Dario	375,361
Costanzo, Roberto	357,879
Lima, Salvatore	305,308
Gonella, Guido	273,593
Barbi, Paolo	270,185
Piccoli, Flaminio	268,808
Diana, Alfredo	256,771
Narducci, Angelo	244,094
Giummarra, Vincenzo	242,960
Rumor, Mariano	235,478
Travaglini, Giovanni	230,987
Zecchino, Ortensio	227,342
Ligios, Giosué	223,050
Ghergo, Alberto	207,595
Cassanmagnago, M. Luisa	185,303
Pedini, Mario	182,568
Lega, Silvio	160,131
Macario, Luigi	157,074
Sassano, Mario	152,281
Bersani, Giovanni	148,235
Colleselli, Arnaldo	136,556
Adonnino, Pietro	134,860
Gaiotti, Paola	134,609
Filippi, Renzo Eligio	128,593
Giavazzi, Giovanni	127,999
Barbagli, Giovanni	127,572

Modiano, Marcello

Italian Communist Party (24 seats)

	Preference
Berlinguer, Enrico	830,557
Amendola, Giorgio	805,449
Pajetta, Giancarlo	639,472
†Iotti, Nilde	220,600
de Pasquale, Pancrazio	214,145
Papapietro, Giovanni	205,445
Cardia, Umberto	202,175
Carossino, Angelo	191,906
Spinelli, Altiero	185,348
Galluzzi, Carlo Alberto	164,882
Ippolito, Felice	139,394
d'Angelosante, Francesco	132,649
Fanti, Guido	121,112
Segre, Sergio	118,278
Ferrero, Bruno	95,989
Cinciari, Rodano M. Luisa	94,791
Ceravolo, Domenico	89,064
Baduel Glorioso, Fabriza	81,115
Romagnoli Carettoni, Tullia	81,104
Squarcialupi, Vera	78,310
Barbarella, Carla	76,007
Bonaccini, Aldo	75,359
Gouthier, Anselmo	65,864
Leonardi, Silvio	48,421

Veronesi, Protogene

Socialists (9 seats)

	Preference
Ruffolo, Giorgio	290,233
Craxi, Bettino	286,739
Zagari, Mario	152,002
Lezzi, Pietro	148,318
Pelikan, Jiri	130,569
Dido, Mario	111,555
Gatto, Vincenzo	110,415
Ripa Di Meana, Carlo	71,581
Arfe, Gaetano	58,449

Italian Social Movement (4 seats)

	Preference
Almirante, Giorgio	519,479
Romualdi, Pino	133,224
Buttafuoco, Antonino	67,691
Petronio, Franco	43,585

Social Democrats (4 seats)

Cariglia, Antonio 74,216
Ferri, Mauro 39,537
Orlandi, Flavio 28,427
Puletti, Ruggero 28,091

Radical Party (3 seats)

Pannella, Marco 97,955
Sciascia, Leonardo 66,013
Bonino, Emma 51,445

Liberals (3 seats)

Pininfarina, Sergio 258,542
Bettiza, Enzo 223,678
Cecovini, Manlio 42,787

Republican Party (2 seats)

Agnelli, Susanna 101,232
Visentini, Bruno 58,669

Proletarian Party (1 seat)

Castellina, Luciana 15,027

Proletarian Democracy (1 seat)

Capanno, Mario 23,891

S. Tyrol People's Party (1 seat)

Dalsass, Joachim 125,076

Voting details in Italy's five Regional Constituencies

Italy, North-West

Party	Votes	% turnout	Seats
DC	3,424,012	34·4	8
PCI	2,856,550	28·7	7
PSI	1,240,564	12·4	3
MSI	330,500	3·3	1
PSDI	468,596	4·7	1
PR	410,711	4·1	1
PLI	625,537	6·3	2
PRI	297,702	3·0	1
PDUP	111,030	1·1	–
DP	91,243	0·9	1
UV	79,211	0·8	–
DN	30,409	0·3	–
Totals	9,966,065		25

The following were elected:

Christian Democrats (8 seats)

	Preference
Zaccagnini, Benigno	737,499
Diana, Alfredo	256,771
Narducci, Angelo	244,094
Cassanmagnago, M. Luisa	185,303
Pedini, Mario	182,568
Lega, Silvio	160,131
Macario, Luigi	157,079
Giavazzi, Giovanni	127,999

Italian Communist Party (7 seats)

Pajetta, Giancarlo	639,472
Carossino, Angelo	191,906
Spinelli, Altiero (a)	185,348
Ferrero, Bruno	95,898
Segre, Sergio (b)	89,826
Romagnoli Carettoni, Tullia	81,104
Squarcialupi, Vera	78,310

Socialists (3 seats)

Craxi, Bettino	286,739
Pelikan, Jiri	130,569
Dido, Mario	111,555

Italian Social Movement (1 seat)

Almirante, Giorgio (c)	149,368

Social Democrats (1 seat)

Ferri, Mauro	139,537

Radical Party (1 seat)

Pannella, Marco	97,955

Liberals (2 seats)

Pininfarina, Sergio	258,542
Bettiza, Enzo	223,678

Republican Party (1 seat)

Agnelli, Susanna	101,232

Proletarian Democracy (1 seat)

Capanna, Mario	23,891

(a) Owing to option, substituted by Aldo Bonaccini.
(b) Owing to option, substituted by Silvio Leonardi.
(c) Owing to option, substituted by Franco Petronio.

Italy, North-East

Party	Votes	% turnout	Seats
DC	2,583,631	36·7	6
PCI	2,134,276	30·3	5
PSI	751,055	10·7	2
MSI	189,671	2·7	–
PSDI	323,278	4·6	1
PR	251,059	3·6	1
PLI	259,519	3·7	1
PRI	195,457	2·8	–
PDUP	59,779	0·8	–
DP	38,343	0·5	–
SVP	196,199	2·8	1
UV	46,917	0·7	–
DN	17,607	0·2	–
Totals	7,046,791		17

The following were elected:

Christian Democrats (6 seats)

	Preference
Selva, Gustavo	398,401
Piccoli, Flaminio	268,808
Rumor, Mariano	235,478
Bersani, Giovanni	148,235
Colleselli, Arnaldo	136,556
Gaiotti, Paola	134,609

Italian Communist Party (5 seats)

Iotti, Nilde	220,600
Fanti, Guido	121,112
Ceravolo, Domenico	89,064
Baduel, Maria Fabrizia	81,115
Gouthier, Anselmo	65,864

Socialists (2 seats)

Ripa di Meana, Carlo	71,581
Arfe, Gaetano	58,449

Social Democrats (1 seat)

Orlandi, Flavio	28,427

Radical Party (1 seat)

Pannella, Marco (a)	58,044

Liberals (1 seat)

Bettiza, Enzo	76,393

S. Tyrol People's Party (1 seat)

Dalsass, Joachim	125,076

(a) Owing to option, substituted by Leonardo Sciascia.

Italy, Central

Party	Votes	% turnout	Seats
DC	2,260,770	31·7	5
PCI	2,594,140	36·4	6
PSI	742,559	10·4	1
MSI	393,050	5·5	1
PSDI	282,144	4·0	1
PR	262,828	3·7	1
PLI	186,911	2·6	–
PRI	206,241	2·9	1
PDUP	117,753	1·7	1
DP	48,339	0·7	–
UV	12,432	0·2	–
DN	20,928	0·3	–
Totals	7,128,095		17

The following were elected:

Christian Democrats (5 seats)

	Preference
Gonella, Guido	273,593
Sassano, Mario	152,281
Adonnino, Pietro	134,860
Filippi, Renzo Eligio (a)	128,593
Barbagli, Giovanni	127,999

Italian Communist Party (6 seats)

Berlinguer, Enrico	830,557
Galluzzi, Carlo Alberto	164,882
Spinelli, Altiero	129,014
Segre, Sergio	118,278
Cinciari Rodano, M. Luisa	94,791
Barbarella, Carla	76,007

Socialists (1 seat)

Zagari, Mario 152,002

Italian Social Movement (1 seat)

Romualdi, Pino 133,224

Social Democrats (1 seat)

Puletti, Ruggero 28,029

Radical Party (1 seat)

Pannella, Marco (b) 81,777

Republican Party (1 seat)

Visentini, Bruno 58,669

Proletarian Party (1 seat)

Castellina, Luciana 15,027

(a) Proclaimed elected following appeal against the provisional poll result which had given Sergio Romano Ercini as last of the elected with 126,233 votes.
(b) Owing to option, substituted by Emma Bonino.

Italy, South

Party	Votes	% turnout	Seats
DC	3,058,327	41·8	7
PCI	1,883,435	25·7	4
PSI	761,748	10·4	2
MSI	691,571	9·4	1
PSDI	315,490	4·3	1
PR	207,951	2·8	–
PLI	107,390	1·5	–
PRI	107,396	1·5	–
PDUP	80,242	1·1	–
DP	48,230	0·7	–
UV	14,851	0·2	–
DN	45,301	0·6	–
Totals	7,321,932		15

The following were elected:

Christian Democrats (7 seats)

	Preference
Colombo, Emilio	860,147
Antoniozzi, Dario	375,361
Costanzo, Roberto	357,879
Barbi, Paolo	270,185
Travaglini, Giovanni	230,987
Zecchino, Ortensio	227,342
Ghergo, Alberto	207,595

Social Democrats (1 seat)

Cariglia, Antonio	74,216

Italian Communist Party (4 seats)

Amendola, Giorgio	805,449
Papapietro, Giovanni	205,445
Ippolito, Felice	139,394
d'Angelosante, Francesco	132,649

Socialists (2 seats)

Ruffolo, Giorgio	290,233
Lezzi, Pietro	148,318

Italian Social Movement (1 seat)

Almirante, Giorgio	519,479

Italy, Islands

Party	Votes	% turnout	Seats
DC	1,426,610	40·6	3
PCI	875,590	24·9	2
PSI	361,744	10·3	1
MSI	299,713	8·5	1
PSDI	122,052	3·5	–
PR	150,292	4·3	–
PLI	90,255	2·6	–
PRI	89,730	2·6	–
PDUP	36,185	1·0	–
DP	24,422	0·7	–
UV	11,874	0·3	–
DN	27,500	0·8	–
Totals	3,515,967		7

The following were elected:

Christian Democrats (3 seats)

	Preference
Lima, Salvatore	305,308
Giummarra, Vincenzo	242,960
Ligios, Giosué	223,050

Italian Communist Party (2 seats)

de Pasquale, Pancrazio	211,145
Cardia, Umberto	202,175

Socialists (1 seat)

Gatto, Vincenzo	110,415

Italian Social Movement (1 seat)

Buttafuoco, Antonio	67,691

LUXEMBOURG

Polling date: June 10 (Voting compulsory and coinciding with a general election.)

Electorate: 212,740 Turnout: 88·9%

Votes cast: 974,991 (Electors had six votes each)

Seats: 6

Party	Votes	% of turnout	Seats
Christian Socialist Peoples' Party	352,296	36·1	3
Democratic Party	274,307	28·1	2
Socialist Workers Party	211,106	21·7	1
Socialist Democrat Party	68,289	7·0	—
Communist Party	48,813	5·0	—
Others	20,180	2·1	—
Totals	974,991	—	6

Voting system: National list, PR, for one national constituency.

The following were elected:

Christian Socialist Peoples' Party (3 seats):
*Pierre Werner
*Jacques Santer
*Fernand Boden

Fischbach, Marc
Estgen, Nicolas
Spautz, Jean

Democratic Party (2 seats):
*Gaston Thorn
Mrs Colette Flesch

Hamilius, Jean

Socialist Worker Party (1 seat):
Victor Abens

*Resigned; replacements named beneath rule

THE NETHERLANDS

Polling date: June 7 Electorate: 9,799,761
Votes cast: 5,667,303 Turnout: 57·8%
Seats: 25

Party	Votes	% of turnout	Seats
Christian Democrats (CDA)	2,017,743	35·6	10
Labour (PvdA)	1,722,240	30·4	9
Liberal (VVD)	914,787	16·1	4
Democrats '66 (Independents)	511,567	9·0	2
Staatkundig Gereformeerde Partij (SGP)	126,412	2·2	—
Communist (CPN)	97,343	1·7	—
Pacifistisch Socialistische Partij (PSP)	97,243	1·7	—
Politieke Partij Radicalen (PPR)	92,055	1·6	—
Gereformeerd Politiek Verbond (GPV)	62,610	1·1	—
Others	24,903	0·4	—
Totals	5,667,303	—	25

Voting system: National list, PR, with whole country as one constituency.

The following were elected:

Christian Democrats (10 seats):
B. Beumer
Willem Vergeer
Teun Tolman
E. C. A. M. Boot
Harry Notenboom
Sj. Jonker
Frans van der Gun
J. J. M. Penders
J. R. H. Maij-Weggen
J. L. Janssen van Raay

Labour (9 seats):
Anne Vondeling
Ien van den Heuvel Blank
Piet Dankert
Johan van Minnen
Wim Albers
Annie Krouwel-Vlam
Bob Cohen
Hemme Muntingh
Eisso Woltjer

Liberals (4 seats):
Cornelius Berkhouwer
Hans R. Nord
H. J. Louwes
Aart Geurtsen

Democrats' 66 (2 seats):
A. de Goede
Mevr. S. Dekker

UNITED KINGDOM
England, Scotland and Wales

Polling date: June 7 Electorate: 40,529,970
Votes cast: 12,873,930 Turnout: 31·8%
Seats: 78

Party	Votes	% of turnout	Seats
Conservative	6,508,492	50·6%	60†
Labour	4,253,247	33·0%	17
Liberal	1,690,638	13·1%	—
Scot Nat	247,836	1·9%	1
PI Cymru	83,399	0·6%	—
Others	90,318	0·8%	—
Totals	12,873,930	—	78

Voting system: Simple majority – first past the post.

The following were elected:

Conservative (60 seats):
Neil Balfour
Robert Battersby
Peter Beazley
Lord Bethell
Miss Beata Brooks
Sir Frederick Catherwood
Richard Cottrell
David Curry
Ian Dalziel
John de Courcy Ling
Basil de Ferranti
The Marquess of Douro
William Newton Dunn
The Baroness Elles
Adam Fergusson
Miss Norvella Forster
Eric Forth
Lord Harmar-Nicholls
David Harris
Miss Gloria Hooper
William Hopper
Brian Hord
Paul Howell
Alisdair Hutton
Christopher Jackson
Robert Jackson
Stanley Johnson
Edward Kellett-Bowman
Mrs Elaine Kellett-Bowman
John Marshall
Robert Moreland
James Moorhouse
Sir David Nicholson
Tom Normanton
Lord O'Hagan
Ben Patterson
Andrew Pearce
Sir Henry Plumb
Derek Prag
Peter N. Price
Christopher Prout
James Provan
John Purvis
Sir Brandon Rhys Williams
†Miss Shelagh Roberts
James Scott-Hopkins
Madron Seligman
Dr Alexander Sherlock
Richard Simmonds
Anthony Simpson
Tom Spencer
James Spicer
Sir John Stewart-Clark
John M. Taylor
Fred Tuckman
Amedee Turner QC
Alan Tyrrell QC
Sir Peter Vanneck
Sir Frederick Warner
Michael Welsh

†Election of Miss Roberts ruled invalid. By-election in September, 1979. She was re-elected.

Labour (17 seats):
Gordon Adam
Richard Balfe
Roland Boyes
Mrs Janey Buchan
Richard Caborn
Mrs Barbara Castle
Kenneth Collins
Derek Enright
Michael Gallagher
Winston James Griffiths
Brian Key
Alfred Lomas
Thomas Megahy
Miss Joyce Quin
Mrs Ann Clwyd Roberts
Alan Rogers
Barry Seal

Scottish National Party (1 seat):
Mrs Winifred Ewing

Constituency Results

A more detailed table of voting in England, Scotland and Wales is at the end of the constituency results.

The following abbreviations have been used for political parties standing in the European elections:

Anti-CM – Anti-Common Market; AWE – Against Wealth Extremes; Community Dem – Community Democrat; C – Conservative Party; CR – Centre Right; Ecology – Ecology Party; EFP – European Federal Party; IACM – Independent Anti-Common Market; Ind – Independent; Ind C – Independent Conservative; IM – International Marxist; L – Liberal Party; Lab – Labour Party; Lab and Co-op – Labour and Co-operative; Meb Kernow – Mebyon Kernow; Scot Nat – Scottish National Party; UACM – United Anti-Common Market; Wessex Reg – Wessex Regionalist.

Full results in the 78 constituencies under the first past the post system, were:

BEDFORDSHIRE

Electorate: 515,237

Bedford; Hemel Hempstead; Hitchin; Luton East; Luton West; Mid-Bedfordshire; South Bedfordshire.

Beazley, P. (C)	102,054
Elliott, M. N. (Lab)	48,454
Roberts, P. (L)	21,943
Shrive, T. H. (CR)	1,198
C majority	53,600

Total vote 173,649 (33·7%): C 58·8%; Lab 27·9%; L 12·6%; CR 0·7%. C maj 30·9%.

BIRMINGHAM, NORTH

Electorate: 537,957

Aldridge-Brownhills; Birmingham, Erdington; Birmingham, Perry Barr; Birmingham, Stechford; Sutton Coldfield; Warley East; Warley West; West Bromwich East; West Bromwich West.

Forth, M. E. (C)	68,507
Jackson, P. M. (Lab)	60,163
Hooper, E. C. A. (L)	14,583
C majority	8,344

Total vote 143,253 (26·6%): C 47·8%; Lab 42·0%; L 10·2%. C maj 5·8%.

BIRMINGHAM, SOUTH

Electorate: 509,529

The Birmingham constituencies of Edgbaston; Hall Green; Handsworth; Ladywood; Northfield; Selly Oak; Small Heath; Sparkbrook; Yardley.

Forster, Miss N. F. (C)	66,012
Bore, A. (Lab)	60,775
Batchelor, A. J. (L)	12,160
C majority	5,237

Total vote 138,947 (27·3%): C 47·5%; Lab 43·7%; L 8·8%. C maj 3·8%.

BRISTOL

Electorate: 526,254

The Bristol constituencies of North East, North West, South, South East and West; Chippenham; Kingswood; South Gloucestershire.

Cottrell, R. (C)	100,160
Naysmith, J. D. (Lab)	59,443
Heppell, J. (L)	25,308
C majority	40,717

Total vote 184,911 (35·1%): C 54·2%; Lab 32·1%; L 13·7%. C maj 22·1%.

CAMBRIDGESHIRE

Electorate: 497,317

Cambridge; Cambridgeshire; Huntingdonshire; Isle of Ely; Peterborough; Wellingborough.

Catherwood, Sir F. (C)	94,497
Mackie, M. L. (Lab)	42,038
O'Loughlin, M. W. B. (L)	23,501
C majority	52,459

Total vote 160,036 (32·2%): C 59·0%; Lab 26·3%; L 14·7%. C maj 32·7%.

CHESHIRE, EAST

Electorate: 504,770

Crewe; Hazel Grove; Knutsford; Macclesfield; Newton; Runcorn; Warrington.

Normanton, T. (C)	89,640
Davies, D. W. (Lab)	50,324
Bingham, V. N. (L)	19,952
C majority	39,316

Total vote 159,916 (31·7%): C 56·1%; Lab 31·5%; L 12·5%. C maj 24·6%.

CHESHIRE, WEST

Electorate: 505,896

Bebington and Ellesmere Port; Birkenhead; City of Chester; Nantwich; Northwich; Wallasey; Wirral.

Pearce, A. (C)	93,589
Bailey, A. E. (Lab)	47,276
Green, R. M. (L)	23,816
C majority	46,313

Total vote 164,681 (32·6%): C 56·8%; Lab 28·7%; L 14·5%. C maj 28·1%.

CLEVELAND

Electorate: 537,002

Cleveland and Whitby; Hartlepool; Richmond (Yorks); Scarborough; and the four Teesside seats of Middlesbrough, Redcar, Stockton, Thornaby.

Vanneck, Sir P. (C)	76,514
Wistrich, E. (Lab)	51,688
Pitts, M. (L)	18,125
Hill, S. (Anti CM)	4,960
C majority	24,826

Total vote 151,287 (28·2%): C 50·6%; Lab 34·2%; L 12·0%; Anti CM 3·3%. C maj 16·4%.

CORNWALL AND PLYMOUTH

Electorate: 489,803

Bodmin; Falmouth and Camborne; North Cornwall; the Plymouth seats of Devonport, Drake and Sutton; St Ives; Truro.

Harris, D. A. (C)	94,650
Leather, D. (Lab)	36,681
Spring, G. (L)	23,105
Jenkin, R. (Meb Kernow)	10,205
Goldsmith, E. R. (Ecology)	5,125
Ash, Dr A. E. M. (UACM)	1,834
C majority	57,969

Total vote 171,600 (35·0%): C 55·2%; Lab 21·4%; L 13·5%; Meb Kernow 5·9%; Ecology 3.0%; UACM 1.1%. C maj 33.8%.

COTSWOLDS

Electorate: 509,749

Banbury; Cheltenham; Cirencester and Tewkesbury; Gloucester; Mid-Oxon; Oxford; Stroud.

Plumb, Sir H. (C)	109,139
Honeybone, J. A. (Lab)	37,713
Burton, Miss M. (L)	27,916
Bennett, D. C. T. (UACM)	11,422
C majority	71,426

Total vote 186,200 (36·5%): C 58·6%; Lab 20·3%; L 15·0%; UACM 6·1%. C maj 38·3%.

CUMBRIA

Electorate: 531,948

Barrow-in-Furness; Carlisle; Lancaster; Morecambe and Lonsdale; North Fylde; Penrith and the Border; Westmorland; Whitehaven; Workington.

Kellett-Bowman, Mrs M. E. (C)	104,471
Little, H. (Lab)	62,485
Graham, Miss E. (L)	16,631
Burrows, E. (Ind)	1,596
C majority	41,986

Total vote 185,183 (34·8%): C 56·4%; Lab 33·7%; L 9·0%; Ind 0·9%. C maj 22·7%.

DERBYSHIRE

Electorate: 528,643

Belper; Bolsover; Derby North; Derby South; High Peak; Ilkeston; South East Derbyshire; West Derbyshire.

Spencer, T. (C)	81,046
Denby, Miss M. J. (Lab)	62,347
Blackburn, D. (L)	15,775
C majority	18,699

Total vote 159,168 (30·1%): C 50·9%; Lab 39·2%; L 9·9%. C maj 11·7%.

DEVON

Electorate: 533,237

Exeter; Honiton; North Devon; Tiverton; Torbay; Totnes; West Devon.

O'Hagan, Lord (C)	127,032
Pinney, A. (L)	41,010
Scott, R. C. J. (Lab)	37,380
C majority	86,022

Total vote 205,422 (38·5%): C 61·8%; L 20·0%; Lab 18·2%. C maj 41·9%.

DURHAM

Electorate: 546,265

Bishop Auckland; Chester-le-Street; Consett; Darlington; Durham; Easington; Houghton-le-Spring; North West Durham.

Boyes, R. (Lab)	81,982
Sheaf, R. (C)	53,043
Foote-Wood, C. (L)	16,094
Lab majority	28,939

Total vote 151,119 (27·7%): Lab 54·2%; C 35·1%; L 10·6. Lab maj 19·1%.

ESSEX NORTH EAST

Electorate: 503,434

Braintree; Colchester; Maldon; Saffron Walden; South East Essex; Southend East; Southend West.

Curry, D. (C)	99,137
O'Brien, C. (Lab)	33,496
Phillips, A. (L)	26,298
Smedley, W. O. (UACM)	4,497
C majority	65,641

Total vote 163,428 (32·5%): C 60·7%; Lab 20·5%; L 16·1%; UACM 2·8%. C maj 40·2%.

ESSEX SOUTH WEST

Electorate: 474,239

Basildon; Brentwood and Ongar; Chelmsford; Epping Forest; Harlow; Thurrock.

Sherlock, A. (C)	78,059
Coughlan, J. P. (Lab)	46,244
Kitching, D. (L)	20,516
C majority	31,815

Total vote 144,819 (30·5%): C 53·9%; Lab 31·9%; L 14·2%. C maj 22·0%.

GREATER MANCHESTER NORTH

Electorate: 502,422

Ashton-under-Lyne; Bury and Radcliffe; Manchester Gorton; Middleton and Prestich; Oldham East; Oldham West; Rochdale; Stalybridge and Hyde.

Castle, Mrs B. A. (Lab)	79,920
Grantham, C. C. (C)	62,450
Steed, M. (L)	16,910
Lab majority	17,470

Total vote 159,280 (31·7%): Lab 50·2%; C 39·2%; L 10·6%. Lab maj 11·0%.

GREATER MANCHESTER SOUTH

Electorate: 498,530

Cheadle; the Manchester seats of Ardwick, Blackley, Central, Moss Side, Openshaw, Withington and Wythenshawe; Stockport North; Stockport South.

Harmar-Nicholls, Lord (C)	70,688
Mills, J. A. D. (Lab)	63,214
Doherty, J. B. (L)	14,869
C majority	7,474

Total vote 148,771 (29·8%): C 47·5%; Lab 42·5%; L 10·0%. C maj 5·0%.

GREATER MANCHESTER WEST

Electorate: 526,602

Altrincham and Sale; Bolton East; Bolton West; Eccles; Farnworth; Leigh; Salford East; Salford West; Stretford.

Hopper, W. (C)	67,127
Nurse, P. (Lab)	66,825
Weddell, E. A. O. G. (L)	21,021
C majority	302

Total vote 154,973 (29·4%): C 43·3%; Lab 43·1%; L 13·6%. C maj 0·2%.

HAMPSHIRE WEST

Electorate: 580,647

Basingstoke; Eastleigh; New Forest; Salisbury; Southampton Itchen; Southampton Test; Winchester.

de Ferranti, B. (C)	114,978
Matthew, J. W. (L)	45,786
Jariwala, P. S. (Lab)	34,472
C majority	69,192

Total vote 195,236 (33·6%): C 58·9%; L 23·5%; Lab 17·7%. C maj 35·4%.

HEREFORD AND WORCESTER

Electorate: 522,406

Bromsgrove and Redditch; Hereford; Kidderminster; Leominster; South Worcestershire; West Gloucestershire; Worcester.

Scott-Hopkins, J. S. R. (C)	106,271
Jones, R. H. J. (Lab)	49,888
Otter, R. G. (L)	25,421
C majority	56,383

Total vote 181,580 (34·8%): C 58·5%; Lab 27·5%; L 14·0%. C maj 31·0%.

HERTFORDSHIRE

Electorate: 524,320

East Hertfordshire; Hertford and Stevenage; St Albans; South Hertfordshire; South West Hertfordshire; Watford; Welwyn and Hatfield.

Praq, D. (C)	97,174
Dore, A. J. K. (Lab)	49,619
Cobbold, D. L. (L)	46,757
C majority	47,555

Total vote 193,550 (36·9%): C 50·2%; Lab 25·6%; L 24·2%. C maj 24·6%.

HUMBERSIDE

Electorate: 510,529

Bridlington; Brigg and Scunthorpe; Haltemprice; Howden; and the three Kingston-upon-Hull seats of Central, East, West.

Battersby, R. (C)	79,551
Wheaton, M. A. (Lab)	56,521
Walker, R. (L)	17,643
C majority	23,010

Total vote 153,715 (30·1%): C 51·8%; Lab 36·8%; L 11·5%. C maj 15·0%.

KENT EAST

Electorate: 559,857

Ashford; Canterbury; Dover and Deal; Faversham Folkestone and Hythe; Maidstone; Thanet East; Thanet West.

Jackson, C. (C)	117,267
Holmes, J. C. M. S. (Lab)	40,060
Morris, A. (L)	20,190
Coulon, D. (NCMR)	3,788
C majority	77,207

Total vote 181,305 (32·4%): C 64·8%; Lab 22·1%; L 11·1%; NCMR 2·1%. C maj 42·6%.

KENT WEST

Electorate: 569,412

Dartford; East Surrey; Gillingham; Gravesend; Rochester and Chatham; Royal Tunbridge Wells; Sevenoaks; Tonbridge and Malling.

Patterson, B. (C)	113,961
Humphries, A. J. (Lab)	46,482
Blow, S. (L)	27,127
C majority	67,479

Total vote 187,570 (32·9%): C 60·8%; Lab 24·8%; L 14·5%. C maj 36·0%.

LANCASHIRE CENTRAL

Electorate: 533,829

Blackpool North; Blackpool South; Chorley; Preston North; Preston South; South Fylde; Westhoughton; Wigan.

Welsh, M. J. (C)	91,355
Taylor, I. J. (Lab)	63,709
Sanders, Rev D. (L)	13,821
C majority	27,646

Total vote 168,885 (31·6%): C 54·1%; Lab 37·7%; L 8·2%. C maj 16·4%.

LANCASHIRE EAST

Electorate: 465,080

Accrington; Blackburn; Burnley; Clitheroe; Darwen; Heywood and Royton; Nelson and Colne; Rossendale.

Kellett-Bowman, T. E. (C)	77,087
Walsh, M. (Lab)	62,729
Easton, P. (L)	12,268
Tyrall, F. (Dem)	2,473
C majority	14,358

Total vote 154,557 (33·2%): C 49·9%; Lab 40·6%; L 7·9%; Dem 1·6%. C maj 9·3%.

LANCASHIRE WEST

Electorate: 557,354

Crosby; Huyton; Ince; Ormskirk; St Helens; Southport; Widnes.

Price, P. N. (C)	79,888
Jeuda, B. S. (Lab)	60,399
Gibb, J. (L)	12,116
Farrell, B. (Ind)	3,486
C majority	19,489

Total vote 155,889 (28·0%): C 51·2%; Lab 38·7% L 7·8%; Ind 2·2%. C maj 12·5%.

LEEDS

Electorate: 478,676

Batley and Morley; the six Leeds seats of East, North East, North West, South, South East and West; Pudsey.

Enright, D. A. (Lab)	62,475
Price, P. C. (C)	54,405
Austick, D. (L)	20,005
Lab majority	8,070

Total vote 136,885 (28·6%): Lab 45·6%; C 39·7%; L 14·6%. Lab maj 5·9%.

LEICESTER

Electorate: 512,809

Carlton; Leicester East; Leicester South; Leicester West; Melton; Newark; Rushcliffe.

Tuckman, F. A. (C)	91,675
Middleton, Rev K. F. (Lab)	57,811
Watson, G. G. (L)	17,027
C majority	33,864

Total vote 166,513 (32·5%): C 55·1%; Lab 34·7%; L 10·2%. C maj 20·3%.

LINCOLNSHIRE

Electorate: 542,558

Gainsborough; Grantham; Grimsby; Holland with Boston; Horncastle; Lincoln; Louth; Rutland and Stamford.

Newton Dunn, W. F. (C)	104,460
James, C. A. (Lab)	44,616
Phillips, C. (L)	20,815
C majority	59,844

Total vote 169,891 (31·3%): C 61·5%; Lab 26·3%; L 12·3%. C maj 35·2%.

LIVERPOOL

Electorate: 462,673

Bootle and the Liverpool seats of Edge Hill, Garston, Kirkdale, Scotland Exchange, Toxteth, Walton, Wavertree, and West Derby.

Hooper, Miss G. (C)	49,646
Harrison, T. J. (Lab)	42,419
Clark, P. (L)	17,650
C majority	7,227

Total vote 109,715 (23·7%): C 45·2%; Lab 38·7%; L 16·1%. C maj 6·6%.

LONDON CENTRAL

Electorate: 512,432

The three Camden seats of Hampstead, Holborn and St Pancras South, and St Pancras North; City of London and Westminster South; City of Westminster, Paddington; City of Westminster, St Marylebone; Hammersmith, Fulham; Hammersmith North; Kensington and Chelsea, Chelsea; Kensington and Chelsea, Kensington.

Nicholson, Sir D. (C)	84,915
Gresham, P. J. (Lab)	45,721
Browne, R. (L)	19,010
Porritt, J. (Ecology)	6,448
C majority	39,194

Total vote 156,094 (30·5%): C 54·4%; Lab 29·3%; L 12·2%; Ecology 4·1%. C maj 25·1%.

LONDON EAST

Electorate: 541,938

Barking; Barking, Dagenham; the three Havering seats of Hornchurch, Romford and Upminster; Newham, North-East; the three Redbridge seats of Ilford North, Ilford South, and Wanstead and Woodford.

Tyrrell, A. R. (C)	77,940
O'Neill, P. D. (Lab)	64,925
Blackburn, D. (L)	16,782
C majority	13,015

Total vote 159,647 (29·5%): C 48·8%; Lab 40·7%; L 10·5%. C maj 8·2%.

LONDON NORTH

Electorate: 523,484

Barnet Finchley; the three Enfield seats of Edmonton, North, Southgate; the three Haringey seats of Hornsey, Tottenham, Wood Green; the three Islington seats of Central, North, and South and Finsbury.

Marshall, J. (C)	74,042
Little, K. W. (Lab)	59,077
Brass, L. S. (L)	15,838
C majority	14,965

Total vote 148,957 (28·5%): C 49·7%; Lab 39·7%; L 10·6%. C maj 10·0%.

LONDON NORTH EAST

Electorate: 518,912

The three Hackney seats of Central, North and Stoke Newington, South and Shoreditch; Newham North-West; Newham South; Tower Hamlets Bethnal Green and Bow; Tower Hamlets Stepney and Poplar; the three Waltham Forest seats of Chingford, Leyton and Walthamstow.

Lomas, A. (Lab)	61,044
Stanbrook, C. (C)	36,200
Bancroft, R. (L)	8,839
Lab majority	24,804

Total vote 106,083 (20·4%): Lab 57·5%; C 34·1%; L 8·3%. Lab maj 23·4%.

LONDON NORTH WEST

Electorate: 506,740

The three Barnet seats of Chipping Barnet, Hendon North, Hendon South; the three Brent seats of East, North and South; the three Harrow seats of Central, East and West.

Bethell, Lord (C)	87,596
Gordon, Mrs M. (Lab)	49,268
Bridge, G. J. (L)	21,618
C majority	38,328

Total vote 158,482 (31·3%): C 55·3%; Lab 31·1%; L 13·6%. C maj 24·2%.

LONDON SOUTH

Electorate: 500,072

The four Croydon seats of Central, North East, North West and South; Merton Mitcham and Morden; Merton Wimbledon; Sutton and Cheam; Sutton Carshalton.

Moorhouse, J. (C)	98,298
Duncan, G. A. (Lab)	44,967
Pitt, W. H. (L)	23,526
C majority	53,331

Total vote 166,791 (33·4%): C 58·9%; Lab 27·0%; L 14·1%. C maj 32·0%.

LONDON SOUTH EAST

Electorate: 499,315

The three Bexley seats of Bexleyheath, Erith and Crayford, Sidcup; the four Bromley seats of Beckenham, Chislehurst, Orpington, Ravensbourne; and two of the Greenwich seats — Woolwich East and Woolwich West.

Rhys Williams, Sir B. (C)	94,180
Bundred, S. (Lab)	54,798
Fryer, J. (L)	21,494
Turner, W. E. (AWE)	890
C majority	39,382

Total vote 171,362 (34·3%): C 56·0%; Lab 32·0%; L 12·5%; AWE 0·5%. C maj 23·0%.

LONDON SOUTH INNER

Electorate: 508,306

Greenwich; Lambeth Norwood; Lambeth Streatham; the three Lewisham seats of Deptford, East and West; the three Southwark seats of Bermondsey, Dulwich, Peckham.

Balfe, R. (Lab)	67,830
Butterfill, J. (C)	60,652
Insole, R. (L)	10,509
Lab majority	7,178

Total vote 138,991 (27·3%): Lab 48·8%; C 43·6%; L 7·6%. Lab maj 5·2%.

LONDON SOUTH WEST

Electorate: 511,719

Kingston upon Thames; Kingston upon Thames Surbiton; Lambeth Central; Lambeth Vauxhall; Richmond upon Thames Richmond; Richmond upon Thames Twickenham; the four Wandsworth seats of Battersea North, Battersea South, Putney, Tooting.

Roberts, Miss S. (C)	83,498
Hart, A. (Lab)	51,742
Fogarty, B. (L)	21,251
Varah, Rev C. (Ind)	3,613
Eustace, S. S. (EFP)	497
C majority	31,756

Total vote 160,601 (31·4%): C 52·0%; Lab 32·2%; L 13·2%; Ind 2·2%; EFP 0·3%. C maj 19·8%.

The election of Miss Roberts was subsequently declared invalid because of her membership of the Occupational Pensions Board, from which she resigned. A by-election was held in September 1979.

LONDON WEST

Electorate: 530,687

The three Ealing seats of Acton, North, Southall; the three Hillingdon seats of Hayes and Harlington, Ruislip-Northwood, Uxbridge; and two Hounslow seats of Brentford and Isleworth, Feltham and Heston.

Hord, B. (C)	89,433
Daly, J. (Lab)	67,193
Cohen, R. (L)	17,077
Ali, T. (IM)	1,635
C majority	22,240

Total vote 175,338 (33·0%): C 51·0%; Lab 38·3%; L 9·7%; IM 0·9%. C maj 12·7%.

MIDLANDS CENTRAL

Electorate: 480,949

The four Coventry seats of North East, North West, South East, South West; Solihull; Stratford-on-Avon; Warwick and Leamington.

de Courcy Ling, J. (C)	94,606
Hunt, D. V. (Lab)	46,557
Davis, Miss V. M. (L)	15,859
Benfield, K. M. (Ecology)	6,380
C majority	48,049

Total vote 163,402 (34·0%): C 57·9%; Lab 28·5%; L 9·7%; Ecology 3·9%. C maj 29·4%.

MIDLANDS EAST

Electorate: 476,743

Blaby; Bosworth; Loughborough; Meriden; Nuneaton; Rugby.

Taylor, J. M. (C)	85,098
O'Sullivan, T. (Lab)	53,935
Gopsill, G. A. (L)	14,819
C majority	31,163

Total vote 153,852 (32·3%): C 55·3%; Lab 35·1%; L 9·6%. C maj 20·3%.

MIDLANDS WEST

Electorate: 541,295

Dudley East; Dudley West; Halesowen and Stourbridge; Walsall North; Walsall South; and the three Wolverhampton seats of North East, South East, South West.

Simmonds, R. J. (C)	69,916
Randall, S. J. (Lab)	68,024
Court, A. W. G. (L)	9,936
C majority	1,892

Total vote 147,876 (27·3%): C 47·3%; Lab 46·0%; L 6·7%. C maj 1·3%.

NORFOLK

Electorate: 504,605

Norfolk North; Norfolk North West; Norwich North; Norwich South; Norfolk South; Norfolk South West; Yarmouth.

Howell, P. (C)	102,981
Gray, H. (Lab)	52,406
Baxter, B. (L)	16,805
C majority	50,575

Total vote 172,192 (34·1%): C 59·8%; Lab 30·4%; L 9·8%. C maj 29·4%.

NORTHAMPTONSHIRE

Electorate: 529,239

Aylesbury; Buckingham; Daventry; Harborough; Kettering; Northampton North; Northampton South.

Simpson, A. M. H. (C)	103,638
Gordon, A. (Lab)	47,029
Crooks, S. M. (L)	23,134
C majority	56,609

Total vote 173,801 (32·8%): C 59·6%; Lab 27·1%; L 13·3%. C maj 32·6%.

NORTHUMBRIA

Electorate: 521,530

Berwick-upon-Tweed; Blyth; Hexham; Morpeth; the four Newcastle upon Tyne seats of Central, East, North, West; Wallsend.

Adam, G. J. (Lab)	75,172
Weait, J. (C)	67,066
Scott, G. (L)	25,713
Lab majority	8,106

Total vote 167,951 (32·2%): Lab 44·8%; C 39·9%; L 15·3%. Lab maj 4·8%.

NOTTINGHAM

Electorate: 506,018

Ashfield; Bassetlaw; Beeston; Mansfield; the three Nottingham seats of East, North, West.

Gallagher, M. (Lab)	66,279
Taylor, J. D. (C)	64,728
Chambers, D. J. (L)	13,515
Lab majority	1,551

Total vote 209,250 (28·6%): Lab 31·7%; C 30·9%; L 6·5%. Lab maj 0·7%.

SALOP AND STAFFORD

Electorate: 488,471

Ludlow; Newcastle under Lyme; Oswestry; Shrewsbury; South West Staffordshire; Stafford and Stone; The Wrekin.

Prout, C. J. (C)	90,545
Hopkins, J. S. (Lab)	45,547
Robson, T. G. (L)	16,469
Larney, Mrs P. J. E. (Ind C)	4,804
C majority	44,998

Total vote 157,365 (32·2%): C 57·5%; Lab 28·9%; L 10·5%; Ind C 3·1%. C maj 28·6%.

SHEFFIELD

Electorate: 518,713

Chesterfield; North East Derbyshire; the six Sheffield seats of Attercliffe, Brightside, Hallam, Heeley, Hillsborough, Park.

Caborn, R. G. (Lab)	77,219
Batiste, S. (C)	64,157
Salt, K. (L)	10,951
Lab majority	13,062

Total vote 152,327 (29·4%): Lab 50·7%; C 42·1%; L 7·2%. Lab maj 8·6%.

SOMERSET

Electorate: 547,844

Bath; Bridgwater; North Somerset; Taunton; Wells; Weston-super-Mare; Yeovil.

Warner, Sir F. (C)	120,057
Butt Philip, A. A. S. (L)	48,600
Lovelace, D. R. (Lab)	41,931
C majority	71,457

Total vote 210,588 (38·4%): C 57·0%; L 23·1%; Lab 19·9%. C maj 33·9%.

STAFFORDSHIRE EAST

Electorate: 512,291

Burton; Cannock; Leek; Lichfield and Tamworth; the three Stoke-on-Trent seats of Central, North, South.

Moreland, R. J. (C)	70,836
Tracey, M. P. (Lab)	64,230
Hargreaves, B. (L)	10,409
C majority	6,606

Total vote 145,475 (28·4%): C 48·7%; Lab 44·2%; L 7·2%. C maj 4·5%.

SUFFOLK

Electorate: 521,751

Bury St Edmunds; Eye; Harwich; Ipswich; Lowestoft; Sudbury and Woodbridge.

Turner, A. E. (C)	101,966
Manley, R. (Lab)	45,642
Gladwyn, Lord (L)	21,131
C majority	56,324

Total vote 168,739 (32·3%): C 60·4%; Lab 27·0%; L 12·5%. C maj 33·4%.

SURREY

Electorate: 553,601

Chertsey and Walton; Dorking; Epsom and Ewell; Esher; Guildford; North West Surrey; Reigate; Woking.

Douro, Marquess of (C)	113,786
Mayhew, C. P. (L)	62,272
Cox, J. (Lab)	28,897
Heims, P. A. (IACM)	4,450
C majority	51,514

Total vote 209,405 (37·8%): C 54·3%; L 29·7%; Lab 13·8%; IACM 2·1%. C maj 24·6%.

SUSSEX EAST

Electorate: 535,564

Brighton Kemptown; Brighton Pavilion; Eastbourne; East Grinstead; Hastings; Hove; Lewes; Rye.

Stewart-Clark, Sir J. (C)	123,506
Stevens, A. S. J. (Lab)	33,581
Moore, R. G. (L)	30,847
C majority	89,925

Total vote 187,934 (35·1%): C 65·7%; Lab 17·9%; L 16·4%. C maj 47·8%.

SUSSEX WEST

Electorate: 563,865

Arundel; Chichester; Havant and Waterloo; Horsham and Crawley; Mid-Sussex; Shoreham; Worthing.

Seligman, M. (C)	131,077
Walsh, Dr J. M. M. (L)	35,593
Whipp, B. J. (Lab)	26,894
Vince, L. N. (UACM)	5,303
C majority	95,484

Total vote 198,867 (35·3%): C 65·9%; L 17·9%; Lab 13·5%; UACM 2·7%. C maj 48·0%.

THAMES VALLEY

Electorate: 528,167

Beaconsfield; Chesham and Amersham; Eton and Slough; Spelthorne; Windsor and Maidenhead; Wokingham; Wycombe.

Elles, Lady (C)	110,788
Ennals, J. A. F. (Lab)	39,865
Fogarty, M. (L)	24,877
C majority	70,923

Total vote 175,530 (33·2%): C 63·1%; Lab 22·7%; L 14·2%. C maj 40·4%.

TYNE SOUTH AND WEAR

Electorate: 503,764

Blaydon; Gateshead East; Gateshead West; Jarrow; South Shields; Sunderland North; Sunderland South; Tynemouth.

Quin, Miss J. G. (Lab)	73,936
Landau, J. (C)	67,475
Freitag, P. (L)	8,958
Lab majority	6,461

Total vote 150,369 (29·8%): Lab 49·2%; C 44·9%; L 6·0%. Lab maj 4·3%.

UPPER THAMES

Electorate: 527,786

Abingdon; Devizes; Henley; Newbury; Reading North; Reading South; Swindon.

Jackson, P. (C)	103,488
Gray, P. H. (Lab)	39,900
Ainslie, J. (L)	30,907
C majority	63,588

Total vote 174,295 (33·0%): C 59·4%; Lab 22·9%; L 17·7%. C maj 36·5%.

WESSEX

Electorate: 555,098

Bournemouth East; Bournemouth West; Christchurch and Lymington; North Dorset; Poole; South Dorset; Westbury; West Dorset.

Spicer, J. W. (C)	130,744
Goss, J. M. (L)	42,910
Duncan, W. M. (Lab)	31,220
Thynn, A. (WREF)	1,706
C majority	87,834

Total vote 368,544 (37·2%): C 63·3%; L 20·8%; Lab 15·1%; WREF 0·8%. C maj 42·5%.

WIGHT AND HAMPSHIRE EAST

Electorate: 575,991

Aldershot; Fareham; Farnham; Gosport; Isle of Wight; Petersfield; Portsmouth North; Portsmouth South.

Johnson, S. P. (C)	128,414
Seear, Lady (L)	35,248
Bennett, L. F. (Lab)	34,901
C majority	93,166

Total vote 198,563 (34·5%): C 64·7%; L 17·8%; Lab 17·6%. C maj 46·9%.

YORKSHIRE NORTH

Electorate: 483,639

Barkston Ash; Goole; Harrogate; Ripon; Skipton; Thirsk and Malton; York.

Balfour, N. R. (C)	98,464
Singleton, F. B. (Lab)	41,408
Brooks, Mrs K. C. (L)	26,814
C majority	57,056

Total vote 166,684 (34·5%): C 59·1%; Lab 24·8%; L 16·1%. C maj 34·2%.

YORKSHIRE SOUTH

Electorate: 530,714

Barnsley; Dearne Valley; Doncaster; Don Valley; Penistone; Rotherham; Rother Valley.

Key, B. M. (Lab)	83,490
Robinson, M. N. F. (C)	46,656
Capstick, W. (L)	13,025
Lab majority	36,834

Total vote 143,171 (27·0%): Lab 58·3%; C 32·6%; L 9·1%. Lab maj 25·7%.

YORKSHIRE SOUTH WEST

Electorate: 501,478

Colne Valley; Dewsbury; Hemsworth; Huddersfield East; Huddersfield West; Normanton; Pontefract and Castleford; Wakefield.

Megahy, T. (Lab)	75,473
Chambers, Miss J. F. (C)	52,157
Waudby, Mrs P. (L)	17,850
Lab majority	23,316

Total vote 145,480 (29·0%): Lab 51·9%; C 35·9%; L 12·3%. Lab maj 16·0%.

YORKSHIRE WEST

Electorate: 497,380

Bradford North; Bradford South; Bradford West; Brighouse and Spenborough; Halifax; Keighley; Shipley; Sowerby.

Seal, B. H. (Lab)	76,552
St Oswald, Lord (C)	73,555
Cherry, J. M. S. (L)	15,460
Lab majority	2,997

Total vote 165,567 (33·3%): Lab 46·2%; C 44·4%; L 9·3%. Lab maj 1·8%.

GLASGOW

Electorate: 534,414

The Glasgow seats opf Cathcart, Central, Craigton, Garscadden, Govan, Hillhead, Kelvingrove, Maryhill, Pollok, Provan, Queen's Park, Shettleston, Springburn.

Buchan, Mrs J. O. (Lab)	73,846
Vaughan, Mrs B. (C)	41,144
Leslie, G. (Scot Nat)	24,776
Attwooll, Miss E. (L)	11,073
Lab majority	32,702

Total vote 150,839 (28·2%): Lab 49·0%; C 27·3%; Scot Nat 16·4%; L 7·3%. Lab maj 21·7%.

HIGHLANDS AND ISLANDS

Electorate: 298,802

Orkney and Shetland; Western Isles; Caithness and Sutherland; Ross and Cromarty; Inverness; Moray and Nairn; Banff; Argyll.

Ewing, Mrs W. M. (Scot Nat)	39,991
Johnston, D. R. (L)	36,109
Joughin, M. (C)	30,776
Watson, J. G. (Lab)	10,846
Scot Nat majority	3,882

Total vote 117,722 (39·4%): Scot Nat 34·0%; L 30·7%; C 26·1%; Lab 9·2%. Scot Nat maj 3·3%.

LOTHIANS

Electorate: 537,420

Midlothians; West Lothian; the Edinburgh seats of Central, East, Leith, North, Pentlands, South, West.

Dalziel, I. (C)	66,761
Mackie, A. A. (Lab)	61,180
Stevenson, D. (Scot Nat)	29,935
Smith, R. L. (L)	29,518
C majority	5,581

Total vote 187,394 (34·9%): C 35·6%; Lab 32·6%; Scot Nat 16·0%; L 15·8%. C maj 3·0%.

SCOTLAND MID AND FIFE

Electorate: 538,483

Central Fife; Dunfermline; East Fife; Kirkcaldy; Clackmannan and East Stirlingshire; West Stirlingshire; Stirling, Falkirk and Grangemouth; Kinross and West Perthshire; Perth and East Perthshire.

Purvis, J. (C)	66,255
Panko, Mrs M. (Lab)	58,768
McIntyre, Dr R. D. (Scot Nat)	45,426
Calder, J. M. (L)	18,112
C majority	7,487

Total vote 188,561 (35·0%): C 35·1%; Lab 31·2%; Scot Nat 24·1%; L 9·6%. C maj 4·0%.

SCOTLAND NORTH EAST

Electorate: 481,680

East Aberdeenshire; West Aberdeenshire; Aberdeen North; Aberdeen South; North Angus and Mearns; South Angus; Dundee West; Dundee East.

Provan, J. (C)	51,930
Mackie of Banshie, Lord (L)	38,516
Clyne, D. E. (Lab)	38,139
Bell, C. (Scot Nat)	28,886
C majority	13,414

Total vote 57,471 (32·7%): C 33·0%; L 24·5%; Lab 24·2%; Scot Nat 18·3%. C maj 8·5%.

SCOTLAND SOUTH

Electorate: 450,761

Berwick and East Lothian; Roxburgh, Selkirk and Peebles; Dumfries; Galloway; South Ayrshire; Ayr; Central Ayrshire; Lanark.

Hutton, A. (C)	66,816
Foy, P. N. (Lab)	43,145
MacGibbon, I. (Scot Nat)	28,694
Wallace, J. (L)	16,825
C majority	23,671

Total vote 155,480 (34·5%): C 43·0%; Lab 27·7%; Scot Nat 18·5%; L 10·8%. C maj 15·2%.

STRATHCLYDE EAST

Electorate: 463,656

Bothwell; East Kilbride; Kilmarnock; Hamilton; North Lanarkshire; Rutherglen; Coatbridge and Airdrie; Motherwell and Wishaw.

Collins, K. D. (Lab)	72,263
Carse, Miss M. (C)	41,482
Murray, G. (Scot Nat)	21,013
Watts, Dr D. (L)	10,325
Lab majority	30,781

Total vote 145,083 (31·3%): Lab 49·8%; C 28·6%; Scot Nat 14·5%; L 7·1%. Lab maj 21·2%.

STRATHCLYDE WEST

Electorate: 495,799

East Renfrewshire; West Renfrewshire; Greenock and Port Glasgow; Paisley; East Dunbartonshire; Central Dunbartonshire; West Dunbartonshire; Bute and North Ayrshire.

Fergusson, A. (C)	65,608
Friel, Miss V. (Lab)	63,781
Slesser, C. G. M. (Scot Nat)	29,115
Fraser, T. R. L. (L)	17,995
C majority	1,827

Total vote 176,499 (35·6%): C 37·2%; Lab 36·1%; Scot Nat 16·5%; L 10·2%. C maj 1·0%.

MID AND WEST WALES

Electorate: 489,816

Cardigan; Brecon and Radnor; Pembroke; Carmarthen; Llanelli; Gower; Swansea East; Swansea West.

Clwyd Roberts, Mrs A. (Lab)	77,474
Lloyd, D. G. (C)	67,226
Moseley, H. (Pl Cymru)	22,730
Thomas, C. (L)	17,628
Windsor-Williams, H. D. (Ind)	1,826
Lab majority	10,248

Total vote 186,884 (38·2%): Lab 41·5%; C 36·0%; Pl Cymru 12·2%; L 9·4%; Ind 1·0%. Lab maj 5·5%.

NORTH WALES

Electorate: 493,181

Anglesey; Caernarvon; Conway; Denbigh; West Flint; East Flint; Merioneth; Wrexham; Montgomery.

Brooks, Miss B. (C)	74,173
Dillon, T. A. (Lab)	46,627
Jones, I. W. (Pl Cymru)	34,171
Wyn-Ellis, Miss N. (L)	21,989
C majority	27,546

Total vote 176,960 (35·9%): C 41·9%; Lab 26·3%; Pl Cymru 19·3%; L 12·4%. C maj 15·6%.

SOUTH WALES

Electorate: 535,752

Neath; Aberavon; Ogmore; Pontypridd; Barry; four Cardiff seats of North West, North, West, South East.

Griffiths, W. J. (Lab)	77,784
Terlezki, S. (C)	66,852
Greaves, J. (L)	17,811
Williams, D. J. (Pl Cymru)	14,029
Lab majority	10,932

Total vote 176,476 (32·9%): Lab 44·1%; C 37·9%; L 10·1%; Pl Cymru 7·9%. Lab maj 6·2%.

SOUTH EAST WALES

Electorate: 545,152

Rhondda; Aberdare; Merthyr Tydfil; Caerphilly; Ebbw Vale; Bedwellty; Abertillery; Pontypool; Newport; Monmouth.

Rogers, A. R. (Lab)	93,093
Robinson, Mrs A. (C)	51,478
Jones, M. D. (Pl Cymru)	12,469
Pope, A. (L)	10,534
Kelly, B. (Ind)	2,182
Lab majority	41,615

Total vote 169,756 (31·1%): Lab 54·8%; C 30·3%; Pl Cymru 7·3%; L 6·2%; Ind 1·3%. Lab maj 24·5%.

UNITED KINGDOM (excluding Northern Ireland)

	C	Lab	L	Scot Nat Pl Cymru	Others	Totals
ENGLAND	5,817,991	3,536,301	1,444,203	—	86,310	10,884,805
% turnout	53·5	32·5	13·3	—	0·8	—
Number of MEPs	*54	12	—	—	—	66
SCOTLAND	430,772	421,968	178,473	247,836	—	1,279,049
% turnout	33·7	33·0	14·0	19·4	—	—
Number of MEPs	5	2	—	1	—	8
WALES	259,729	294,978	67,962	83,399	4,008	710,076
% turnout	36·6	41·5	9·6	11·7	0·6	—
Number of MEPs	1	3	—	—	—	4
TOTALS	6,508,492	4,253,247	1,690,638	331,235	90,318	12,873,930
% turnout	50·6	33·0	13·1	2·6	0·7	—
Number of MEPs	*60	17	—	1	—	78

*The election of Miss Shelagh Roberts as Conservative MEP for London, South-West, was declared invalid because of her membership, at the time she stood in the elections, of the Occupational Pension Board. A by-election was held in September, 1979.

United Kingdom by-election: September 20, 1979

LONDON SOUTH WEST

Roberts, Miss S. (C)	41,096
Hart, A. (Lab)	32,632
Mayhew, C. (L)	23,842
Smedley, O. (Anti-CM and Free Trade Party)	1,830
Massey, D. (UDP)	305
C majority	8,464

Total vote 99,705 (19·3%): C 41·2%; Lab 32·7%; L 23·9%; Anti-CM 1·8%; UDP 0·3%. C maj 8·5%.

NORTHERN IRELAND

Electorate	1,029,490	
Total Poll	586,060	56·9%
Spoiled Votes	13,821	2·4% of poll
Total Valid Poll	572,239	55·6%
Seats	3	
Quota	143,060	
Candidates	13	

First preferences	Number	Percentage	Seats
Alliance	39,026	6·81	—
Dem U	170,688	29·82	1
Independent	33,962	5·93	—
Liberal	932	0·16	—
Off UU	125,169	21·87	1
Repub Clubs	4,418	0·77	—
SDLP	140,622	24·57	1
UCC	9,383	1·64	—
UL	6,122	1·06	—
UPNI	3,712	0·64	—
UU	38,198	6·67	—

Voting system: PR, using single transferable vote in multi-member constituencies.

The quota is calculated by dividing the total number of valid votes by the number of seats plus one, and then adding one to the result.

The following were elected:

Rev. Ian Paisley, Dem U
John Hume, SDLP
John Taylor, Off UU

Vote analysis (elected members):

	Votes	Multiple of quota
Paisley	170,688	1·19
Hume	140,622	0·98
Taylor	68,185	0·47

Abbreviations include: Dem U – Democratic Unionist; Off UU – Official Ulster Unionist; Repub Clubs – Republican Clubs; SDLP – Social Democratic and Labour Party; UCC – United Community Campaign; UL – United Labour; UPNI – Unionist Party of Northern Ireland; UU – Ulster Unionist.

Details of 6 counts in Northern Ireland

NAME	PARTY	1st Count	2nd Count		3rd Count		4th Count		5th Count		6th Count	
		Votes	Transfer of Paisley's Surplus	Result	Transfer of Bleakley's, Brennan's, Cummings', Devlin's, Donnelly's and Murray's Votes	Result	Transfer of Devlin-McAliskey's Votes	Result	Transfer of Napier's Votes	Result	Transfer of West's Votes	Result
Bleakley, David	UCC	9,383	+ 218	9,601	−9,601	—	—	—	—	—	—	—
Brennan, Brian	Repub Clubs	3,258	+ 5	3,263	−3,263	—	—	—	—	—	—	—
Cummings, Eddie	UPNI	3,712	+ 125	3,837	−3,837	—	—	—	—	—	—	—
Devlin, Paddy	UL	6,122	+ 24	6,146	−6,146	—	—	—	—	—	—	—
Devlin-McAliskey, Bernadette	Ind	33,969	+ 7	33,976	+2,130	36,106	−36,106	—	—	—	—	—
Donnelly, Francis	RCMP	1,160	+ 4	1,164	−1,164	—	—	—	—	—	—	—
Hume, John	SDLP	140,622	+ 55	140,677	+5,396	*146,073*	—	*146,073*	—	*146,073*	—	*146,073*
Kilfedder, Jim	UU	38,198	+12,424	50,622	+3,364	53,986	+ 638	54,624	+14,760	69,384	+ 3,174	72,558
Murray, James	Liberal	932	+ 16	948	− 948	—	—	—	—	—	—	—
Napier, Oliver	Alliance	39,026	+ 378	39,404	+6,299	45,703	+ 5,561	51,264	−51,264	—	—	—
Paisley, Ian	Dem U	*170,688*	−27,628	*143,060*	—	*143,060*	—	*143,060*	—	*143,060*	—	*143,060*
Taylor, John	Off UU	68,185	+ 9,044	77,229	+2,979	80,208	+ 198	80,406	+16,001	96,407	+57,059	*153,466*
West, Harry	Off UU	56,984	+ 4,179	61,163	+ 789	61,952	+ 188	62,140	+ 3,776	65,916	−65,916	—
Non-transferable:			1,149	1,149	+4,003	5,152	+29,521	34,673	+16,727	51,400	+ 5,683	57,083

Candidatures reflected party attitudes

The choice of British candidates made by groups of constituency officials and activists for the European direct elections may be fairly reckoned to tell a story about the socio-economic composition of the Conservative and Labour parties in Britain, and also about the political division in Britain on commitment to membership of the European Community.

Forced to take a view on the so-called "dual mandate" well ahead of the Westminster general election that took place on May 3, Conservative leaders did nothing to encourage candidates to try to win seats in both Parliaments, but left MPs and their Westminster constituency associations to agree between themselves. In the event, four Westminster MPs were adopted as European candidates, along with five Peers (three of whom had served as nominated MEPs).

Mr James Scott-Hopkins, however, who had been named by Mrs Thatcher as leader-designate of the Europe Conservative Group after Mr Paul Channon had failed to find a European constituency, resigned his Westminster seat to stand on June 7 for Hereford and Worcester. Avoidance of a rigid rule against the dual mandate has ensured that the Conservative Group will benefit in the new European Parliament from experience gained since Peter Kirk led the first nominated delegation to Strasbourg in January, 1973.

Labour's national executive committee, partly out of anti-Community motives and partly out of a painful experience of governing in a "hung" Parliament at Westminster since March, 1974, forbade the dual mandate, and any Westminster MPs wishing to stand in the European direct elections was required to retire at the next domestic general election. Sir Geoffrey de Freitas, throughout the post-war years a considerable political figure in Europe, and Dr Colin Phipps, a highly qualified oil expert and farmer, made themselves available for choice as European candidates, and neither was selected. Nor was a single peer who had experience of the European Parliament, although one or two, like Lord Bruce of Donington, had been leading members of main committees.

Consequently, the 78 Labour candidates standing in British seats included not one who had ever served in the European Parliament, and the only popularly familiar name in the party list was that of Mrs Barbara Castle, former Cabinet Minister in Sir Harold Wilson's administrations and an anti-Community member of the party's national executive committee. Nevertheless, the Labour roll-call proved to be less resolutely anti-European Community than had been expected; it included, for instance, the name of Dr Ernest Wistrich, who as the director of the European Movement in Britain has to be counted among the most able and zealous of Europeanists since the early days of the campaign for United Kingdom entry to the Community.

For obvious reason, Conservative leaders and party managers found it much easier than Labour to draw up a panel of European candidates who, even after taking the hurdle of constituency selection meetings, would make a balanced team matching the job specification for work in the European Parliament and on its new committees: industrialists, farmers, lawyers, linguists, and so on. In the event, 20 of the 78 Conservative candidates were directors or had City connections; 11 were professional men or executives; nine were farmers and nine were journalists or broadcasters; six were lawyers; and no fewer than seven were employed by the European Community in or outside Britain.

The list included only two university lecturers and one teacher. That stood in sharp contrast with the Labour list, where 32 out of 78 candidates were officially described as teachers. Only five Labour candidates appeared to be manual workers, although seven others were in political or trade union jobs. Business and management produced 10 Labour names, and the professions seven. But Labour also had a clergyman standing, and one housewife among eight women. (The Conservative constituencies selected 10 women, some for manifestly winnable or even blue chip seats.)

The Conservative list of candidates for Europe included several men of mark and name in and outside politics. Among them were Sir Peter Vanneck, a former Lord Mayor of the City of London; Sir Fred Catherwood, one-time chief economic advisor to the Labour Government's Department of Economic Affairs and director general of the National Economic Development Council; Sir Henry Plumb, for nearly a decade president of the National Farmers' Union and vice-president of the International Federation of Agricultural Producers; Sir Fred Warner, former Ambassador to Tokyo and the United Nations; Mr Basil de Ferranti, deputy chairman of Ferranti Ltd and immediate past president of the European Economic and Social Committee in the Community; and Mr Madron Seligman, marketing director for a firm with 60 world-wide companies and the oldest Oxford friend of Mr Edward Heath.

All in all, the rival lists of candidatures clearly reflected the Conservative acceptance of the United Kingdom's destiny within the European Community and the Labour Party's ambivalence on such questions as Westminster sovereignty, European big business, and economic self decision.

The following is an analysis of the professions and trades of the Conservative and Labour candidates, although the qualification must be made that some could be placed in more than one group:

Conservative: Company directors or City of London, 20; journalists and communicators, nine; House of Commons, four; Community officials, seven; professional and executive, 11; House of Lords, five; law, six; Civil Service and administration, two; farmers, nine; lecturers, two; management consultant, one; medical practitioner, one; teacher, one; hotelier, one.

Labour: Teachers (university and other), 32; engineers, three; politics and trade unions, seven; business and management, 10; social services administration, three; professional, seven; manual workers, five; local government or Civil Service, three; journalism and communications, four; housewife, psychologist, clergyman, and self employed, one each.

N.B. In the European elections, unlike Westminster elections, members of the House of Lords and clergymen of Established Churches qualified to stand.

The first session at Strasbourg

National parties adjust to multinational influences

When the directly-elected European Parliament met for the first time in the Palais de l'Europe, Strasbourg, on July 17, 1979, the official agenda comprised a considered mixture of ceremony and down-to-earth practical business such as the election of a President and 12 vice-presidents and a wrangle over the size of party groups. Not surprisingly, though, in the event, rather fewer than 410 MEPs who had the added authority of democratic election, and coming fresh from the hustings, were above all set on showing that it was to be a Parliament with a difference by forming new alliances, by establishing the balance of power in the Chamber, by renaming old groups and creating a new one, by disputing the chairmanship of committees, and by democratic exploitation of the Parliament's procedural rules.

The opening week, therefore, showed democracy in action. From the sublime sonority of the ceremonial, there was a collapse into procedural wrangles that again and again brought an interruption of the first plenary session; and some of more than 700 journalists in attendance took their chance to show the Parliament in a poor light, not least the British journalists, who chose to forget that Westminster sometimes goes about its work in a mysterious or infuriating way.

The main groups had met in Luxembourg the preceding week to settle their tactics. The Christian Democratic Group, with 108 members in the chamber, decided to take the name of the European People's Party. The British Conservative Group, by a majority in private session of 48 votes to 10, announced that they would be known in the Parliament as the European Democratic Group. That name ran in line with Mrs Thatcher's decision some time ago to join in the creation of the European Democratic Union, in which Right-Centre parties in and outside the EEC could combine against parties of the Left, but there were a few MEPs in the group who, having been elected as Conservatives a month before and feeling no shame about the word, resented a tactical dissociation from their party heritage.

Of course, tactically the argument for a change of name is grounded on the fact that the word "Conservative" has no place in continental politics, and would be a deterrent to any Right-Centre continental politician looking for friends and a party home, much as the name Christian Democrat has overtones that put off the Conservatives from more than loose ad hoc alliances within the European Parliament.

The changes of name may be reckoned, therefore, to be one of the early adjustments of national parties to multinational influences, and probably ought to be welcomed for that reason at any rate by convinced Europeanists. But certainly a Conservative politician of long experience, like Lord Harmar-Nicholls, and his nine dissident colleagues, thought it unwise to fight elections and by-elections under one name and operate as a party group under another. As critics of the change argued, Conservatives in the European Parliament should take care to ensure that the policies they promoted were consistent with Conservative Government policies at Westminster.

After the fairly predictable renaming of two of the three largest groups in the Parliament, there came the unexpected formation of a new group made up of minor parties and independents under the formal name of the Group for the Technical Coordination and Defence of Groups and non-attached members. It consists of anti-Market Danes, Italians, Belgian Francophones, and Volksunie, a dozen strong. The portents became clear during the first Strasbourg session.

Minor parties and independents with strong national or even nationalist interests had combined to win the marked parliamentary benefits of recognition as a group, with consequent facilities, finance, and membership of the Parliament's managerial bureau. They made it their first task to obstruct any attempt by the larger groups to raise the membership qualification for the recognition of a parliamentary group after the doubling of membership by direct elections, and under the leadership of Sgr Marco Pannella, a lawyer and journalist who founded the Italian Radical Party, they gave early warning during the week that they were masters of the rule book and parliamentary filibustering.

Moreover, some of the group appear to have an interest in reducing the new Parliament to impotence, or obstructing its work. Some of the old parliamentary hands, who provide the element of continuity between the old Parliament and the new, foresaw that Sgr Pannella and his friends would be the awkward squad that every democratic forum needs, or at any rate gets.

There were other changes that, in effect, revised the result of the direct elections between June 7–10. M François Mitterand, leader of the French Socialists, formally withdrew and was replaced by another name from the Socialist list; Mr Gaston Thorn, the former Prime Minister of Luxembourg, resigned to join in attempts to form a new Luxembourg Government; and Mr Finn Lynge, a former Catholic priest and now the Siumut party MEP for Greenland, with a commitment to carry his country out of the Community, joined the Socialist Group, raising the group's total membership to 112 compared with the European People's Party (or Christian Democrat) tally of 108.

Miss Shelagh Roberts, the British Conservative whose election for London South-West had been declared void on the technicality that she sat at the time on the Occupational Pensions Board, did not take her seat, and the British Conservative strength was thereby reduced to 59, with the support of three Danes and one Official Ulster Unionist. A by-election in London South-West was held in September, 1979.

Mrs Winifred Ewing, of the Scottish National Party, who served in the defunct nominated Parliament as a very active independent, decided to accept an invitation to join the Chirac Gaullists who mainly constitute the European Progressive Democrats Group, although Irish and Danish members are included. She explained that her duty was "to protect the interests of my vast constituency, the Highlands and Islands of Scotland, the largest in Europe, the size of Belgium, and suffering from regional problems of all kinds". To do that in the enlarged Parliament she had to belong to a group, with the advantages that would bring, including membership of the Parliament's regional committee. She was promptly elected one of the Group's vice-chairmen.

Mr Thomas Maher, a farmer's leader from the Republic of Ireland who was elected as an Independent, made a similar decision. He attached himself to the Liberal Group, although he explained that he did not necessarily commit his votes.

Such are examples of the changes in group names and group affiliations that have already occurred as the new European Parliament lifts off from its launching pad, and perhaps it is needful to warn, in a reference book, that similar changes may occur during the five-year life of the Parliament. Where the list system operates, MEPs may resign to go into national governments or for other reasons, and the next name will be taken from the list to replace them. On a fixed-term election MEPs may even change party or group allegiances, and there will be little that can be done about it. In Britain, of course, resignation or death of a MEP will necessitate a by-election on the first-past-the-post electoral system, although a British MEP could leave his Group and not have to resign.

One of the first lessons of direct elections between June 7–10 was quickly confirmed by the inaugural meeting of the Parliament: the Right-Centre parties and groups (the European People's Party or Christian Democrats, the European Democrats or British Conservatives, the Liberal and Democrat Group, and the Progressive Democrats or Gaullists and allies), with more than 250 out of 410 seats or more than 60 per cent., could in combination easily swamp the largest single group, the Socialists, with their 112 seats. (The Socialist Group, incidentally, alone covers all the countries of the Nine.)

The "anti-Marketeers" of the British Labour Party who have held for 20 years that the Six and then the Nine would work against the Left, through a Right-wing Parliament, multinational bureaucracy, and multinational industry, may think that their fears have been fulfilled. Such thinking played a part in the Socialist Group's decision to challenge the election of Mme Simone Veil, the French Giscardian candidate in the election who joined the Liberal Group, to the presidency.

Leaders of the Groups in the outgoing Parliament, preparing for their successors, had provisionally encouraged the Liberals to expect the presidency, and Mme Veil, alike for personal and political reasons, had to be reckoned an extremely strong candidate. Her chances improved when the British Conservatives decided not to run in competition, in spite of some backbench pressure that a "marker" ought to be put down. On the other hand, the Gaullists continued their dispute with President Giscard d'Estaing by fielding a Chirac candidate, apparently to show that Mme Veil, the former Giscardian Minister, would need their votes to receive an absolute majority of the votes cast.

In the event, there were five candidates: Mme Veil, Sgr Mario Zagari (Socialist), Sgr Giorgio Amendola (Communist), M Christian de la Malene (Gaullist), and Sgra Emma Bonino (Radical member of the new and assertive minority and independent group). Mme

Veil lay well ahead on the first ballot, in which 191 votes were needed for an absolute majority of the 380 valid votes cast:

Mme Veil	183
Sgr Zagari	118
Sgr Amendola	44
M de la Malene	26
Sgra Bonino	9

After a short suspension of the sitting for tactical discussions M de la Malene, the Chirac standard bearer, and Sgra Bonino withdrew; and some, though not all, French votes were released for Mme Veil in what was to prove the decisive second ballot, in which 377 valid votes were cast and the requirement for an absolute majority was 189 votes:

Mme Veil	192
Sgr Zagari	138
Sgr Amendola	47

By a majority of merely three votes over the requirement, Mme Veil was declared the first President of the new Parliament by another remarkable Frenchwoman, Mme Louise Weiss, who at 86 years had presided ad interim and delivered with great spirit a ceremonial speech notable for its high rhetorical style and historic allusion.

Another distinguished woman politician, Mrs Barbara Castle, called a Press conference with Mr Ernest Glinne, the new Belgian leader of the Socialist Group, to lodge a protest against Mme Veil's election to the presidency on party lines. Sitting on the grass in the evening sunshine, Mrs Castle with much charm argued that the President should be more nearly akin to the Speaker of the House of Commons in the manner of election and in presidential practice, although not all the Westminster journalists present immediately recognised her theory of Speakership. At any rate, she was correct to draw a distinction between a Speaker who carefully keeps at arm's length from the business managers at Westminster, and a President of the European Parliament who heads the managerial bureau and also serves as the Parliament's "ministerial" negotiator with the Council of Ministers.

Yet it remained difficult to see how Westminster practice could be married to the procedures of a Parliament that has been run very differently and given quite different powers and parallel institutions to deal with. The complaints of Mr Glinne and Mrs Castle boiled down to a protest against Mme Veil's appointment as President being fixed for a 30-month term – half the term of the new Parliament. The Right-Centre Groups, allowing for reservations by the Chirac MEPs, had their way.

The new European Parliament, like most Parliaments, is not without a proportion of members who nurture the conspiracy theory of politics, or indeed a proportion of deeply experienced members who now and then justify the theory. Consequently, Mme Veil's nomination, and the manoeuvrings behind the scenes to secure its majority backing, aroused a private suspicion in some quarters that President Giscard d'Estaing's influence had been at work, although the more public criticism was that in a Chamber containing many lifelong politicians and more than 50 former Ministers, she presented herself for election as a President with no backbench experience.

The extremely experienced Sgr Pannella and his mixed band of colleagues, with their exploitation of procedure and the rule book, set out to prove the point by forcing the suspension of sittings and threatening time-consuming roll-call votes. An important objective of their campaign was to establish their rights to be recognised as a multinational and multi-party group and thereby qualify for a place on the managerial bureau of the Parliament, where much horsetrading takes place and the deals over appointments and the agenda are struck.

Nor was Mme Veil's election the only occasion for manoeuvring. The British Conservative Group, not only feeling their muscle as the third largest group in the new Chamber but also by convention entitled to two chairmanships of parliamentary committees, were determined to ensure the appointment of Sir Henry Plumb, for nearly a decade President of the English National Farmers' Union and an established figure in the agricultural machine in Brussels, as chairman of the agricultural committee. In a chamber that contained more than 40 agricultural specialists his qualifications for the post could not be equalled.

But his nomination could be seen by the French as a manoeuvre to place in a key position a British Conservative who would have both the expertness and the will to promote the policies of all the main parties in United Kingdom politics to speed the reform of the common agricultural policy, with its claim to more than 70 per cent. of the Community budget, with its financing of surplus production, and with the burden it places on members of the Nine that are importers rather than exporters of food. The formidable

M Jacques Chirac and his colleagues united for "defending French interests in Europe" wanted a Frenchman in the post, and there were apparently French members of other parties who shared their suspicions and their aim about the intentions of British Conservatives to place Sir Henry in a chairmanship of crucial importance.

No experienced parliamentarian, above all no experienced Westminster parliamentarian, should have been surprised that the leaders and members of a new Parliament spent the early days testing their strength, looking for allies, bidding or even bluffing that they held high cards, and generally falling short of their public rhetoric about history in the making as the first multinational parliament the world has known took shape. That is the way of democratic parliaments; and sometimes procedural adroitness and deals behind the scenes have succeeded where high principle and idealism have failed.

Nevertheless, the founding fathers of the European idea and ideal may well have been restive, if not shocked, that the inaugural session should have inspired so very little concentrated thought about the role of the Parliament, its relations with other Community institutions (the summit meetings, the Council of Ministers, and the Commission), its influence upon, if not control over, the Community budget, its powers under the Treaty of Rome, its democratic decision on where the Parliament should sit, and how it should transact its business in the most efficient way.

Yet those fundamental questions for the new Parliament were not entirely disregarded. Mme Veil, in her presidential speech, and the Group leaders, at least glanced at the problem of the Parliament's existing limited powers and the question whether in the fullness of time the Parliament will want, or be driven to fight for, increased powers out of a sense of "the new legitimacy" deriving from "universal elections". The speeches proved to be cautious.

Passages from Mme Veil's address gave rise to two different interpretations by two of the ablest British correspondents. The *Financial Times* heading ran: "Veil cool on extending powers of Parliament"; the *Economist* observer in Strasbourg, however, reported: "Mrs. Veil made a rousing presidential speech in which she showed that she means to fight for the Parliament's rights, and will not bow to the wishes of the French Government, as some Euro-MPs feared." Let Mme Veil speak for herself in her own language. In her speech she said:

"Parce qu'il est élu au suffrage universel et qu'il tirera ainsi de cette élection une autorité nouvelle, ce Parlement aura un rôle particulier à jouer pour permettre aux Communautés européennes de parvenir à ces finalités et de relever ainsi les défis auxquels elles sont confrontées. A cet égard, l'élection historique du mois de juin 1979 a soulevé en Europe un espoir, un immense espoir. Les peuples qui nous ont élus ne nous pardonneraient pas de ne pas savoir assumer cette responsabilité combien lourde, mais aussi combien exaltante.

"Cette responsabilité, le Parlement européen aura à l'exercer dans toutes ses délibérations. Je voudrais cependant souligner combien à mon sens son autorité nouvelle le conduira à renforcer son action sur deux terrains: d'une part, exercer plus démocratiquement sa fonction de contrôle, d'autre part jouer plus vigoureusement un rôle d'impulsion dans la construction communautaire.

"Issu de l'élection directe, le Parlement européen sera en mesure de jouer pleinement sa fonction de contrôle démocratique, qui est la fonction primordiale de toute Assemblée élue.

"Il lui appartient en particulier, du fait des pouvoirs qui lui sont conférés par les traités, de délivrer l'autorisation budgétaire au nom des citoyens de la Communauté. C'est désormais dans la Communauté, comme dans tous les Etats qui la constituent, l'Assemblée élue par le peuple qui vote le budget. Le budget est l'acte le plus important qui relève des compétences de ce Parlement, qui a le pouvoir de l'amender, voire de le rejeter en totalité.

"Je voudrais rappeler l'importance du dialogue budgétaire aux différents stades, aussi bien de l'élaboration du projet que de son adoption définitive. C'est une procédure complexe, lourde, supposant des délais, des navettes entre le Conseil et l'Assemblée, mais cette complexité et ces aller-retour ont pour contrepartie la possibilité de faire entendre notre voix.

"A diverses conditions toutefois: d'une part, à condition que nous soyons présents, puisque la présence est nécessaire. D'autre part, il est bien évident que notre force sera d'autant plus grande qu'elle sera plus unanime et aussi plus dépourvue de tout esprit de démagogie ou d'irréalisme.

"Le première tâche inscrite au programme de ce Parlement consistera d'ailleurs en l'examen en première lecture de l'avant-projet de budget pour 1980, qui nous occupera incessamment.

"Si l'on examine de façon plus globale l'exercice des pouvoirs budgétaires du Parlement élu au suffrage universel direct, un point me paraît à souligner. Je veux dire qu-un Parlement responsable ne doit pas se borner, à l'occasion de l'élaboration du budget, à arrêter un montant de dépenses, mais doit aussi prendre en considération la perception des recettes. Cela n'est d'ailleurs que parfaitement conforme à la vocation démocratique qui est la nôtre. Nous savons qu'historiquement c'est par l'autorisation de la perception des recettes que se sont constitués les premiers parlements du monde.

"La question peut d'autant moins être éludée que nous savons que c'est au cours de cette législature que le budget de la Communauté européenne atteindra le plafond de 1% de T.V.A. fixé par les traités pour la perception des resources propres. Dans les années à venir, le problème des recettes sera donc le problème primordial à prendre en compte, et ce Parlement, en tant que représentant de tous les citoyens, c'est-à-dire de tous les contribuables de la Communauté, sera nécessairement amené à jouer un rôle de premier plan en vue de sa solution.

"Le Parlement doit également être un organe de contrôle de politique générale au sein de la Communauté. Ne croyons pas en effet que les limitations proprement institutionnelles de ses compétences peuvent empêcher un Parlement, tel que le nôtre, de faire entendre à tout moment, et quel que soit le domaine de l'action communautaire, la voix que lui confère l'autorité politique issue de son élection.

"Il appartient aussi à notre Parlement de jouer un rôle d'impulsion dans la construction de l'Europe. Cela est particulièrement vrai à un moment où, ainsi que nous l'avons dit, l'Europe a d'abord besoin d'un complément de solidarité. Ce nouveau Parlement permettra aux voix de tous les citoyens de la Communauté de s'exprimer sur la scène européenne, contribuera en même temps à faire mieux ressentir aux différentes catégories d'entre eux les exigences de la solidarité européenne, au-delà des préoccupations immédiates, toujours légitimes, mais qui ne doivent jamais dissimuler les intérêts fondamentaux de la Communauté.

"Nous n'ignorons pas, bien entendu, l'organisation des pouvoirs, telle qu'elle existe dans la Communauté et confère à chaque institution son autonomie.

"Les fonctions d'initiative d'une part, de décision législative d'autre part, sont attribuées par les traités à la Commission et au Conseil. Cette autonomie de chacune des institutions, nécessaire au bon fonctionnement des Communautés, n'empêche pas que ces institutions agissent fondamentalement en collaboration les unes avec les autres, et c'est dans le cadre de cette collaboration que l'élan nouveau que représente pour la Communauté la légitimité nouvelle de cette Assemblée doit être un facteur efficace d'impulsion.

"C'est donc dans un renforcement du travail en commun avec les autres institutions que notre Parlement jouera plus efficacement son rôle pour les progrès de l'Europe. Il devra le faire aussi bien dans le cadre des consultations – qui peuvent être données sans limite –, que dans le cadre de la nouvelle procédure de concertation qui doit permettre au Parlement de participer effectivement aux décisions législatives des Communautés.

"La voix de notre Assemblée, forte de sa légitimité, portera dans toutes les instances de la Communauté, et notamment au niveau le plus élevé de la décision politique. Je pense en particulier à ce sujet au Conseil Européen. Comme il est naturel et normal dans une assemblée démocratique telle que la nôtre, nous divergeons par les programmes que nous souhaitons mettre en oeuvre, par les idées que nous voulons défendre et même quant à notre propre rôle.

"Gardons-nous cependant du travers qui nous conduirait à faire de notre Assemblée le forum des divisions et des rivalités. Trop souvent déjà, les Communautés européennes donnent à nos opinions publiques l'image d'insititutions bloquées, incapables de parvenir dans les délais nécessaires à des décisions.

"Notre Parlement aura pleinement satisfait les espoirs qu'il a fait naître si, loin d'être le lieu de résonance des divisions internes de l'Europe, il parvient à exprimer et à faire percevoir par la Communauté l'élan de solidarité si nécessaire aujourd'hui.

"Pour ce qui me concerne, c'est la totalité de mon temps et de mes forces que j'entends consacrer à la tâche qui est devant nous. Je n'ignore pas que, bien qu'issus d'une civilisation commune et formés par une culture nourrie aux mêmes sources, nous n'avons nécessairement ni les mêmes conceptions de la société, ni les mêmes aspirations.

"Pourtant, je suis convaincue que le pluralisme de notre Assemblée peut constituer un facteur d'enrichissement de nos travaux et non un frein à la progression de la construction de l'Europe. Quelles que soient nos différences de sensibilité, je pense en effet que nous partageons la même volonté de réaliser une Communauté fondée sur un patrimoine commun et un respect partagé des valeurs humaines fondamentales. C'est dans cet esprit que je vous invite à aborder fraternellement les travaux qui nous attendent.

"Puissions-nous ainsi, au terme de notre mandat, éprouver le sentiment d'avoir fait progresser l'Europe. Puissions-nous surtout avoir pleinement répondu à l'espérance que suscite cette Assemblée, non seulement chez les Européens, mais parmi tous ceux qui, dans le monde, sont attachés à la paix et à la liberté."

Thus said Mme Veil, the president and former French Minister in President Giscard d'Estaing's administration. Mr Glinne, leader of the Socialist Group, though much concerned with making French party points about irregularities in validating Giscardian votes after the June 10 election, supported the argument for parliamentary involvement in decisions of heads of government and Prime Ministers at summit conferences (which are no part of the Community's Treaty institutions).

But no Group leader, in his inaugural speech, challenged the agreement of the summit conference that direct elections and the so-called new democratic legitimacy should not lead to parliamentary delusions of grandeur involving an increase in Parliament's powers. Dr Martin Bangemann, the Liberal leader, was for the time being more concerned to press, in the terms of the Rome Treaty, for a uniform system of direct elections in 1984 to correct the anomaly that the British Liberal Party, on first-past-the-post, won not one seat although Proportional Representation would have allotted them 10 seats. (Mr Russell Johnston, Mr Christopher Mayhew, and other British Liberals, during the luncheon interval, mounted a demonstration by occupying 10 seats in the otherwise empty hemicycle, and then held a Press conference to make their rational point.)

For his part, Mr James Scott-Hopkins, leader of the British Conservatives and European Democrats, accepted that direct elections were not primarily intended to give the European Parliament more power, but he also indicated the scope for parliamentary development in the new circumstances, without trespassing on the powers of national governments. Here are extracts from his speech:

"The principal tasks for this Community over the next five years are a second enlargement to include Greece, and subsequently Portugal and Spain, and to maintain the Community's progress towards closer monetary integration, already mentioned by previous speakers, and the greater stability that will bring, of which the EMS is perhaps but a first stage. Now who in this Chamber here really feels confident that this Parliament will have real influence unless we really fight hard for it on the big decisions to be taken in these particular areas? What consideration, for instance, has been given to the role that we in this Parliament should play, in the management of EMS at any stage? And what influence has this Parliament so far had on the course of the enlargement negotiations? We were informed. We had an opportunity of listening, but *after* the events had taken place. Or indeed again, what infiuence has this Parliament had on the crucial question of the adjustment of the weighted majority voting system in the Council? The answer to all these questions is, I fear, 'very little, if any' and however eloquent and well-reasoned our speeches may be, our influence will continue to be negligible unless we exercise it with great skill and determination. Unless we can do this we will continue as we are and as we have been in the past.

"The point of these elections was not primarily to give this institution more power, but to give the citizens of the Community a greater say in the decisions which affect them. From now on, when the views of the Parliament are set aside, it is the views of the people who elected us that are being ignored, not just us, and I would emphasise this point both to the Council and to the Commission. And the governments know, and the Commission will soon find out, that this is not the kind of democracy that we are all led to defend and something which can or will continue indefinitely.

"Our responsibility to our electors is to work efficiently and to this end we must not be hindered by precedent in deciding what procedures we should adopt to exercise a mandate that we have been given. I believe, for example, that we shall need to review before long the system of committees, with rapporteurs, reports and so on. Indeed one might even look at closely the system of confidentiality and secrecy which exists in these committees to the exclusion of the press and others.

"I also believe that we should give a very high priority to working out satisfactory relations with our colleagues in national parliaments, both within the Community and elsewhere, especially those in the applicant states and in bodies such as the Council of Europe and others working in that field. And I hope we can take up with these appropriate authorities all the matters which have a direct bearing on the efficiency of Parliament and our work as individual Members, and notably perhaps the question of a permanent site for all our activities.

"These problems and much else, must be among the task we set ourselves for the first five years. The effectiveness of our solutions, the skill with which we deploy our limited powers, will be the crucial test for the future.

"Although, as I have said, the period of establishing ourselves will not be an easy one, we would be foolish to think it will, we will not yield to the temptation of concerning ourselves solely with our internal problems and affairs. One effect of the European election campaign has been to present the European Parliament as an institution whose decisions have a direct relevance to the policies developed and applied by the Community to the ordinary citizen and thus have a great bearing on the lives of all our electors. As the 1984 elections approach, we shall find ourselves under great pressure to demonstrate that we have kept the promises that we all of us in our different way have made this year and that accordingly this institution, this Parliament, is something which is worth the electors voting for and continuing to support.

"And this means that we must concern ourselves not only with the big institutional questions, but also with those relatively unglamorous issues of local, technical but nevertheless specific concern. Mr Tindemans has mentioned some of them and they are of great importance, because they are the issues which affect people in their homes. And we will find ourselves dealing with local and sectoral lobbies; we shall be worried about whether or not a particular region or a particular industry is getting a fair deal. This is right and proper and in my view the proper responsibilities that we should be taking on. They are essential to Paliament's work if this institution and its Members are not to drift into remoteness and irrelevance. Our interest needs to be built up over the whole range of the Community's activities.

"I should probably point out at this stage that I am not suggesting that we should take over in areas more properly the concern of national parliaments; that would not be the right approach. And it is wrong in any case to assume that any extension of our powers would automatically be at the expense of national parliaments. Let me give you two quick examples: in matters relating to the negotiation and the conclusion of the Community's external agreements, which are becoming increasingly important given our position as the largest trading bloc in the world, there is inadequate provision for any form of democratic control either in the drawing up of the Commission's negotiating mandate or at the conclusion of these negotiations. National parliaments have little, if any, power in this particular area and it is one into which the European Parliament could move without presenting any formal challenge to the Council of Ministers or to any national parliament.

"A different example arises in the case of the Council of Ministers; individually, of course, ministers are responsible to their national parliaments, and they should remain so, of course. But the Council itself is responsible to no one. Its prime duty as a Community Institution must be to the Community, and there is no one to whom it is accountable in the performance of this duty. In the past, my group and others have on several occasions criticized the way in which the Council sets about its work: its excessive secrecy, the inadequate answers to Members' questions, as well as the enormous length of time it takes to get those questions answered; the unassailable but nonetheless powerful influence of the officials of COREPER who work extremely hard – I sometimes wonder what they do. Although recent events in my country mean that there has been the most welcome change in the composition of the Council, we shall continue politely but firmly to seek to hold the Council to account for the decisions it reaches or more often – unfortunately – fails to reach. I wonder if the President-in-Office of the Council has any idea how many of Parliament's reports, flowing from Commission proposals, are still awaiting decision in the Council or have been shelved.

"From what I have said, Madam President, I think it will be clear, that on some occasions Parliament will need to use its united strength and to exert pressure where pressure is needed. I think the evidence is that we really must move along these lines."

Mr Roy Jenkins, President of the Commission, took a high line about the role of the Parliament and an extremely sombre view of the decade in which it would develop. He said:

"The first task before this House, in my view, collectively and individually, is to carry to the people of Europe those issues which are of concern and of importance to all within the Community. Your concern and your opportunity are to ensure that Community issues, not the narrow lines of national politics, dominate the discussion. It is an opportunity to demonstrate to millions of our citizens that their votes really mattered and to convince those who abstained – regrettably my own country comfortably carried off the wooden spoon of discredit in this respect – that the Community and its Parliament are living organs of concern for the issues which touch closely on their daily lives. To achieve this, it will be necessary for this House to engage itself directly with the major problems which confront the Community and its Member States.

"I will not hide from this House my view that we stand on the threshold of a sombre decade. Our difficulties were great enough a year ago. The prospects for sustained growth and employment were at best uncertain. Now the resurgence of the energy crisis, wholly predictable in substance if not in time, has made us painfully aware of the most important constraint on the future of our economy. We have sustained a major transfer of real resources, of real income, away from us as a result of the recent oil price increases.

"That is something which we cannot just pretend has not happened. In these circumstances, on constant policies, predictions would necessarily show lower growth, higher inflation and more unemployment. That is a reason, not for supineness, but for the urgent evolution of new policies to mitigate, and then, over as short a period as possible, to overcome our present vicissitudes. I will return to these matters tomorrow, when I hope to report to you on the European Council at Strasbourg, the Tokyo Summit and the issues associated with them, which will be dominant throughout the span of this Parliament. But what is absolutely clear is that the ability of the Community to survive and to prosper depends on our joint determination to preserve what we have already achieved, to build on this, and, above all, to keep a vision and commitment to make progress towards a greater European unity. That vision – a constant reaffirmation of our will to move forward – matters, I think, far more than rather sterile blueprints about the exact form of political organisation at which we shall ultimately arrive. That will not, in my belief, be something that can be found in the traditional text-books of political science. We cannot simply look it up under a model labelled 'federal' or 'confederal'. It will have an unique character of its own arising out of a balance between our need for unity on major issues and our strong and even disparate national traditions. But of one thing I am absolutely certain: there is a much greater danger of advancing too slowly rather than too fast.

"This House, Madam President, has an essential role to play in this process. Of course, the relationships between the different institutions of the Community are complex and created in a spirit of balance. No one institution is dependent upon another: each has its prerogatives; each has its duties; each has its obligations. Within that balance, it is the concern and the duty of the Commission to act as the motor of the Community, to initiate policy and also to undertake the management and execution of existing policies. We should not only defend the frontiers of Community competence, but also, with a proper sense both of adventure and realism, endeavour to push them forward where a practical and relevant case can be established.

"Having said that, however, it is clear that this Parliament, resting as it does on a wide popular support and commanding a new democratic authority, represents a most important evolution for the Community. It is right that it should exercise to the fullest possible extent its powers to question and to subject to criticism the way in which the Commission exercises its powers and the way in which the Council of Ministers reaches or does not reach its decisions. We need the spur of constructive advice and imagination, and we will welcome all your efforts in that direction.

"It is right too that the Parliament, as a major partner with the Commission and the Council in the formulation of the Community's budget, should assert itself in the development of the financial muscle which underlies Community policies. This is an area of potentially great significance for the internal development of the Community where this House will have an essential influence. Equally, it is, I believe, right that the Parliament should aim to broaden the basis of popular support for Community Institutions and create a greater sense of involvement in their policies.

"Against this background, the Commission regards it as an obligation and priority to do all within its power to create and to sustain a positive relationship with this House. First, I and my colleagues will make ourselves available to the fullest possible extent to the Parliament and to its committees. We hope to have early discussions about ways and means of securing the Commission's maximum participation in and assistance at your various forms of deliberations. Second, we believe that it is important from the outset that there should be the opportunity for wider and earlier discussion of major proposals which we take to the Council. Here it seems to us essential that there should be a greater understanding of important issues at a Community level, and we would be willing to prepare, where appropriate, discussion documents as a basis of Parliamentary debate of broad policy issues in advance of formulating proposals for the Council. Third, the Commission will take the lead in seeking to improve the processes of consultation between the three institutions. We are currently studying how to improve the conciliation procedure which resulted from an earlier Commission initiative.

"It is through the development of procedures of this kind that the positive and creative relationship we want can grow and flourish. Our relationship must be based on the special character of our different Institutions, each with its direct responsibilities towards the collective interest of the Community. You can count on us to do all in our power to deepen and intensify that relationship. On it will depend much of the future evolution not only of the Parliament and the Commission but of the Institutions of the Community as a whole."

On the last day of the first plenary session, the new Parliament, in accordance with the Community's budgetary cycle, had a foretaste of one of its main powers – the approval or total rejection of the budget as introduced by the Commission and amended by the Council of Ministers. Presenting the budgetary proposals for 1980, Mr Christopher Tugendhat, Commissioner for the budget, delivered a strong warning that one of the preoccupations of the MEPs would be the early exhaustion of the EEC's "own resources", which as now defined consist of customs duties, levies on trade in foodstuffs, and up to one per cent. of VAT. In 1979 the Community VAT rate is 0.74 per cent.; in 1980 it is estimated at 0.88 per cent.

Thanks to the decisions of agricultural Ministers, said Mr Tugendhat, there was a clear prospect that by 1981 the Community's own resources would be inadequate, and the development of the EEC could be arrested or retarded; and he did not need to add that national governments will be reluctant to increase the VAT commitment, which bears directly on domestic retail prices. The logic could therefore be the maintenance of obligatory spending on agricultural support and the curbing of (say) the regional and social funds or aid connected with external policies. In a time of recession during the 1980s that may harden the determination of many MEPs to press for reforms in the common agricultural policy.

With the enlargement of the directly-elected Parliament to 410 members, compared with 198 relatively long-serving members in the old nominated Parliament, the MEPs understandably were feeling their way, learning the geography of the Palais de l'Europe, mastering the procedure, and consulting the old hands – especially the British contingent that contained very few members with parliamentary experience of any kind because of the attitude of the two main parties to the "dual mandate", and the disinclination of Labour selection committees to choose Labour peers with European experience.

Nevertheless, new members joined with the old in raising questions outside the Chamber about how the European Parliament should develop, how it could live up to the prospectus of curbing the bureaucracy of the Commission and the national arbitrariness of the Council of Ministers and the summit meetings of heads of government and Prime Ministers. They also understandably applied themselves to the question of their financial allowances, since the national governments had pre-empted the decision on their salaries to suit the *amour propre* of national politicians.

It was fairly clear that one of the first campaigns in which the new Parliament may be expected to engage will be for the rationalisation of the meeting place. By the diktat of the Council of Ministers, the Parliament must now meet roughly alternately in Strasbourg and Luxembourg, while committee meetings are mainly held in Brussels to be near the Commission headquarters. For the time being, only the Palais de l'Europe in Strasbourg will accommodate 410 members and it is there plenary sessions must be held until 1980, although Strasbourg's hotels are over-strained and air services to Entzheim are of provincial rather than metropolitan kind.

Another question that only time will settle, is how much time the MEPs will spend on parliamentary business in Strasbourg, Luxembourg, and Brussels, and how much time they will want to spend in their constituencies or coordinating with their domestic parliaments and parties. The more democratically muscular the European Parliament proves to be, the more it will fill available time with democratic activity, although it must be remembered that it is in the nature of the prevailing committee and rapporteur system to spend as much time in committee as in plenary sessions. Good judges estimate that before long MEPs will be devoting three weeks a month to parliamentary business, one way or another, and making sure that their home contacts do not rust unused for the other week. None of the new MEPs will forget that they, unlike their nominated predecessors, are accountable to an electorate, in Britain more than elsewhere.

Moreover, the majority of members of the new Parliament are middle-aged or youngish, with a parliamentary career to make. The average age is 50, compared with 55 in the old Parliament; at an average 45 years the United Kingdom provides the youngest delegation, with Mr Paul Howell, son of a former nominated member, Mr Ralph Howell, as its youngest member at 28. The youngest member of all is Miss Sile de Valera, a granddaughter of the former Irish leader. But about an eighth of the new Parliament consists of former Ministers in national governments, including enough Prime Ministers and senior Ministers to form a Cabinet for any country of the Nine. An assembly that includes Willy Brandt, Jacques Chirac, Edgar Faure, Michel Debre, Pierre Messmer, Leo Tindemans, Emilio Colombo, Mariano Rumor and Mrs Barbara Castle should never be reckoned negligible.

The European Parliament

The biographical information on the members of the European Parliament has been compiled from information supplied to *The Times* by the Directorate-General of Information and Public Relations of the European Parliament and its offices in the EEC member states, the Secretariats of the Political Groups of the Parliament, and Conservative Central Office and Labour Party Headquarters in the United Kingdom. Occupations are those held at the date of the direct elections.

The abbreviations used for the political groups of the EP and the political parties of MEPs in their member states are those set out on pages 8 and 16 of this guide.

ABENS, VICTOR
Luxembourg, Soc (POSL)

Mr Victor Abens, an industrialist, is a member of the assembly of the Council of Europe. Deputy Mayor of Vianden. B October, 1912.

Address: 48, Grand-rue, Vianden. Tel: 84006.

ADAM, GORDON
UK, Northumbria, Soc (Lab)

Mr Gordon Adam, a mining engineer. B March 1934; ed Leeds University. BSc, PhD, CEng. Member, Whitley Bay Borough Council, 1971-74; North Tyneside Metropolitan District Council, since 1973. In general elections fought Tynemouth, 1966, and Berwick-upon-Tweed, February 1974 and November 1973 by-election. Special interests: energy policy, economic planning, industry, unemployment and the arts.

Address: 2 Queen's Road, Whitley Bay, Tyne and Wear, NE26 3BJ. Tel: 0632-528616.

ADONNINO, PIETRO
Italy, EPP (DC)

Sgr Pietro Adonnino, lawyer and university lecturer in fiscal law, is vice-chairman of the Association of Italian Fiscal Experts, member of the International Fiscal Association (IFA), director of the Lawyers' Provident Fund and director of RAI-TV, the Italian television and broadcasting corporation. B November, 1929.

Address: Via di Villa Grazioli, 11, 00198 Roma. Tel: 06-8441330.

AGNELLI, SIGNORA SUSANNA
Italy, LD (PRI)

Signora Susanna Agnelli became a Republican Party member of the Italian Parliament in 1976. Mayor of Monte Argentaria since 1974. Vice-chairman of the Italian committee for the International Year of the Child. B April, 1922; married with six children.

Address: 58019 Porto S. Stefano (Grosseto).

AIGNER, HENRICH
Germany, EPP (CSU)

Herr Henrich Aigner has been a member of the Bundestag since 1957 and of the European Parliament, since 1961; head of CDU/CSU delegation until June 1979. Former senior executive officer, Bavarian Ministry of Agriculture; vice-chairman, Deutsche Stiftung in Berlin; member, Management Committee of Catholic Central Agency for Development Aid. Curator, German-Brazil Society. B May, 1924. Married with three children.

Address: Kaiser-Wilhelm-Ring 14, 8450 Amberg (Oberpfalz). Tel: 22 883 and 23 128.

ALBER, SIEGBERT
Germany, EPP (CDU)

Herr Siegbert Alber has been a member of the Bundestag since 1969 and of the European Parliament since 1977. Read law and became junior legal official and public prosecutor; after election to the Bundestag became parliamentary official for CDU political group in the Baden-Württemberg Landtag. Since 1971, chairman of the Stuttgart CDU; member, North Württemberg district executive and Baden-Württemberg "Land" CDU executive. Since 1970, member, Parliamentary Assembly, Council of Europe and of WEU; chairman of the committees on budgets of both bodies. B July, 1936. Married with one child.

Address: Gammertinger Strasse 35, 7000 Stuttgart 80. Tel: 725445.

ALBERS, WILLEM
Netherlands, Soc (PvdA)

Mr Willem Albers has been a member of the European Parliament since 1974. B November, 1920. Trained as chemical analyst. In local politics at Zutphen. Member, Dutch Parliament, since 1973.

Address: Paulus Potterstraat 33, 7204 CP Zutphen. Tel: 05750-15267.

ALMIRANTE, GIORGIO
Italy, Ind (MSI-DN)

Sgr Giorgio Almirante has been an Italian MP since 1948. Journalist. One of the founders of the Italian Social Movement and is its National Secretary. Has been member of several parliamentary committees including the Committees on Home Affairs, Constitutional Affairs (four times) and Education. During the fourth legislature, he was the most fervent opposer to the regional electoral Bill. Chairman of the party's parliamentary group. B June, 1914; arts degree.

Addresses: Camera dei Deputati, 00100 Roma. Via Quattro Fontane 109, 00100 Roma. Tel: 4740382.

AMENDOLA, GIORGIO
Italy, Comm (PCI)

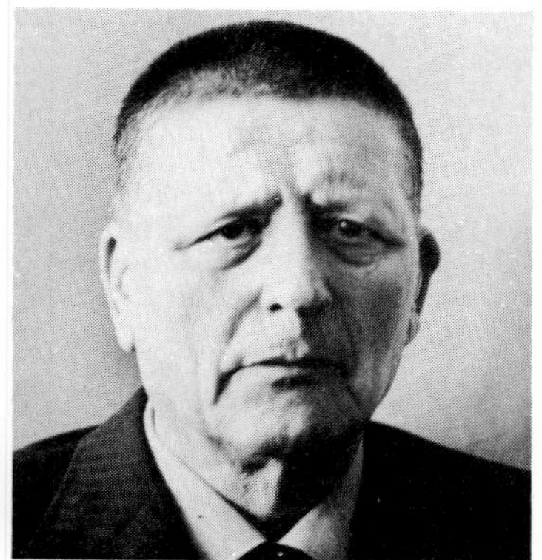

Sgr Giorgio Amendola was re-elected chairman of the Communist and Allies Group of the European Parliament in July, 1979, the office he held in the outgoing Parliament which he joined in 1976. Journalist. Italian MP from 1948. Party member since 1929. Communist representative on the Military Council of 1943. Member of the Central Committee and party leadership. Twice member of the Finance and Treasury Committee; five times member of the Committee on the Budget and State Economic Participation. Author of *Storia del Partito Comunista Italiano*. B November, 1907; degree in law.

Address: Via delle Botteghe Oscure 4, 00186 Roma.

ANSART, GUSTAVE
France, Comm (PCF)

M Gustave Ansart was elected a vice-chairman of the Communist and Allies Group of the European Parliament, in July, 1979. Deputy for the Nord. Member of the outgoing nominated European Parliament and of the political bureau of the French Communist Party. Metal worker. B March 1923.

Address: Fédération du PCF, 18 rue Inkermann, 59000 Lille. Tel: 57 33 48.

ANSQUER, VINCENT
France, DEP (DIFE)

M Vincent Ansquer, company director, is a former minister. Deputy for the Vendee. B January, 1925. Graduate in law; graduate of Ecole nationale de la France d'Outre-mer.

Address: 4 Place de Lattre de Tassigny, 92300 Levallois-Perret.

ANTONIOZZI, DARIO
Italy, EPP (DC)

Sgr Dario Antoniozzi, a lawyer, was a member of the European Parliament, 1972–1976; vice-chairman, European People's Party, since 1976. Member of Parliament since 1953; many times Under-Secretary of State for Transport, for Posts and Telecommunications, for Tourism and Entertainment, for the Merchant Marine and for Agriculture and Forestry. Minister for Tourism and Entertainment, then Minister for Cultural Assets and the Environment. Former National Councillor for the DC; assistant political secretary in 1976, and director of the Office for International Relations. B December, 1923.

Address: Via Nomentana 373, 00162 Roma. Tel: 837078-8391627.

ARFE', GAETANO
Italy, Soc (PSI)

Sgr Gaetano Arfe', was elected an Italian Senator in 1972 and an MP in 1976. University teacher of Modern History; Professorship in Risorgimento History at the University of Florence. Member of party since 1945. Director of *Avanti,* 1966–76. Vice-chairman, Committee on Education and the Fine Arts. Member, Committee on Constitutional Affairs; Council of Europe since 1976. B November, 1925; degree in arts and in philosophy.

Address: Via IV Novembre 116, 00187 Roma. Tel: 6786515.

ARNDT, RUDI
Germany, Soc (SPD)

Herr Rudi Arndt is a former minister and former Mayor of Frankfurt. Chairman of South Hesse SPD and member of the SPD Federal Executive. Barrister. B March, 1927.

Address: Mörfelder Landstrasse 273, 6000 Frankfurt am Main 70. Tel: 631473.

BADUEL GLORIOSO, SIGNORA MARIA
Italy, Comm (PCI)

Signora Maria Baduel Glorioso was President of the Economic and Social Committee of the EEC, 1978–79. B July 1927; law graduate. Member of the Studies Office of CISL (Confederation of Italian Workers' Trade Unions), 1963–65; Head of CISL's International Office since 1965.

Address: Via dell 'Arte 91, 00144 Roma.

BAILLOT, LOUIS
France, Comm (PCF)

M Louis Baillot, an engineer, is a member of the Central Committee of the French Communist Party. B May, 1924.

Address: Comité Central du PCF, 2 Place du Colonel Fabien, 75940 Paris Cedex 19. Tel: 238 66 55.

BALFE, RICHARD
UK, Inner London South, Soc (Lab)

Mr Richard Balfe is political secretary to the Royal Arsenal Co-operative Society. B May, 1944; ed Brook Secondary Modern, Sheffield, and London School of Economics. BSc Hons, Fellow of the Royal Statistical Society and of the Royal Institute of Public Administration. Member, Greater Lonon Council, 1973–77. Prospective parliamentary candidate, Paddington, South, 1970. Member, London Regional Executive of Labour Party. Special interests: social policy, economic policy, foreign affairs and the third world. Married.

Address: 10 Genoa Road, London SE20 8ES. Tel: 01-778 5629.

BALFOUR, NEIL
UK, Yorkshire North, ED (C)

Mr Neil Balfour is a director of the European Banking Co Ltd; barrister (Middle Temple). Contested Hillingdon, Hayes and Harlington, in the October 1974 general election; Chester-le-Street, 1973 by-election and February 1974 election. B August 1944; ed Ampleforth College; Sorbonne and University College, Oxford. Married with one son and two step-daughters.

Address: 24 The Little Boltons, London SW10 9LP. Tel: 01-377 8092.

BANGEMANN, MARTIN
Germany, LD (FDP)

Herr Martin Bangemann was elected chairman of the Liberal and Democratic Group of the European Parliament in July 1979; deputy chairman since 1975, and member of the Parliament since 1973. FDP member, Bundestag, since 1972; chairman of the European working party of FDP parliamentary party. Deputy chairman, Federation of European Liberals and Democrats. B November, 1934. Barrister. Member, national executive, FDP and deputy "Land" chairman since 1969; 1974–78 "Land" chairman of Baden-Wurttemberg FDP. Secretary-General of FDP, 1974–75; member, bureau of FDP since 1978. Married with five children.

Address: Sannentalstrasse 9, 7418 Metzingen. Tel: 50 70.

BARBAGLI, GIOVANNI
Italy, EPP (DC)

Sgr Giovanni Barbagli, a surveyor, was a member of Arezzo Municipal Council, 1964–70. Director of the National Farmers' Confederation; member, Tuscan Regional Council, since 1970; chairman, Regional Union of Agricultural Cooperatives, since 1975; chairman, Regional Council's special committee for EEC problems. B June, 1931.

Address: Via Lorenzotti 30, 52100 Arezzo. Tel: 26.790-441617.

BARBARELLA, SIGNORA CARLA
Italy, Comm (PCI)

Signora Carla Barbarella worked from 1965–72 at Euratom and then at the Council of Ministers of the EEC, as principal administrator. Official of the National Alliance of Smallholders. Member of the staff of the Emilia-Romagna Regional Administration. Has been working at party headquarters since 1974 in the Agrarian Section. Member, steering committee of CESPE (Centre for Studies in International Politics). B February, 1940; degree in political science.

Address: Via dei Giubbonari 74, 00188 Roma. Tel: 6567101.

BARBI, PAOLO
Italy, EPP (DC)

Sgr Paolo Barbi is a former Under-Secretary of State for Industry, Commerce and the Arts, and, later, for the Budget. B August, 1919. Graduate in philosophy; professor; journalist. Member, National Council, Christian Democrats, since 1949, and member of party Executive, 1951–52 and 1954–69; party secretary, province of Naples, 1955–58. Member, Chamber of Deputies, from 1958, and of Senate from 1976. Deputy Chairman, Italian section, European Teachers' Association. Married with five children.

Address: Via Vincenzo Padula 2, 80123 Napoli. Tel: 081-7695427.

BATTERSBY, ROBERT
UK, Humberside, ED (C)

Mr Robert Battersby has been a principal administrator with the European Commission since 1973, working on aspects of EEC fisheries policy and before that on European Coal and Steel Community loans to the British Steel Corporation and to the British private steel sector. Previously sales director, GKN Contractors Ltd. B 1924; ed First Park Grammar School, Sheffield; Edinburgh University and Cambridge University; also studied at Sorbonne and Toulouse University. Married with three children.

Addresses: West Cross, Rockshaw Road, Merstham, Surrey RH1 3BZ. Tel: 01-649 3783. 28 First Avenue, Bridlington, N Humberside. Tel: 72489.

BAUDIS, PIERRE
France, LD (UFE)

M Pierre Baudis has been chairman of the Committee of Finance in the French National Assembly. Mayor of Toulouse; Secretary-General of the Association of Mayors of French towns. B May, 1916; Doctor of Law, diploma of the Ecole libre des Sciences Politiques, Toulouse. Administrative officer, Ministry of Finance, 1946–58 and 1967–68. Deputy for the Haute-Garonne, 1958–78. Member, Conseil Général of the Toulouse-Centre canton, 1961, being re-elected in 1967, 1973 and 1979. Chairman, parliamentary working party on problems of repatriates, 1968.

Address: 28, rue Maurice Fonvieille, 31000 Toulouse.

BEAZLEY, PETER
UK. Bedfordshire, ED (C)

Mr Peter Beazley has had 31 years' service with Imperial Chemical Industries, 17 of them spent abroad in Frankfurt, Brussels, Portugal, South America and South Africa. Research Fellow, Royal Institute of International Affairs. B 1922; ed Highgate School and St John's College, Oxford. Specialist knowledge of European economy, finance and industry, German political and economic organisation, especially labour relations, Soviet Union and Soviet bloc industry and economy especially technology transfer from West. Married with three children.

Address: 14 The Combe, Ratton, Eastbourne, Sussex BN29 9DB. Tel: 0323-54460.

BERKHOUWER, CORNELIUS
Netherlands, LD (VVD)

Mr Cornelius Berkhouwer was President of the European Parliament, 1975–77; former Vice-President, and former chairman of the Liberal group. Member since 1963. Elected a vice-chairman of the Liberal and Democratic Group, July, 1979. B January 1919; ed Alkmaar Grammar School and Amsterdam Municipal University. Director of several companies. Member of the Second Chamber. Married with one child.

Address: Stationsweg 56, Heiloo (Alkmaar). Tel: 072-332791.

BERLINGUER, ENRICO
Italy, Comm (PCI)

Sgr Enrico Berlinguer has been a member of the Italian Parliament since 1968, and Secretary-General of the Italian Communist Party since 1972. Member of the party since 1943, of its Central Committee, since 1945; and of leadership, since 1948. Secretary-General, Communist Youth Federation, 1949–56; chairman, World Federation of Democratic Youth, 1950–53. Has held other positions within party: Regional Vice-Secretary for Sardinia, Chief of Central Organisation Department and National Vice-Secretary (1969). Has been member, Parliamentary Committee on Foreign Affairs, three times. B May, 1922.

Address: Via delle Botteghe Oscure 4, 00189 Roma. Tel: 6711

BERSANI, GIOVANNI
Italy, EPP (DC)

Sgr Giovanni Bersani is a lawyer and has been a member of the Christian Democrat National Council since 1947. B July, 1914. Member, Chamber of Deputies, 1948–76; member of Senate since 1976. Member, European Parliament, since 1960 (former Vice-President). Under-Secretary of State, Ministry of Labour and Social Security, 1952–53. Regional director of the Italian Christian Workers' Society since 1946 and National Vice-Chairman since 1951. Founder and President of MCL (Workers' Christian Movement).

Address: Via delle Lame 118, 40136 Bologna. Tel: 23 74 19.

BETHELL, LORD
UK, London North West, ED (C)

Lord Bethell has been a member of the European Parliament since 1975; specialised in problems of consumer. Co-author of booklet "Consumers in Europe – a Conservative view". B July 1938; ed Harrow and Pembroke College, Cambridge. On editorial staff of *The Times Literary Supplement*, 1962–64; a script editor in BBC Drama Department, 1964–67. A Lord-in-Waiting (Government whip and a junior Government spokesman), House of Lords, 1970–71. Freelance writer and a translator from Russian and Polish.

Address: 73 Sussex Square, London W2 2SS.

BETTIZA, VINCENZO
Italy, LD (PLI)

Sgr Vincenzo Bettiza was elected a vice-chairman of the Liberal and Democratic Group of the European Parliament in July, 1979; member of the outgoing nominated Parliament. Journalist; on editorial board of *Il Nuovo Giornale*. Senator, 1976. Was correspondent of *La Stampa* and *Corriere della Sera* in various capitals of the world, including Moscow. B June, 1927; married with one child.

Address: c.o. 11 Giornale Nuovo, Piazza di Pietra 26, 00186 Roma. Tel: 6787841.

BEUMER, BOUKE
Netherlands, EPP (CDA)

Mr Bouke Beumer became a member of the Second Chamber in 1975. Director of N.W. Overijssel Regional Council, 1962–66; Burgomaster of Midwolda, 1966–75. Member of the ARP (Anti-Revolutionary Party) executive and of the association for the education and care of the mentally retarded. B November, 1934; studied economics at Rotterdam, 1952–58.

Address: Hoofdstraat 157, Hoogezand.

BLANEY, NEIL
Ireland, TCDG (Ind)

Mr Neil Blaney was Minister for Local Government in the Republic of Ireland, 1957-66; Minister for Posts and Telegraphs, 1957, and Minister for Agriculture and Fisheries, 1966-70. Has farming and business interests. B October 1922; ed St Eunan's College, Letterkenny, Co Donegal. First elected to Dáil Eireann for Donegal, 1948, and was returned as a Fianna Fáil deputy up to and including the 1969 election. Expelled from the party, 1971; in 1973 election was one of two non-party candidates elected. Member, Donegal County Council, 1948-57 (chairman, 1955-57). President, Football Association of Ireland, 1968-73 and a patron since 1973.

Addresses: Leinster House, Kildare St., Dublin 2. Tel: 789911, Ext 303. 485 Howth Road, Dublin 5. Tel: 313085.

BLUMENFELD, ERIK
Germany, EPP (CDU)

Herr Erik Blumenfeld has been a member of the Bundestag since 1961, the European Parliament since 1973, and the North Atlantic Assembly, since 1971. Deputy chairman, Hamburg "Land" CDU (chairman 1958-68). B March 1915. Owner of Messrs Blumenfeld and Co. Member, supervisory board of Albingia Rechtsschutz-Versicherungs AG, Hamburg; vice-president, Hamburg Chamber of Commerce, 1946-54. Member, Hamburg city Parliament, 1946-55 and 1966-70; President, German-Israeli Association; chairman, German group on Parliamentary Council of the European Movement; chairman, Kuratorium für staatspolitische Bildung, Hamburg. Married.

Address: Chilehause B III, 2000 Hamburg 1. Tel: 040-321381.

BOCKLET, REINHOLD
Germany, EPP (CSU)

Herr Reinhold Bocklet, lecturer in political science at the Geschwister-Scholl Institute (Munich University) since 1976. Committee member, CDU-CSU Youth Organisation (JU) for Bavaria since 1969 and of same organization at Federal Republic level since 1973; deputy Federal chairman of this organization and JU representative in the EC working-party of the European Young Christian-Democrats since 1977. Member, SCU Regional Association for Upper Bavaria, since 1975. B April, 1943. Married.

Address: Mitterweg 14, 8031 Olching-Geisselbullach. Tel: 08142-13748.

BØGH, THE REV JØRGEN
Denmark, TCDG (Folkebevaegelsen)

The Rev Jørgen Bøgh, aged 62, dean of Aarhus. Fought European elections on list of anti-EEC coalition movement. For many years, member of the SDP but disagreed with that party on Common Market issue. He has been a teacher at the Askov High School; headmaster of the "free" teachers' training school at Ollerup; and leader of civil defence training, 1952-62. During the German Occupation, he was involved in the formation of the Danish Youth Council.

Address: Kystvej 47, 8000 Aarhus C. Tel: 06-121674.

BONACCINI, ALDO
Italy, Comm (PCI)

Sgr Aldo Bonaccini, a member of the Economic and Social Committee of the EEC, was secretary of the Trade Union of Metallurgical and Mechanical Workers, and thereafter of the Trade Union of Chemical Workers (Province of Milan). Secretary, Workers' Association of Milan, and later of Lombardy. Member, CGIL (Federation of Italian Trade Unions) since 1969, in charge of economic and international politics; and of European Confederation of Trade Unions. Serves on the party's Central Committee. B June, 1920; degree in political science.

Address: Via Raffaele Balestra 44, 00100 Roma.

BONDE, JENS-PETER
Denmark, TCDG (Folkebevaegelsen)

Mr Jens-Peter Bonde, editor, contested the European elections on the list of the anti-EEC coalition movement in Denmark. He was largely responsible for starting up the movement's journal, *Det ny Notat* (The New Report) which he produced with other enthusiasts in a disused hairdresser's salon in Noerrebro, Copenhagen. From his youth, Mr Bonde has been a radical and for a time was chairman of Radical Youth. Member of Denmark's Communist Party. B March, 1948.

Address: Baldersgade 77, 2200 København N.
Tel: (01) 81 83 15.

BONINO, SIGNORA EMMA
Italy, TCDG (PR)

Signora Emma Bonino has been an Italian MP since 1976. Member and coordinator of the Centre for Information on Sterilization and Abortion since 1975. Member of Committee on Labour – Social Security. Secretary, Parliamentary Group of Partito Radicale. B March, 1948.

Address: Via Giulia 167, 00186 Roma.
Tel: 06-6799745.

BOOT, MRS ELISE
Netherlands, EPP (CDA)

Mrs Elise Boot, a member of the academic staff of the Europe Institute, University of Utrecht, serves on the National Council and executive of the European Movement in the Netherlands, and the central executive of the International European Movement. Member of the executive of the Union of European Federalists, and of the Faculty of Laws. Member, Utrecht Provincial Executive; CDA women's consultative section, Utrecht; YWCA working party, Europe; Association of Women Graduates; the International Affairs section, Dutch Council of Churches; the Catholic Council for Church and Community, and the Association for European Law. B August, 1932.

Address: Kerkdwarsstraat 5, 3581 RG Utrecht. Tel: (030) 31 77 80.

BOSERUP, MS BODIL
Denmark, Comm (SF)

Ms Bodil Boserup, lecturer at Copenhagen University, was elected treasurer of the Communist and Allies Group at the European Parliament, in July, 1979. Member, Copenhagen City Council. First became prominent in the Socialist People's Party in 1972 in debates on the EEC. Strongly against the Common Market, she is pressing for greater attention to be given to women's causes. Member of party executive. B June, 1921.

Address: Damstien 32, 2720 Vanløse. Tel: 01-740402.

BOYES, ROLAND
UK, Durham, Soc (Lab)

Mr Roland Boyes, Assistant Director of Durham County Social Services Department. B February, 1937. BSc (Econ), MSc. Member, Easington District Council, 1973–76; Peterlee Town Council, 1968–73 and since 1976. Married, two sons. Special interests: social services, education and new towns. A school manager of four schools; chairman of a comprehensive school. Member, executive committee, Northern Regional Labour Party; honorary secretary/agent, Easington Constituency Labour Party.

Address: 12 Spire Hollin, Peterlee, Co Durham. Tel: 0783 863917.

BRANDT, WILLY
Germany, Soc (SPD)

Herr Willy Brandt was Chancellor of the Federal Republic of Germany, 1969–74. Holder of the Nobel Peace Prize. Member of the Bundestag. Chairman of the SPD, of the Socialist International and the Independent Commission for International Development Questions. B December, 1913. Journalist.

Address: Erich-Ollenhauer-Haus, Ollenhauerstrasse 1, 5300 Bonn 12. Tel: (02221) 5321.

BROOKES, MISS BETA
UK, North Wales, ED (C)

Miss Beta Brookes is secretary to a tourism and catering company; formerly social worker with Denbighshire County Council. B 1931; ed Lowther College, Abergele, University of Wales and Alliance Française, Paris. Awarded American State Department Scholarship to study politics in United States. Parliamentary candidate for Widnes, 1955; Warrington, 1963 by-election; and Manchester Exchange, 1964. Member, European affairs committee, Council of Professions Supplementary to Medicine. Special interests: health, agriculture, tourism.

Address: The Cottage, Wayside Acres, Bodelwyddan, nr Rhyl, North Wales. Tel: St Asaph 583189.

BUCHAN, MRS JANEY
UK, Glasgow, Soc (Lab)

Mrs Janey Buchan is chairman of the Labour Party in Scotland and recently was chairman of the Scottish Gas Consumers' Council. For many years she was chairman of a local consumer group. Glasgow housewife and regional councillor, being vice-chairman of Strathclyde Regional Council's education committee. Married to Mr Norman Buchan, Labour MP for West Renfrewshire, with one son, a Fleet Street journalist. Member of ASTMS.

Address: 72 Peel Street, Glasgow G11 5LR, Scotland. Tel: 041-339 2583.

BUCHOU, HUBERT
France, DEP (DIFE)

M Hubert Buchou, a farmer, is President of the Fédération nationale des Sociétés d'aménagement foncier et d'établissement rural (SAFER); Vice-President of the Economic and Social Council of the EEC, and former Vice-President of the Fédération nationale des syndicats d'exploitants agricoles (FNSEA). B January, 1925.

Address: 276, Cami Salié, 64000 PAU.
Tel: 02 65 81.

BUTTAFUOCO, ANTONIO
Italy, Ind (MSI–DN)

Sgr Antonio Buttafuoco was elected to the Italian Parliament in 1972. Party member since its foundation; member of Central Committee. Member of the Sicilian Regional Assembly, 1951–71, being chairman of the parliamentary group, 1958–63. Deputy Secretary, Sicilian Regional Assembly, 1963–67. Town councillor for eight years. Mayor of Nissoria since 1968. Chairman, board of directors of Nissoria's bank Cassa Rurale ed Artigiana S. Giuseppe. B April, 1923; degree in political and social sciences.

Address: Via Zara 4, 94013 Leonforte (Enna).
Tel: 0935/61737-61621.

CABORN, RICHARD
UK, Sheffield, Soc (Lab)

Mr Richard Caborn has been elected chairman of the UK Labour Party group of members of the European Parliament. A fitter; full-time convenor of shop stewards with the British Steel Corporation in Sheffield. Member of Sheffield, Attercliffe, Constituency Labour Party; vice-chairman, Sheffield Trades Council and Sheffield Labour Party. B October, 1943; ed Hurlfield Comprehensive School and Sheffield Polytechnic. Married with one daughter and one son.

Address: 29 Quarry Vale Road, Sheffield S12 3EB. Tel: 0742 393802.

CAILLAVET, HENRI
France, LD (UFE)

M Henri Caillavet was a member of the nominated Parliament, being chairman of its Committee on Agriculture. Senator for Lot-et-Garonne; former district councillor and mayor. Vice-chairman, Committee on Cultural Affairs, in the Senate; rapporteur of opinions on press, information and television issues. Chairman, Finance Committee, Aquitaine Regional Assembly; France-Iran Parliamentary Friendship Group, and France-Israel Parliamentary Friendship Group. Former member, North Atlantic Assembly and WEU. B February, 1914.

Address: 28 rue Borghèse, 92200 Neuilly-sur-Seine. Tel: 637 43 20.

CALVEZ, CORENTIN
France, LD (UFE)

M Corentin Calvez has, since 1964, been head of the general centralisation department of a leading European oil company – Antar, Paris, Member, Economic and Social Council, 1968; Secretary-General of CGC (Management and Staff Confederation), 1969; general representative of the CGC, 1973–79; member CNESER (National Council for Higher Education and Research), 1976 Secretary-General, International Management Staff Confederation. 1976; member, management board, ELF-ERAP, 1978. Former French Rugby Federation referee; honorary chairman, Sports Association of La Baule. B June, 1920; ed Conservatoire National des Arts et Métiers, Paris.

Address: 27, avenue du Languedoc, 78450 Villepreux. Tel: 055 22 20.

CAPANNA, MARIO
Italy, TCDG (DP)

Sgr Mario Capanna was one of the leaders of the '68 student protest movement. Regional Councillor for Lombardy. B January, 1945; degree in philosophy.

Address: Via Giovanni Lanza 3, 20121 Milano.

CARDIA, UMBERTO
Italy, Comm (PCI)

Sgr Umberto Cardia, a member of the Italian Parliament from 1968, was a radio-television journalist from 1945 until he resigned in 1950 to join *L'Unita*. Director of the Association of Journalists. Party member since 1946; on Central Committee since 1958. Town councillor of Cagliari, 1952; Regional councillor, 1953. Secretary of the Communist Federation of Cagliari, 1957; Secretary, party's regional committee of Sardinia, since 1963; chairman, Communist group at the Regional Council, 1964–66. Member, Parliamentary Committee on Foreign Affairs. Married with three children. B September, 1921; degree in modern arts.

Address: Viale Merello 53, Cagliari.

CARIGLIA, ANTONIO
Italy, Soc (PSDI)

Sgr Antonio Cariglia was an Italian MP, 1963–76. Freelance journalist; official of the Court of Auditors. Former National Secretary, Italian Union of Labour (UIL). Member of party's national leadership and former party Vice-Secretary. Permanent member, Bureau of the Socialist International. Served as chairman, Committee on Foreign Affairs and the Committee on Affairs of the Council Presidency. B March, 1924; degree in political science.

Address: Via del Leone 13, 00186 Roma.
Tel: 67 81 570 and 47 58 940.

CAROSSINO, ANGELO
Italy, Comm (PCI)

Sgr Angelo Carossino, a factory worker, was Mayor of Savona, 1957–68; party Regional Secretary, 1967–75; Regional Councillor for Liguria, 1970; and became chairman of the Regional Council for Liguria in 1975. Elected member of the Central Committee at the XI Party Congress, he entered the party leadership at the XIV Party Congress. B February, 1929.

Address: Via Privata Lanfranco 34\B, Casa A/1, 17011 Albisola Capo (SV). Tel: 019-44364.

CASSANMAGNAGO CERRETTI, SIGNORA MARIA LUISA
Italy, EPP (DC)

Signora Maria Luisa Cassanmagnago Cerretti was elected a Vice-Chairman of the European People's Party Group (formerly CD) in July, 1979. Member, European Parliament, since 1976, and of Italian Chamber of Deputies, 1972-79. Organiser of the Christian Democrat Women's Movement in the province of Milan and member of the National Executive of the Women's Movement since 1963. Adviser to Milan provincial administration on problems of social assistance and security. B April, 1929; graduate in economics and commerce.

Address: Via Emanuele Filiberto 190, 00185 Roma. Tel: 7577607.

CASTELLINA, SIGNORA LUCIANA
Italy, TCDG (PDUP)

Signora Luciana Castellina has been a member of the Italian Parliament since 1976. Journalist; member of managing committee of the daily newspaper *Il Manifesto.* Member of her party's Central Committee. Vice-Chairman of the parliamentary group. Member of the Committee on Justice and the Interparliamentary Committee on the general guidance and supervision of the broadcasting services. B August, 1929; degree in jurisprudence.

Address: Partito di Unità Proletaria per il Comunismo, Via Tomacelli 166/b, 00186 Roma.

CASTLE, MRS BARBARA
UK, Greater Manchester North, Soc (Lab)

Mrs Barbara Castle, leader of the UK Labour Party group in the European Parliament and a vice-chairman (from July 1979) of the Socialist Group, was Secretary of State for Social Services, 1974–76. Member, national executive committee, Labour Party, 1950–79, being party chairman in 1958–59 and vice-chairman, 1957–58. Labour MP for Blackburn, 1955–79; previously for Blackburn East, 1950–55, and Blackburn, 1945–50. Minister of Overseas Development, 1964–65; Minister of Transport, 1965–68; First Secretary of State and Secretary of State for Employment and Productivity, 1968–70. Journalist. B October, 1911.

Address: 19G John Spencer Square, London N.1. Tel: 01-359 2012.

CATHERWOOD, SIR FREDERICK
UK, Cambridgeshire, ED (C)

Sir Frederick Catherwood has been appointed chairman of the European Parliament's External Economic Relations Committee. Director-General of the National Economic Development Council, 1966–71; previously Chief Economic Adviser, Department of Economic Affairs. Ex-managing director of John Laing and Son Ltd, of which he is currently director. Chartered accountant. Former chairman, British Overseas Trade Board, British Institute of Management, Mallinson-Denny Ltd and Wittenborg Automat Ltd. B January 1925; ed Shrewsbury School; Clare College, Cambridge. Married with three children.

Addresses: 25 Woodville Gardens, London W5 2LL; Sutton Hall, Balsham, Cambridgeshire.

CECOVINI, MANLIO
Italy, LD (PLI)

Sgr Manlio Cecovini, a lawyer, is Mayor of Trieste. Member, and former chairman, of the council of 'Ente Sona Industriale di Trieste'. Magistrate in Milan and Trieste from 1938, State Attorney from 1949, and head of regional office of Friuli-Venezia Giulia from 1962. In 1978 elected to regional council of Friuli-Venezia Giulia. B January, 1914; married with two children.

Address: Fraz. Padriciano 74, 34012 Trieste. Tel: (040) 226135.

CERAVOLO, DOMENICO
Italy, Comm (PCI)

Sgr Domenico Ceravolo was secretary, Italian Socialist Party's Federation of Padova, 1951–63. Member, Socialist Party's Central Committee until he moved to the Socialist Party for Proletarian Unity. In 1972 he was one of the supporters of the move to join the Italian Communist Party. Member, Communist Party's Central Committee; Group chief at the regional level. B September, 1928; degree in biology.

Address: Via Buonarroti, 35027 Noventa Padovana (PD). Tel: 049-628335.

CHAMBEIRON, ROBERT
France, Comm (PCF)

M Robert Chambeiron, former high official; director of a cultural organisation. Secretary-General of l'Union progressiste. B May, 1915.

Address: 16, rue Gustave Zédé, 75016 Paris. Tel: 647 7189.

CHARZAT, MME GISÈLE
France, Soc (PS)

Mme Gisèle Charzat is a teacher. B 1941.

Address: 63, rue Lauriston, 75016 Paris. Tel: 55 35 784.

CHIRAC, JACQUES
France, DEP (DIFE)

M Jacques Chirac was Prime Minister of France, 1974-76. Mayor of Paris; President of Rassemblement pour la République (RPR). Former conseiller referendaire of Cour des Comptes. Deputy for the Corrèze. B November, 1932. Graduate in political science; graduate of Ecole nationale d'administration.

Address: 1, Place Hôtel de Ville, 75004 Paris.

CHOURAQUI, MME NICOLE
France, DEP (DIFE)

Mme Nicole Chouraqui is Assistant Secretary-General of Rassemblement pour la République (RPR). Elected a vice-chairman of the European Progressive Democrats Group in July, 1979. Head of a women's centre for economic education. B 1939; graduate in political science.

Address: 123, rue de Lille, 75007 Paris.

CINCIARI RODANO, SIGNORA MARIA
Italy, Comm (PCI)

Signora Maria Cinciari Rodano was an Italian MP, 1948–63, and became a Senator, 1968. Party member since 1946. Rome City Councillor, 1946–56. Member and then National Chairman, Union of Italian Women. Member of Parliamentary Committees on: Home Affairs, Education and the Fine Arts, Employment and Social Security, Constitutional Affairs and Foreign Affairs. Vice-Chairman of the Lower House in the IV Legislature. Member, steering committee of the parliamentary group. B January, 1921; married with five children.

Address: Via delle Botteghe Oscure 4, 00188 Roma. Tel: 6711.

CLINTON, MARK
Ireland, EPP (F-Gael)

Mr Mark Clinton was Minister of Agriculture in the Republic of Ireland, 1973–77. B February, 1915; ed Christian Brothers' School, Dublin (Diploma in social science and agricultural science). Formerly estate manager. Fine Gael opposition front bench spokesman on local government, agriculture and defence. Dáil deputy for Dublin County, 1961–69, and for Dublin County North, 1969–77. Member, Dublin County Council 1955–73 (chairman 1957–59 and 1968–69); Dublin County Committee of Agriculture, 1955–73, (chairman 1965–68).

Address: Inisfail, Newcastle, Co Dublin. Tel: (01) 281493.

COHEN, ROBERT
Netherlands, Soc (PvdA)

Mr Robert Cohen is a former principal in the cabinets of Mr Mansholt and Mr Lardinois when EEC Commissioners; former Chef de Cabinet for Commissioner Vredeling; "development" director at the Commission. B March, 1920; studied political and social sciences at Amsterdam.

Addresses: E Speeckaertlaan 87, 1200 Brussels: Tel: 771.52.45. Traay 233, Driebergen. Tel: 03438-3518.

COLLA, MARCEL
Belgium, Soc (BSP)

Mr Marcel Colla is a former Chef de Cabinet at the Ministry of Economic Affairs. Alderman at Deurne, Antwerp. B September, 1943; studied sociology.

Address: Bosuil 27, 2100 Deurne. Tel: 031/24.35.39.

COLLESELLI, ARNALDO
Italy, EPP (DC)

Sgr Arnaldo Colleselli, President of the Italian-German Association of the Inter-Parliamentary Union, was a Deputy from 1958 and has been a Senator since 1972. Former Under-Secretary, Ministry of Agriculture and Forestry. Since 1953, President of the Provincial Federation and, subsequently, of the Regional Federation of Farmers of the Veneto Region. Town councillor, Belluno; President of the hill-farmers community. B September, 1918; graduated from the Catholic University of Milan.

Address: Via Garibaldi 45/B, 32100 Belluno. Tel: 0437-23998 and 0437-25750.

COLLINS, KENNETH
UK, Strathclyde East, Soc (Lab)

Mr Kenneth Collins, deputy leader, Labour Party group of European Parliament, has been appointed chairman of the Parliament's Committee on Environment, Public Health and Consumer Protection. Lecturer; councillor at East Kilbride since 1973. B August, 1939; ed Glasgow University and Strathclyde University. BSc(Hons geography), MSc. Member, board of East Kilbride Development Corporation; Association of Lecturers in Scottish Central Institutions; former chairman, North-East Glasgow's Children's Panel; vice-chairman, East Kilbride Constituency Labour Party. Married with one daughter and one son.

Address: 11 Clamps Terrace, East Kilbride, Strathclyde, Scotland. Tel: East Kilbride 37282.

COLLOMB, FRANCISQUE
France, EPP (UFE)

M Francisque Collomb, an industrialist, is Senator and Mayor of Lyon. B December, 1910.

Address: 59, rue Duquesne, 69006 Lyon. Tel: 24 28 00.

COLOMBO, EMILIO
Italy, EPP (DC)

Sgr Emilio Colombo was President of the European Parliament from March, 1977, to June, 1979. Prime Minister of Italy, 1970–72. Between 1955 and 1976 he was Minister of agriculture, of external trade, of industry, of the Treasury, for the budget, and of finance. Member, Chamber of Deputies, since 1948. Member, European Parliament since 1976 (chairman of political affairs committee, 1976-77). B April, 1920.

Address: Piazza S. Apollinare 33, 00186 Roma. Tel: 65 73 10.

COMBE, FRANCIS
France, LD (UFE)

M Francis Combe, a baker, is President of the Assemblée Permanente des Chambres de Métiers (APCM – Permanent Assembly of Trades and Crafts) and President of the International Union of Crafts and Small and Medium Enterprises (UIAPME). B May, 1926.

Address: 12, avenue Marceau, 75008 Paris. Tel: 225 45 77.

COPPIETERS, MAURITZ
Belgium, Ind (VU)

Mr Mauritz Coppieters is Senator for Dendermonde-Sint-Niklaas. B May, 1920; studied history and law.

Address: Meesterstraat 161, 2770 Nieuwkerken (Sint Niklaas-Waas). Tel: 031/76 57 64.

COSTANZO, ROBERTO
Italy, EPP (DC)

Sgr Roberto Costanzo, a graduate in social science, is national Vice-President of the Confederation of Italian Cooperatives. Former provincial party secretary. Former town and provincial councillor; a regional councillor since 1970. Chairman, Association for Rural Tourism. Chairman, EEC tobacco committee. Member, National Academy of Agriculture. B 1930.

Address: Via Nicola Calandra 25, 821000 Benevento. Tel: 0824-28864.

COTTRELL, RICHARD
UK, Bristol, ED (C)

Mr Richard Cottrell is a television reporter. B July, 1943; ed Court Fields Secondary School, Wellington, Somerset, and technical college. Special interests: economics and business. Married with two children.

Address: Combeside, Back Lane, Croscombe, Wells, Somerset.

CRAXI, BETTINO
Italy, Soc (PSI)

Sgr Bettino Craxi was elected national party secretary in 1976; Italian MP since 1968 being chairman of the PSI parliamentary group. Freelance journalist and author. Town councillor, 1960–70. Former President, Institute for the Science of Public Administration. Party representative in the Socialist International. Member of Committee on Defence; on Foreign Affairs; and Emigration. B February, 1934.

Address: Via Foppa 5, 20144 Milano.

CRESSON, MME EDITH
France, Soc (PS)

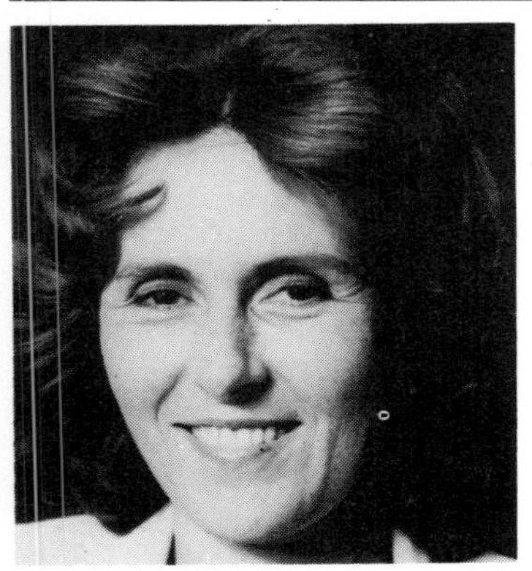

Mme Edith Cresson is an agricultural engineer. B 1934; studied economics.

Address: 5, rue Clémont Marot, 75008 Paris. Tel: 35 99 788.

CRONIN, JEREMIAH
Ireland, DEP (F-Fáil)

Mr Jeremiah Cronin, a Deputy for Cork North-East since 1965, was Minister for Defence, 1970–73, and Parliamentary Secretary to the Minister for Agriculture and Fisheries, 1966–70. Company director in auctioneering and insurance. B September 1925; ed Christian Brothers' Secondary School, Fermoy. Member, Cork County Council, 1967–69 and since 1974; Cork County Committee of Agriculture, 1967–69 and since 1974. Has been Secretary, Irish Sugar Beet Growers' Association (Mallow Sugar Factory area). Founder member, Mallow Industrial Development Association. Married with two sons and three daughters.

Addresses: Home — 71 Main Street, Mallow, C Cork. Business — West End, Mallow, Co Cork. Tel: (022) 21361 and (022) 21630.

CROUX, LAMBERT
Belgium, EPP (CVP-EVP)

Mr Lambert Croux was a member of the Belgian Parliament, 1967–77; became a Senator, 1977. Member, national party executive and national bureau of the Christelijke Volkspartij (CVP) 1975–77. B 1927; degree in economic sciences, Doctor of Law. Industrial legal adviser at Alken since 1954. Chairman, Association of CVP delegates from municipalities and provinces, since 1978; vice-chairman, European Union of CD delegates from local and regional authorities. Chairman, Limburg Economic Council, 1972–77, and Limburg GOM (Regional Development Society), 1975–77.

Address: Stationsstraat 19, 3820 Alken. Tel: 011-312.537.

CURRY, DAVID
UK, Essex North East, ED (C)

Mr David Curry, a journalist, was in 1975 appointed Brussels correspondent of *The Financial Times* covering EEC and Benelux affairs with special mandate to cover industrial, business and financial matters and the European Parliament. He had been editor of the international business and company sections of *The Financial Times;* in 1976 he became Paris correspondent, and in 1978 was appointed Foreign News Editor in London. Contested Morpeth in both 1974 general elections. B June, 1944; ed Ripon Grammar School and Corpus Christi College, Oxford. Married with three children.

Address: The Old Maltings, Arkesden, nr Saffron Waldon, Essex CB11 4HB. Tel: Clavering 368.

DALSASS, JOACHIM
Italy, EPP (SVP)

Sgr Joachim Dalsass, a doctor in jurisprudence, was an official in the Trento regional administration from 1953–1956 responsible for cooperatives and the fire service. Member, Regional Council of the South Tyrol, since 1956; deputy Councillor for Social Welfare for South Tyrol, 1956–1960; member, regional executive in charge of public works 1960–1972; in charge of agriculture, forestry, hunting and fishing, 1972–78. Deputy chairman, South Tyrol People's Party since 1969; President, South Tyrol Regional Council, since 1978. B December, 1926.

Address: 49040 Petersberg (Post Aldein). Tel: 616591.

DALZIEL, IAN
UK, Lothians, ED (C)

Mr Ian Dalziel is senior manager (corporate finance) with a merchant bank, with special responsibility for development of relations with European institutions. B 1947; ed Daniel Stewart's College, Edinburgh, and St John's College, Cambridge. Member, Richmond-upon-Thames Council. Married with two children.

Address: 21 Greenhill Gardens, Edinburgh 1H10 4BL. Tel: (031) 447 3441 and 01-600 4585 (London office).

DAMETTE, FÉLIX
France, Comm (PCF)

M Félix Damette is an assistant geography master. B 1936.

Address: Comité Central du PCF, 2, Place du Colonel Fabien, 75940 Paris Cedex 19. Tel: 238 66 55.

DAMSEAUX, ANDRÉ
Belgium, LD (PRL)

Mr André Damseaux has been appointed a Vice-Chairman of the Liberal and Democratic Group of the European Parliament. Deputy for Verviers; a former chairman of the Party of Reform and Liberty of Wallonia (PRLW). Was a member of the nominated European Parliament. Merchant. B March, 1937; graduate in diplomatic and political science. Leader of French-speaking PLP group in Cultural Council, 1973; member, Belgian Olympic Committee; chairman, Charles Rogier Centre.

Address: 30, rue des Hougnes, 4800 Verviers.
Tel: 087-22 11 67.

D'ANGELOSANTE, FRANCESCO
Italy, Comm (PCI)

Sgr Francesco d'Angelosante is an Italian Senator. Lawyer. Party member since 1942. Town councillor of Penne. Former member of the Committees on Defence and Foreign Affairs. Twice member of the Committee of Inquiry into indictment proceedings.

Address: Via Regina Elena 62, 65100 Pescara.
Tel: 23124.

DANKERT, PIETER
Netherlands, Soc ((PvdA)

Mr Pieter Dankert has been a member of the European Parliament since 1977. Member of Dutch Parliament; former member, Assembly of Council of Europe and the WEU Assembly. Former PvdA international secretary. B January, 1934. Trained teacher; Dip Ed history.

Address: Hoogstraat 1, 1135 BZ Edam.
Tel: 02993-71668.

DAVERN, NOEL
Ireland, DEP (F-Fáil)

Mr Noel Davern, a farmer, was elected for Tipperary South in the 1969 general election. B December 1945; ed Christian Brothers' School, Cashel; Franciscan College, Gormanstown, Co Meath. Member, Dáil and Seanad Joint Restaurant Committee, 1970–73; Cashel Gaelic Athletic Association Club; Cashel Rugby Club, Cashel Sportsfield Committee.

Address: Tannersrath, Clonmel, Co Tipperary. Tel: (052) 22991.

DEBATISSE, MICHEL
France, EPP (UFE)

M Michel Debatisse, a farmer, is a former President of the Fédération Nationale des Syndicats d'Exploitants Agricoles (FNSEA). B April, 1929.

Address: 8, Avenue Marceau, 75008 Paris. Tel: 225 5154.

DEBRÉ, MICHEL
France, DEP (DIFE)

M Michel Debré, was Prime Minister of France, 1959–62. Deputy for Reunion; Mayor of Amboise. B January, 1912.

Address: 36, rue de Bellechasse, 75007 Paris. Tel: 550 4084.

DE CLERCQ, WILLY
Belgium, LD (PVV-ELD)

Mr Willy de Clercq is chairman of the Partij voor Voijheid en Vooruitgang (PVV) and a vice-chairman of the European Liberal Democrats (ELD). Lawyer. Representative for Ghent-Eeklo. Under Secretary of State for the Budget, 1960; leader of PVV parliamentary party, 1965; Deputy Prime Minister and Minister of Finance, 1966 and again in 1973; President of EEC Council of Ministers of Finance, first half of 1973; Minister of Finance, 1974–77. B July, 1927. Married with two children.

Address: Baron Cyriel Buyssestraat 12, 9000 Gent. Tel: 091-22 59 47 and 091-22 80 69.

DE COURCY LING, JOHN
UK, Midlands Central, ED (C)

Mr John de Courcy Ling, farmer and Lloyds underwriter, was formerly a senior diplomat, his last appointment being as Counsellor, British Embassy, Paris, 1974–77. B October, 1933; ed King Edward's School, Edgbaston, and Clare College, Cambridge. Foreign Office, 1959; Second Secretary, Santiago, 1963–66; First Secretary, Nairobi, 1966–69; Chargé d'Affaires, Chad, 1973. Married with four children.

Address: Bellehatch Farm, Henley-on-Thames, Oxfordshire, RG9 4AW. Tel: Henley (4912) 3878.

DE FERRANTI, BASIL
UK, Hampshire, West, ED (C)

Mr Basil de Ferranti was elected a Vice-President of the European Parliament in July, 1979. President, Economic and Social Committee, European Communities, 1976–79, member since 1973. Joint vice-chairman, European Democrat group, European Parliament, July, 1979. Deputy chairman, Ferranti Ltd. B July, 1930; ed Eton and Trinity College, Cambridge. Conservative MP for Morecambe and Lonsdale, 1958–64; Parliamentary Secretary, Ministry of Aviation, 1962. Deputy managing director, International Computers and Tabulators, 1963; managing director, 1964. Director, International Computers Ltd, until 1972. Married with four children.

Address: Millbank Tower, Millbank, London SW1P 4QS. Tel: 01-834 6611.

DE GOEDE, ARIE
Netherlands, Ind (D'66)

Mr Arie de Goede, a former Secretary of State for Finance, is a former member of the Dutch Second Chamber, the Assembly of the Council of Europe, and the WEU Assembly. B May, 1928; trained in tax law and financial administration.

Address: Brederode 28, Leiderdorp.
Tel: 071-890769.

DE KEERSMAEKER, PAUL
Belgium, EPP (CVP-EVP)

Mr Paul de Keersmaeker has been a member of the European Parliament since 1974. Burgomaster of Asse. Member of Parliament for the Brussels Halle-Vilvoorde district from 1968; member of the Committee for Foreign Affairs and Development and Cooperation, and of the Parliamentary Committee on small traders. Company director. Member, bureau of the CVP Parliamentary Party; chairman, foreign policy working party of the CVP. B July, 1929; doctor of law; notary licenciate.

Address: Broekstraat 4, 1703 Kobbegem (Asse).
Tel: 02-452 60 80.

DEKKER, MRS SUZANNE
Netherlands, Ind (D'66)

Mrs Suzanne Dekker has been a civil servant in the Department for International Energy Affairs at the Ministry of Economic Affairs. B October, 1949; studied law at Groningen.

Address: Burg. Patijnlaan 470, Den Haag.
Tel: 070-45 36 07.

DE LA MALÈNE, CHRISTIAN
France, DEP (DIFE)

M Christian de la Malène unsuccessfully contested the election for the Presidency of the European Parliament in July, 1979. Elected chairman of European Progressive Democrats Group, in July, 1979, a position he held in the outgoing nominated Parliament. Senator for Paris and First Assistant to Mayor of Paris. Former minister. B December, 1920; doctor of law. Sociologist.

Addresses: 31, rue Saint Dominique, 75007 Paris. Hôtel de Ville, 75196 Paris R.P.

DELATTE, CHARLES
France, LD (UFE)

M Charles Delatte, a farmer, has been President of the Caissé Nationale de Crédit Agricole, since 1974. Secretary of the Agricultural Chamber of Cote d'Or. President of the Caissé de Crédit Agricole of Dijon, since 1956; of the National Agricultural Credit Federation, 1968–74; of the National Confederation of Cooperation and Agricultural Credit Friendly Societies, since 1976; and, since 1977, of the International Agricultural Credit Confederation. Chairman, Economic and Social Committee for the Burgundy region, since 1974. B January, 1922; diploma from the Ecole Regionale d'Agriculture de Tomblaine. Married with seven children.

Address: Chemin de Cromois, 21000 Dijon. Tel: (80) 65 28 98.

DELEAU, GUSTAVE
France, DEP (DIFE)

M Gustave Deleau is a member of the Economic and Social Committee of the EEC. Company managing director. President of groupings of small and medium-sized undertakings (PME). B September, 1909.

Address: 50, rue de Crimée, 75019 Paris. Tel: 202 35 15.

DELMOTTE, FERNAND
Belgium, Soc (PSB)

Mr Fernand Delmotte, a former minister, is Senator for Mons-Soignies and Mayor of Lessines. President of the Socialist Group of the Senate. Technician-mechanic. B July, 1920. Was a member of the nominated European Parliament.

Address: 44, Chemin du Foubertsart, 7860 Lessines. Tel: 068-33 29 89.

DELOROZOY, ROBERT
France, LD (UFE)

M Robert Delorozoy, managing director of family retail business, is President of the Permanent Assembly of the Chambers of Commerce and Industry of France. Member of the Economic and Social Council (Finance Section) and chairman of its Private Undertakings Group. Member, Supreme Council for the Middle Classes and of the National Credit Council. President, French Institute of Self-service and Modern Distribution Techniques. Mayor of Choisel (Yvelines).

Address: 2, Rte des Sablières, Choisel, 78460 Chevreuse. Tel: 052 08 87.

DELORS, JACQUES
France, Soc (PS)

M Jacques Delors is a journalist; editor of a weekly newspaper. Delegate of Socialist Party on international economic relations. B July, 1935. Graduate in economic science.

Address: 19, Bd de Bercy, 75012 Paris. Tel: 307 88 83 and 260 93 60.

DEMARCH, MME DANIELLE
France, Comm (PCF)

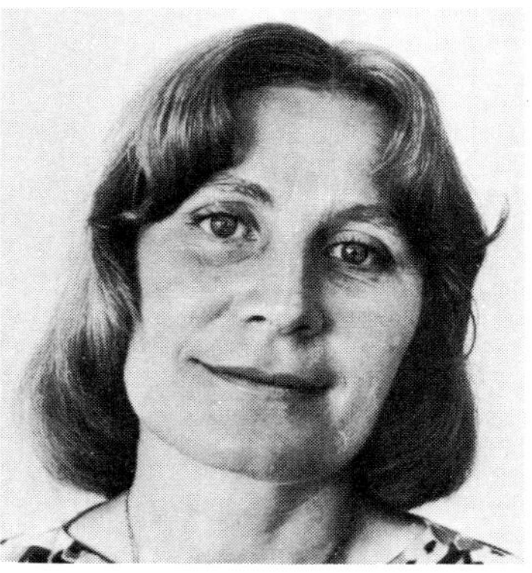

Mme Danielle Demarch, a civil servant, was elected a Vice-President of the European Parliament in July, 1979. Member, Central Committee of French Communist Party. B August, 1939.

Address: Fédération du PCF, Le Colbert – Entree B, Avenue Colbert, 83000 Toulon.

DENIS, JACQUES
France, Comm (PCF)

M Jacques Denis, a painting worker, is a member of the Central Committee of the French Communist Party.

Address: Comité Central du PCF, 2 Place du Colonel Fabien 75940 Paris Cedex 19. Tel: 202 70 10.

DE PASQUALE, FRANCESCO
Italy, Comm (PCI)

Sgr Francesco de Pasquale is Secretary of the Communist Federation of Messina. Town councillor, former chairman of the Regional Council of Sicily. B August, 1925; degree in philosophy.

Address: Via Libertà 161/b, 90100 Palermo. Tel: 295589.

DESMOND, MRS EILEEN
Ireland, Soc (Lab)

Mrs Eileen Desmond, a former civil servant in the Department of Posts and Telegraphs, was first elected to the Dáil in 1965 in a by-election in Mid-Cork; returned in the election that followed, defeated in 1969 and in a by-election in 1972. Elected for Mid-Cork in 1973. B December, 1932; ed Convent of Mercy School, Kinsale. Labour Party opposition spokesman on education, 1965–69; chairman, Women's Representative Committee, since 1975; a senator, Commercial and Industrial Panel, 1969–73. Member, Committee on Procedure and Privileges, 1965–69; Dáil and Seanad Standing Joint Committee on Consolidation Bills, since 1973; Cork County Council, since 1965.

Address: Ballinrea Road, Carrigaline, Co Cork.

DE VALERA, MISS SILE
Ireland, DEP (F-Fáil)

Miss Sile de Valera, formerly a teacher, is a Deputy and the youngest member of the 21st Dáil. That was her first contest for election to a public body. B December, 1954; ed Loreto Convent, Foxrock, Co Dublin; University College, Dublin. Grand-daughter of Eamon de Valera, President of Ireland 1959–73.

Address: Charton, Kerrymount Avenue, Foxrock, Co Dublin. Tel: (01) 894129.

DIANA, ALFREDO
Italy, EPP (DC)

Sgr Alfredo Diana, an agronomist and farmer, was president of the Italian General Federation of Agriculture, 1969–77; currently member of its executive board and chairman, National Economic Council. Deputy chairman, National Economic and Labour Council (CNEL). Member, Council of the Directors-Managers Catholic Union. President of the Institute of Experimental Fruitgrowing. Director of Montedism, Standa and other important Italian companies. President, West Rome Rotary Club. B June, 1930. Married with four children.

Address: Via M Mercati 38, 00197 Roma. Tel: 874312.

DIDO', MARIO
Italy, Soc (PSI)

Sgr Mario Dido' is national secretary of CGIL (Federation of Italian Trade Unions); member, Economic and Social Committee of the EEC, and of the Confederation of European Trade Unions. B November, 1926.

Address: Via Filippo Civinini 37, 00197 Roma.

DIENESCH, MME MARIE-MADELEINE
France, DEP (DIFE)

Mme Marie-Madeleine Dienesch is International Vice-Presient of the European Union of Women. Former minister; former ambassador. Deputy for Côtes-du-Nord. B April, 1914. Agrégée in literature.

Address: 9 rue du Commandant Coupeaux, 22600 Loudeac..

DILIGENT, ANDRÉ
France, EPP (UFE)

M André Diligent, a lawyer and official of press company, was Vice-President of the Democratic Centre in Italy from 1973, being elected Secretary-General of the Centre des démocrates sociaux (CDS) at its convention in Lyons in October, 1977 B May, 1919. Elected member of Parliament for the Nord in 1958; defeated in 1962. Member of the Senate, 1965–74, becoming wellknown for his work to combat illicit advertising on television and his fight to ensure impartiality of information.

Address: 207, Bd Saint Germain, 75007 Paris. Tel: 5447250(1).

DONNEZ, GEORGES
France, LD (UFE)

M Georges Donnez, a lawyer, has been Mayor of St-Amand-les-Eaux since 1953. Deputy for the Nord (19th Division, St-Amand), 1973–78. Vice-president of the Mouvement démocrate socialiste de France (MDSF). B June, 1922; ed Lycée St-Amand-les-Eaux; Faculty of Law, Lille Licencié in law; member of the bar of Valenciennes since 1946. Member of the Conseil Général of the St-Amand-Rive Gauche canton, 1958, re-elected in 1964, 1970 and 1976.

Address: 51 Grand Place, 59230 Saint-Amand-les-Eaux.

d'ORMESSON, OLIVIER
France, EPP (UFE)

M Olivier d'Ormesson, journalist and farmer. Conseiller général for Val-de-Marne; Mayor of Ormesson-sur-Marne. B August, 1918; graduate in economic and commercial science.

Address: avenue Olivier d'Ormesson, 94 Ormesson sur Marne. Tel: 576 95 28 and 576 01 36..

DOURO, MARQUESS OF
UK, Surrey, ED (C)

The Marquess of Douro has been an executive director of Deltec Banking Corporation Ltd, an American investment company, since 1973 and deputy chairman of Thames Valley Broadcasting (a commercial radio station) since 1975. B August, 1945; ed Eton and Christ Church, Oxford. Son of the 8th Duke of Wellington. Contested Islington, North, in the October 1974 general election. Farmer. Member, Basingstoke Borough Council. Married with one son.

Address: 11 Copthall Avenue, London EC2R 7LU. Tel: 01-628 4761. Apsley House, Piccadilly, London W1.

DRUON, MAURICE
France, DEP (DIFE)

M Maurice Druon, former minister, Deputy for Paris. B April, 1918; graduate in literature and political science. Writer; member of the Académie française.

Address: 73 rue de Varennes, 75007 Paris. Tel: 551 93 35.

DUNN, WILLIAM NEWTON
UK, Lincolnshire, ED (C)

Mr William Newton Dunn is purchasing controller in the fertiliser division of Fisons Ltd. B October, 1941; ed Marlborough College; Gonville and Caius College, Cambridge, and the Sorbonne. Contested Carmarthen in February 1974 general election and Cardiff West in October 1974 election. Deputy chairman, Lambeth Vauxhall Conservative Association, 1973; former chairman, Bow Group European energy policy study group. Special interests: shipping (being a former shipping company executive), energy and agriculture (fertilisers).

Tel: Shenton Cottage, Greywell, Basingstoke, Hampshire. Tel: Odiham 2661. Conservative Office, 6 Upgate, Louth, Lincolnshire. Tel: 603713.

ELLES, LADY
UK, Thames Valley, ED (C)

Lady Elles was elected a joint vice-chairman of the European Democrat Group in the European Parliament in July 1979. A Conservative Opposition spokesman on foreign and Commonwealth affairs, House of Lords, 1975–79. Member of the European Parliament, 1973–75. Barrister (Lincoln's Inn). Created a life peer in 1972. B July, 1921; ed London, Paris and Florence; London University (BA Hons). International chairman, European Union of Women, since 1973, and chairman of its British section, 1970–74; former chairman, Conservative Party's International Office.

Address: 75 Ashley Gardens, London SW1. Tel: 828-0175.

ENRIGHT, DEREK
UK, Leeds, Soc (Lab)

Mr Derek Enright has been deputy headmaster and director, sixth form, of Featherstone St Wilfred's Comprehensive School. B August, 1935; ed St Joseph's, Pontefract; St Michael's, Leeds, and Wadham College, Oxford. BA, Diploma of Education in Greats. Member, Pontefract County Council, 1973–77. Treasurer, Pontefract and Castleford CLP and of the West Yorkshire County Party. Former member, Pudsey Borough Council, Leeds Council and Leeds Area Health Authority. AMMA. Press correspondent for his union. Married with two sons and two daughters.

Address: 112 Carleton Road, Pontefract, West Yorkshire WF8 3NQ. Tel: 0977 702096.

ESTGEN, NICOLAS
Luxembourg, EPP (CSV)

Mr Nicolas Estgen, a teacher, served in the Education Ministry of the Duchy; president of L'Action Familiale et Populaire. B 1930.

Address: 1 rue P. Wigreux, Howald. Tel: 48 68 89.

ESTIER, CLAUDE
France, Soc (PS)

M Claude Estier, journalist and editor of a weekly publication, was elected a vice-chairman of the Socialist Group of the European Parliament in July, 1979. B June, 1925. Graduate in political science.

Address: 12, rue Cortot, 75018 Paris. Tel: 705 8290.

EWING, MRS WINIFRED
UK, Highlands and Islands, DEP (Scot Nat)

Mrs Winifred Ewing was elected a vice-chairman of the European Progressive Democrat Group in July 1979; member of European Parliament since 1975. Solicitor. A vice-president of the Scottish National Party; MP for Moray and Nairn, 1974–79; MP for Hamilton, 1967–70. Became SNP spokesman on external affairs and EEC in 1974. B July 1929; ed Queen's Park Senior Secondary School, Glasgow, and Glasgow University. Lecturer in law, Scottish College of Commerce, 1954–56; secretary, Glasgow Bar Association, 1961–67. Married with three children.

Address: 52 Queen's Drive, Glasgow S2, Scotland. Tel: 041-423 8060. Goodwill, Lossiemouth, Morayshire, Scotland.

FANTI, GUIDO
Italy, Comm (PCI)

Sgr Guido Fanti became an Italian MP in 1976. Journalist. Party member since 1945; Secretary of party's Provincial Federation of Bologna (1959). Elected to Central Committee, 1960; member, national leadership, since the XI Congress. Mayor of Bologna, 1966–70. Chairman, Regional Council of Emilia-Romagna, 1970–76. Former member, Presidency of the World Council on Peace. Member, executive committee, World Federation of Twinned Towns. Member of Parliamentary Committees on Public Works and Chairman of Committee for Regional Affairs. Member, parliamentary group's steering committee. B May, 1925.

Address: Corso Vittorio Emanuele 147a, Roma. Tel: 6567777.

FAURE, EDGAR
France, LD (UFE)

M Edgar Faure was Prime Minister of France, 1952 and 1955–56. Lawyer and member of the French Academy. President of the National Assembly, 1973–78. B August 1908. Agrégé in Law (Roman law and history of law) (1962), diploma in modern oriental languages. Advocate at the Paris courts since 1929. Radical-Socialist deputy for the Jura, 1946–58; President of the Conseil General of the Jura, 1949–67; Secretary of State in the Ministry of Finance, 1949–51, then Minister of the Budget. Minister of Finance and Economic Affairs, 1954; Minister of Foreign Affairs, 1955; Minister of Finance, 1958; Minister of Agriculture, 1966–68.

Address: 134 rue de Grenelle, 75007 Paris. Tel: 70546-56 and 5552179.

FAURE, MAURICE
France, Soc (PS)

M Maurice Faure, when a minister, was a signatory of the Treaty of Rome. Deputy for Lot; Mayor of Cahors. Member of the nominated European Parliament. B January, 1922. Agrégé in history and geography. Doctor of Law.

Address: 6, rue Jean Admirat, 46200 Gourdon. Tel: 370258.

FELLERMAIER, LUDWIG
Germany, Soc (SPD)

Herr Ludwig Fellermaier was elected vice-chairman of the Socialist Group of the European Parliament in July, 1979; chairman of group in outgoing nominated Parliament. Businessman. Member of Bundestag. B July, 1930.

Address: Emsstrasse 8, 7910 Neu-Ulm.

FERGUSSON, ADAM
UK, Strathclyde West, ED (C)

Mr Adam Fergusson, author and journalist, was from 1967–77 a feature writer with *The Times* specialising in politics, economics, foreign affairs and environmental matters. B 1932; ed Trinity College, Cambridge. Has done many broadcasts on BBC overseas service on world affairs. Now a freelance journalist, having written for *The Sunday Times, Daily Telegraph, Herald Tribune, Spectator, New Review,* etc. Many publications, including two historical novels. Married with four children.

Addresses: 9 Addison Crescent, London W14: Ladyburn, Maybole, Ayrshire.

FERNANDEZ, GUY
France, Comm (PCF)

M Guy Fernandez, metal worker, serves as a member of the Central Committee of the French Communist Party.

Address: Fédération du PCF, 30, rue Michelet, 89000 Auxerre.

FERRERO, BRUNO
Italy, Comm (PCI)

Sgr Bruno Ferrero is chief of the party group on the town council of Aosta. Secretary, Communist and Allies Group within the European Parliament, 1972–75. Party secretary for the Piedmont Region since 1976; Member, party's Central Committee. B June, 1943; degree in political science.

Address: Via Chiesa della Salute 47, 10100 Torino. Tel: 251058..

FERRI, MAURO
Italy, Soc (PSDI)

Sgr Mauro Ferri, an Italian MP, 1953–76, was Minister of Industry and Commerce in the second Andreotti Government. Lawyer. Former member, Italian Socialist Party's Central Committee and of the leadership of the unified Socialist/Social Democrat Party. On the separation of the two parties, he became Secretary of the Social Democrat Party; head of its Foreign Section. Alderman and then Mayor of Castel San Niccolò, 1944–50. Town councillor of Arezzo, 1951–64, and Provincial councillor, 1951–55. Member of several parliamentary committees including the Committee on Foreign Affairs. B March, 1920.

Address: Via del Casaletto 265, 00151 Roma. Tel: 530416.

FILIPPI, RENZO
Italy, EPP (DC)

Sgr Renzo Filippi is a former civil servant at the Ministry of Foreign Affairs where he specialized in EEC problems. Outgoing Rome City councillor, he was particularly concerned with the preservation of the national heritage. Secretary of the party's area group for the Parioli district of Rome. B September, 1935.

Address: Via Schiaparelli 11, 00197 Roma. Tel: 802167.

FISCHBACH, MARC
Luxembourg, EPP (CSV)

Mr Marc Fischbach, a lawyer, is a member of the national bureau of CSV, secretary of his parliamentary group, and a bureau member of the European People's Party. B 1946.

Address: 2 rue Nic. Welter, Luxembourg. Tel: 47 35 45.

FLANAGAN, SEAN
Ireland, DEP (F-Fáil)

Mr Sean Flanagan was Minister for Lands in the Republic of Ireland, 1969–73; Minister for Health, 1966–69; Parliamentary Secretary to Minister for Industry and Commerce, 1965–66. Elected a vice-chairman of the DEP group, European Parliament, July, 1979. B January, 1922. Solicitor. Deputy for Mayo South, 1951–69 and then for Mayo East until 1977. Member, Dáil and Seanad Joint Committee on EEC Secondary Legislation. Member, Council of Europe, 1952–53, 1957–59 and 1965. Married with two sons and five daughters.

Addresses: 65 St Lawrence Road, Dublin 3 — St Anthony's, Ballaghaderreen, Co Roscommon.

FLESCH, MRS COLETTE
Luxembourg, LD (PD)

Mrs Colette Flesch, Mayor of the City of Luxembourg, has been a member of the European Parliament since 1969 and was chairman, Committee on Development and Cooperation. A vice-chairman, Liberal and Democratic Group. B April, 1937; ed Wellesley College, Wellesley, Massachusetts, and the Fletcher School of Law and Diplomacy, Melford, Massachusetts. Administrator in secretariat of Council of European Communities in Brussels, 1964–69. In 1969 became a member of the Chamber of Deputies; chairman of the parliamentary group of the Democratic Party.

Address: 11a, Boulevard Prince Henri, Luxembourg. Tel: 47 39 10 and 47 961.

FOCKE, FRAU KATHERINA
Germany, Soc (SPD)

Frau Katherina Focke is a former State Secretary and Federal Minister. Member of the Bundestag. Member and director of various private, national and international European organisations. B October, 1922. Political scientist, journalist.

Address: Pferdmengestrasse 34, 5000 Köln 51.

FORSTER, MISS NORVELLA
UK, Birmingham South, ED (C)

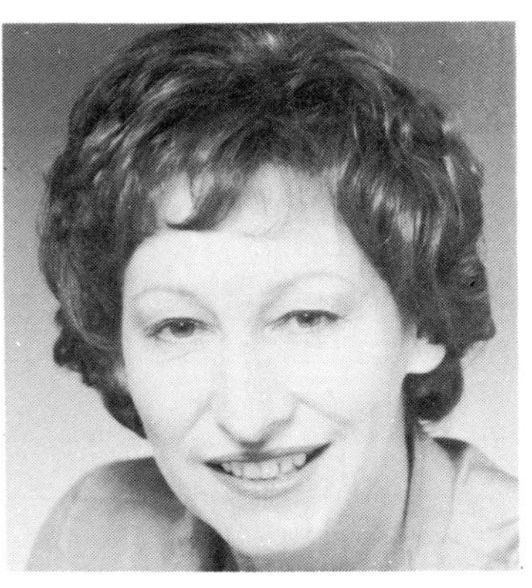

Miss Norvella Forster is chairman and managing director of her own consultancy company specialising in the plastics, packaging, chemical and allied process industries; undertakes research into marketing and management problems. B 1931; ed South Wilts Grammar School, Salisbury, and London University (President of the Union Society). Council member, Bow Group; former member, Hampstead Borough Council; member, London Europe Society and Conservative Group for Europe.

Addresses: Industrial Aids Ltd, 14 Buckingham Palace Road, London SW1W 0QP. Tel: 01-828 5036. 6 Regency House, Regency Street, London SW1. Tel: 01-821 5749.

FORTH, ERIC
UK, Birmingham North, ED (C)

Mr Eric Forth has been audit manager for Rank Xerox, Mitcheldean, Gloucestershire; was a systems development officer. Contested Barking in both 1974 general elections. B September 1944; ed Jordanhill College School, Glasgow, and Glasgow University. Member, Brentwood Urban District Council, 1968–72, being vice-chairman of town centre and health and sewerage committees. Married with two children.

Address: Updown, Merrivale Lane, Ross-on-Wye, Herefordshire. Tel: 4383.

FRIEDRICH, BRUNO
Germany, Soc (SPD)

Herr Bruno Friedrich was elected a Vice-President of the European Parliament in July, 1979. Member of the Bundestag; deputy chairman of SPD in the Bundestag and of the Confederation of Socialist Parties of the EEC. Member, SPD executive. Editor. B May, 1927.

Address: Haus Frankenwarte, 8700 Würzburg.

FRIEDRICH, INGO
Germany, EPP (CSU)

Herr Ingo Friedrich was on the staff of the Institute for Politics and Communications, University of Erlangen-Nuremberg, 1967–70, taking doctor's degree in 1971. Deputy chairman, CSU for Central Franconia region, 1977; CSU chairman, Weissenburg-Gunzenhausen district, since 1972. Chairman, Nuremburg Students' Union, 1964–65. B January, 1942. Married with two children.

Address: Bühringerstrasse 12, 8820 Gunzenhausen. Tel: (09831) 2425.

FRISCHMANN, GEORGES
France, Comm (PCF)

M Georges Frischmann is a member of the Central Committee of the French Communist Party. Post Office worker. B August, 1919.

Address: CGT, 213 rue Lafayette, 75480 Paris Cedex 10.

FRÜH, ISIDOR
Germany, EPP (CDU)

Herr Isidor Früh has been a member of the Bundestag since 1969 and of the European Parliament since 1973. B April, 1922; studied agriculture at University of Hohenheim; doctorate 1958. From 1952–1976, head of the Bad Waldsee rural adult education institute of the Württemberg-Hohenzollern Farmers' Association. Since 1973, chairman, Federal Association of German Fruit Distillers and Small Distillers. Member, CDU, since 1956; chairman of the district agricultural committee; member, "Land" agricultural committee and bureau of the Federal agricultural committee.

Address: Oberer Kirchberg 14,7957 Schemmerhofen 2. Tel: (07356) 615.

FUCHS, KARL
Germany, EPP (CSU)

Herr Karl Fuchs, member of the Bundestag since 1969 and of the European Parliament since 1977. Senior teacher. Deputy chairman, Lower Bavaria Regional Association, since 1972; district councillor, 1966–72; member, Bavarian State Parliament, 1966–69. Married with three children. B September, 1920.

Address: Waldschmidtstrasse 34, 8390 Passau. Tel: (0851) 47281.

FUILLET, MME YVETTE
France, Soc (PS)

Mme Yvette Fuillet has been a member of the Marseilles city council since 1971. Member, national executive bureau, French Socialist Party. B 1923.

Address: Appartement 20, Le Corbusier, 280 Bd Michelet, 13000 Marseille.Tel: 77 21 86.

GABERT, VOLKMAR
Germany, Soc (SPD)

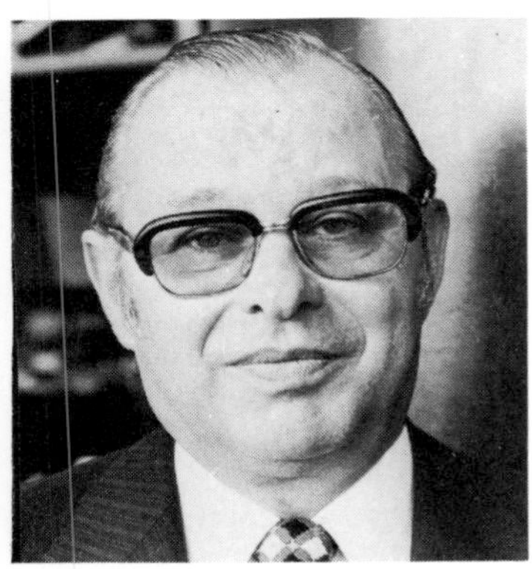

Herr Volkmar Gabert is member and Vice-President of the Bavarian Landtag. Member, SPD executive. Managing director of the Arbeitsgemeinschaft demokratischer Sozialisten im Alpenraum. B March, 1923.

Address: Franz-Fackler-Strasse 39, 8000 Munchen 50. Tel: (089) 150 30 63.

GAIOTTI DE BIASE, SIGNORA PAOLA
Italy, EPP (DC)

Signora Paola Gaiotti de Biase, university lecturer, is a former chairman of the European Women's Union committee on the family. Former member, Italian national committee of Unesco and an Italian representative at the UN conference for International Women's Year. Member of the Ministerial committee for the reform of secondary schooling. B August, 1927; graduate of University of Rome. Married with one son.

Address: Via B Gosio 33, 00191 Roma. Tel: 06/392848.

GALLAGHER, MICHAEL
UK, Nottinghamshire, Soc (Lab)

Mr Michael Gallagher, miner and part-time lecturer for Labour Committee for Europe. B July, 1934; ed Nottingham University (two year miners' day release course), TUC scholarship Coleg Harlech, and then again at Nottingham University (two years' full-time on political, economic and American studies). Member, Mansfield Borough Council, 1970–74, and Nottinghamshire County Council, since 1973 (leader of Labour group). Fought Rushcliffe constituency in February 1974 general election. Member, National Union of Mineworkers. Married with three daughters and two sons.

Address: 31 Woodhouse Road, Mansfield, Nottinghamshire NG18 2AY. Tel: 0623 31659.

GALLAND, YVES
France, LD (UFE)

M Yves Galland is a member of the National Council of UDF (Union for French democracy). Company director. B March, 1941; graduate in law. Member, Comité Directeur and national bureau of Parti Radical-Socialiste. B March, 1941.

Address: 36, rue Sainte Croix de la Bretonnerie, 75004 Paris. Tel: 272 63 38 and 287 95 06.

GALLUZZI, CARLO ALBERTO
Italy, Comm (PCI)

Sgr Carlo Alberto Galluzzi has been an Italian MP since 1963 and a member of the European Parliament since 1976. Accountant. Party official. Member of Italian Parliamentary Committee on Foreign Affairs — emigration matters. Member of party leadership. B December, 1919.

Address: Via Quinto Fabio Pittore 31, 00138 Roma. Tel: 3450542.

GASPARD, MME FRANÇOISE
France, Soc (PS)

Mme Françoise Gaspard is Mayor of Dreux and counsellor to an administrative tribunal. B 1945.

Address: 18, avenue Voisin, 23100 Dreux.
Tel: 465607.

GATTO, VINCENZO
Italy, Soc (PSI)

Sgr Vincenzo Gatto is a former Italian MP (1958–72) and former Senator (1972). Member of party leadership, 1953–64; then became one of the promoters of the PSIUP (Italian Socialist Party for Proletarian Unity), and a Vice-Secretary of same. On its dissolution, returned to the Socialist Party. Served on Committees on Constitutional Affairs, Public Transport and Civil Aviation, Public Works, Communications, and Defence and on Commission on Rules of Procedure. Member, PSI Directorate. B May, 1922.

Address: Viale Eritrea 87, 00199 Roma.
Tel: 834967.

GENDEBIEN, PAUL-HENRY
Belgium, Ind (FDF-RW)

Mr Paul-Henry Gendebien, the deputy for Thuin, is a former president of Rassemblement Wallon. B July, 1939; doctor of law, graduate in economic science. Joint chairman, European Parliament group for the Technical Coordination and Defence of Independent Groups and Members, July 1979.

Address: 18, rue Liégeois, 6530 Thuin.
Tel: 071/59 15 57.

GEURTSEN, AART
Netherlands, LD (VVD)

Mr Aart Geurtsen has been a member of the European Parliament since 1974; member of the Dutch Second Chamber. Lawyer. B January, 1926; studied law at Amsterdam Municipal University. Vice-President of the Benelux Council.

Address: Koningin Julianaweg 118, 3155 AS Maasland. Tel: 01899-13178.

GHERGO, ALBERTO
Italy, EPP (DC)

Sgr Alberto Ghergo, a graduate in economics and commerce, is special commissioner of an Italian sickness fund, of which he was formerly president. Former director-general in Ministry of Labour, and a chef de cabinet and chief personal private secretary to several ministers. Member of the committee for the European Social Fund. B 1946. Married with five children.

Address: Via delle Montagne Rocciose 21, 00144 Roma. Tel: 596353.

GIAVAZZI, GIOVANNI
Italy, EPP (DC)

Sgr Giovanni Giavazzi is a lawyer and since 1978 has been president of the Credito Bergamasco Bank, to which he had been an adviser for 12 years and Vice-President for six. President of the Bergamo Agricultural Association, 1948–52. Elected to Bergamo City Council, 1956, and appointed President of provincial administration, 1964. Married, three children. B April, 1920.

Address: Via Masone 32, 24100 Bergamo. Tel: 035/244106.

GILLOT, ALAIN
France, DEP (DIFE)

M Alain Gillot, an architect, is President of the National Council of Order of Architects. B March, 1927; graduate in architecture.

Address: 4 rue Denfert Rochereau, 92000 Boulogne-sur-Seine. Tel: Mol. 53 27.

GIUMMARRA, VINCENZO
Italy, EPP (DC)

Sgr Vincenzo Giummarra, a lawyer, was formerly assistant in the Faculty of Criminal Case Law at the University of Catania. Member, Sicilian Regional Assembly, since 1955. Several times President of Sicilian Region. Formerly chairman, Central Savings Bank for the Sicilian Provinces. National Adviser of the Farmers' Confederation. B May, 1923.

Address: Via Dante 111, 97100 Ragusa.

GLINNE, ERNEST
Belgium, Soc (PSB)

Mr Ernest Glinne was elected chairman of the Socialist Group at the European Parliament in July, 1979; formerly vice-chairman of the group in the nominated Parliament which he joined in 1968. Member of the Belgian Parliament as deputy for Charleroi. A former Minister of Employment and Labour. B March 1931; graduate in political, administrative and diplomatic science. Member, Bureau of Socialist Party.

Address: 1, Square Salvadore, Allende, 6180 Courcelles. Tel: 071-45 30 66.

GONELLA, GUIDO
Italy, EPP (DC)

Sgr Guido Gonella, university lecturer and journalist, was elected a Vice-President of the European Parliament in July, 1979. Member, Council of Europe, since 1976. Deputy Speaker of the Chamber of Deputies, 1966–72; elected to the Chamber of Deputies in 1948 and to the Senate in 1972. Five times Minister of Justice; also minister reponsible for the reform of government administration. Political Secretary, Democrazia Christiana, 1950–53. Founded *Il Popolo* the official paper of the DC. President, of the National Order of Journalists, since 1955, and Political Editor of *L'Osservatore Romano* for over 10 years. B September, 1905.

Address: Via del Colli della Farnesina 98, 00194 Roma. Tel: 3384286.

GOPPEL, ALFONS
Germany, EPP (CSU)

Herr Alfons Goppel was Prime Minister of Bavaria from 1962–78. Secretary of State, Bavarian Ministry of Justice, 1957; Bavarian Minister of the Interior, 1958–62. Member, CSU group, Bavarian Provincial Assembly, since 1954. Former Mayor of Aschaffenburg. B October, 1905. Married with five children.

Address: Sommerweg 2, 8033 Krailling. Tel: 8574034.

GOUTHIER, ANSELMO
Italy, Comm (PCI)

Sgr Anselmo Gouthier, a lawyer, has been Regional Councillor for Trentino Alto-Adige since 1964. Secretary of the Federation of Bolzano, 1963–75; Regional Secretary, Italian Communist Party, 1969–76. Member, Central Committee, since 1969, and of the Party Secretariat since 1976. B June, 1933; degree in law.

Address: Via Roma 78/13, Bolzano. Tel: 91 64 34.

GREDAL, MS EVA
Denmark, Soc (S)

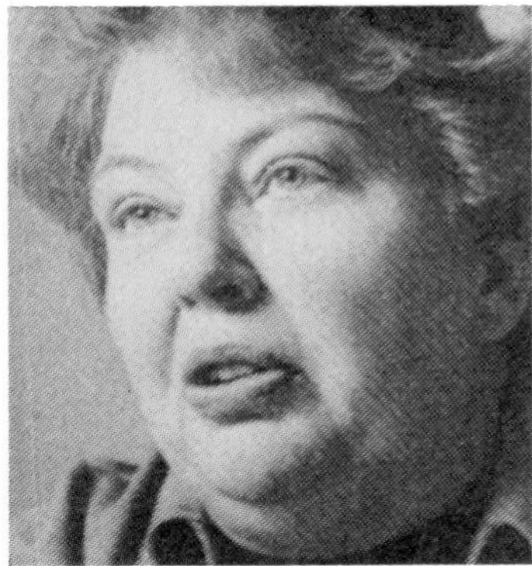

Ms Eva Gredal is a social services adviser. Took her university course at evening school when she was an office worker. In 1954 became a social services adviser; chairman, Danish Social Advice Association, 1959. Elected an MP in 1971 for a Copenhagen constituency and became Minister for Social Affairs in Mr Jens Otto Krag's Social Democratic Party minority government. On the change of government in 1978, she resigned her ministerial post. B February, 1927.

Address: Østbanegade 11, 2100 København Ø. Tel: (01) 260612.

GREMETZ, MAXIME
France, Comm (PCF)

M Maxime Gremetz, a metal worker, is a member of the Secretariat of the Central Committee of the French Communist Party. Deputy for the Somme. B September, 1940.

Address: Comité Central du PCF, 2 Place du Colonel Fabien, 75940 Paris Cedex 19.

GRIFFITHS, WINSTON
UK, South Wales, Soc (Lab)

Mr Winston Griffiths, a comprehensive school teacher. B February, 1943; ed Brecon Boys' Grammar School and Cardiff University College. BA (Hons) History; Diploma in Education. Member, Vale of Glamorgan Borough Council, 1973–76; Dinas Powis Community Council, since 1974. Member of Methodist Church and local preacher. Member, Amnesty International. Nominated by EETPU. Married with one daughter and one son. Secretary of Glamorgan Labour Party.

Address: 27 Murch Road, Dinas Powis, South Glamorgan CF6 4RD, Wales.

GROES, MRS METTE
Denmark, Soc (S)

Mrs Mette Groes, aged 42, lecturer, Aalborg University. Social Democratic Party MP since 1977; specially interested in environmental and energy policies, and consumers' and women's rights. Member, Aalborg City Council, 1974–78. She is critical of some aspects of the EEC; advocates closer involvement of the trade unions in solving European problems.

Address: Gertrud Rasksvej 90, 9210 Alborg SØ. Tel: (08) 141225.

HAAGERUP, NIELS
Denmark, LD (V)

Mr Niels Jørgen Haagerup, editor. Since 1965, has worked for *Berlinske Tidende* as leader writer and commentator on foreign affairs, on which he is accepted as an expert by the Danish Liberal Party (Venstre). Member, Venstre executive committee. Chairman of the party's foreign affairs committee since 1975, and also Danish representative on the executive of the Institute for Strategic Studies in London. Secretary, Danish Foreign Affairs Institute. B October 1925.

Address: Toftegardsvej 11, 3520 Farum.

HABSBURG, OTTO
Germany, EPP (CSU)

Herr Otto Habsburg is a member of the French Academy for Moral and Political Science, the Portuguese Cultural Academy and the Spanish Royal Academy for Moral and Political Science. President, International Council of the European Documentation and Information Centre, 1953–60; subsequently honorary President; President, International Pan-European Union, since 1973. B November, 1912. Married with seven children.

Address: Hindenburgstrasse 15, 8134 Pocking. Tel: 08157/1379.

HAHN, WILHELM
Germany, EPP (CDU)

Herr Wilhelm Hahn is chairman of the German committee of the European Schools Council; president, Germano-Indian Association; general administrator, Institute for Foreign Relations, Stuttgart. B May 1909; holds doctorate of theology and was Professor of Theology and then Vice-Chancellor, Heidelberg University. From 1962–64, member of Bundestag; since 1962 vice-chairman, CDU/CSU Protestant affairs working group; 1964–1978 Minister of Culture. Baden-Württemberg; 1967–1977 member, CDU Federal Executive. Member, Baden-Württemberg Landtag, since 1968. Married with two children.

Address: Im Hofert 3, 6900 Heidelberg. Tel: (06221) 802817.

HAMILIUS, JEAN
Luxembourg, LD (DP)

Mr Jean Hamilius, who replaced Mr Gaston Thorn as an MEP, was Minister of Agriculture and Viticulture and Minister of Public Works; a deputy and municipal councillor for the city of Luxembourg since 1969. Held office at various levels in Democratic Party since 1946. B February, 1927; ed Luxembourg, Brussels University, l'Ecole du Commerce, Solvay, and Cornell University, where he graduated in the school of business and public administration. Worked in Luxembourg steel industry, 1952–53, and then as an independent accountant until 1968, when he became president of the board of a bank in Luxembourg.

Address: 10 Eicherfeld, Luxembourg. Tel: 432119.

HAMMERICH, MS ELSE
Denmark, TCDG (Folkebevaegelsen)

Ms Else Hammerich, aged 42, lecturer at a teachers' training college, fought the European elections on list of the anti-EEC coalition movement. Became interested in social problems under the influence of her father, Cdr Kai Hammerich, who led the Church Army in Denmark and later became director of the Red Cross. She specialises in paedological studies at the Blaagaard Teachers' Training College. Co-author of a series of teaching manuals. For several years has been editor of *Vi Kvinder* (We women).

Address: Glumsøvej 40, 2700 Brønshøj. Tel: (01) 607535.

HÄNSCH, KLAUS
Germany, Soc (SPD)

Herr Klaus Hänsch, political scientist and press officer, is chairman of Mettman local SPD. B December, 1938.

Address: Akazienstrasse 5, 4000 Düsseldorf 22. Tel: 201978.

HARMAR-NICHOLLS, LORD
UK, Greater Manchester South, ED (C)

Lord Harmar-Nicholls, company owner and director, and Lloyds underwriter. Conservative MP for Peterborough 1950–74. B November 1912; ed Queen Mary's Grammar School, Walsall, and Middle Temple. Parliamentary Secretary, Ministry of Agriculture, Fisheries and Food, 1955–58; Parliamentary Secretary, Ministry of Works, 1958–61. President, Federation of Wholesale and Industrial Distributors. Chairman, Malvern Festival Theatre Trust Ltd. Director of J. and H. Nicholls Ltd, Nicholls and Hennessy Hotels Ltd, Cannon Assurance Ltd and Radio Luxembourg (London) Ltd. Chairman, Pleasurama Ltd. Created life peer, 1974. Married with two daughters.

Address: Abbeylands, Weston, Stafford. Tel: 0889-270252 and 01-219 5353.

HARRIS, DAVID
UK, Cornwall and Plymouth, ED (C)

Mr David Harris was chief political correspondent of *The Daily Telegraph*, 1976–79; member of that newspaper's parliamentary and political staffs from 1961. Previously on staffs of *Western Morning News* and other West country newspapers. Former chairman and vice-chairman of Lobby journalists at Westminster, and of Parliamentary branch of the National Union of Journalists. Parliamentary candidate, Mitcham and Morden, February 1974. Member, Greater London Council, for Bromley Ravensbourne, 1968–76. B November, 1937; ed Mount Radford School, Exeter. Married with two children.

Address: Little Trehan Farm, Trehan, Saltash, Cornwall PL12 4QN. Tel: 3720.

HAUENSCHILD, Karl
Germany, Soc (SPD)

Herr Karl Hauenschild, businessman, is chairman of the Chemical, Paper and Pottery Industries Trade Union. Member, Economic and Social Committee of EEC. B August, 1920

Address: Wundramstrasse 16, 3005 Hemmingen (Nds.). Tel: (0511) 421758.

HELMS, WILHELM
Germany, EPP (CDU)

Herr Wilhelm Helms was a member of the Bundestag from 1969 to 1972, when he left the FDP which he had joined in 1963, for the CDU. Farmer. B December 1923. From 1961 to 1972, Mayor and Gemeindedirektor of Heiligenloh. In 1968 became member of FDP provincial executive committee for Lower Saxony; since 1973, member of advisory committee on agricultural policy of the CDU Association in Lower Saxony; member, CDU group, town council of Twistringen, since 1976. Married with two children.

Address: 2832 Twistringen—Bissenhausen.

HENCKENS, JAAK
Belgium, EPP (CVP)

Mr Jaak Henckens has been a member of the Belgian Chamber of Representatives for the Louvain district, since 1965; First Deputy, Chamber of Representatives, 1961–65. Chairman, CVP Parliamentary Party Cultural Council for the Dutch Cultural Community; chairman, committee on national education, Chamber of Representatives. Within CVP youth movement, has been Tienen local chairman, Louvain district chairman and national vice-chairman; local and regional chairman, Tienen CVP; district chairman, Louvain, and member, national bureau. B July 1933; studied law and political and social science.

Address: Getelaan 54, 3300 Tienen.
Tel: (016) 81 32 79.

HERKLOTZ, FRAU LUISE
Germany, Soc (SPD)

Frau Luise Herklotz is a journalist and housewife. B August, 1918. Member, SPD bureau in the Palatinat.

Address: Hasenpfuhlstrasse 7, 6720 Speyer.

HERMAN, FERNAND
Belgium, EPP (PSC)

Mr Fernand Herman is Secretary-General of the Cercles populaires européens (European people's movement). Minister of Economic Affairs, 1975–77; Senator for Brussels, 1977–78, and member of Parliament for Brussels. Director of the National Society for Investment (SNI) confederation of industry, 1964–75. B January 1932; doctor of law and degree in economics at the Catholic University of Louvain.

Address: 22, rue Phillippe le Bon, 1040 Bruxelles.
Tel: 2304105.

HOFF, FRAU MAGDALENE
Germany, Soc (SPD)

Frau Magdalene Hoff is a member of the Federal executive of SPD and its working party on urban planning and housing policy. Civil engineer and lecturer on industrial safety and accident prevention. B December, 1940. Member, Bureau of Hagen Federation of SPD and of Hagen Municipal Council.

Address: Zur Höhe 72 A, 5800 Hagen.
Tel: (02331) 75661 and (02331) 70854.

HOFFMAN, MME JACQUELINE
France, Comm (PCF)

Mme Jacqueline Hoffman, a welder, is a member of the Central Committee of the French Communist Party. B December, 1943

Address: 8, rue Francis de Pressensé, 92800 Puteaux. Tel: 238 66 55.

HOFFMAN, KARL-HEINZ
Germany, EPP (CDU)

Herr Karl-Heinz Hoffman has been an active trade unionist since 1945 starting in IG Chemie, then in IG Bergbau, and now OTV. Elected deputy chairman of OTV (public services and transport) 1968, and re-elected in 1972 and 1976. Member, Economic and Social Committee of EEC, since 1965, being chariman, from 1970, of working party on transport and communications. Member, Konrad-Adenauer Foundation advisory board on trade unions. B February 1928. Federal executive member, from 1969, of CDA social committees. Married with four children.

Address: Hauweg 28, 7067 Plüderhausen.

HOOPER, MISS GLORIA
UK, Liverpool, ED (C)

Miss Gloria Hooper is a solicitor in private practice. B 1939; ed Convent High School, Southampton; Southampton University (president of university Conservative Association) and Universidad Central, Quito, Ecuador. Special interests: education, housing, taxation and international affairs.

Address: 11 Cleveland Row, St James's, London SW1. Tel: 01-839 3929.

HOPPER, WILLIAM
UK, Greater Manchester West, ED (C)

Mr William Hopper is director of a London merchant bank. B 1929; ed Queen's Park Secondary School, Glasgow, and Glasgow University. Author. School governor. Specialised knowledge of tax and finance. Founder and first chairman, Institute for Fiscal Studies, London.

Address: Morgan Grenfell & Co Ltd, 23 Great Winchester Street, London EC2P 2AX. Tel: 01-588 4545. 15 Chepstow Villas, London W11 3DZ. Tel: 01-727 2426

HORD, BRIAN
UK, London West, ED (C)

Mr Brian Hord, a chartered surveyor, contested the constituency of Darlington in both 1974 general elections. B June 1934; ed Reedham School and Purley County Grammar School. Served on Conservative South Eastern area education advisory and CPC committees. Special interests: housing and land, urban development, town planning and the environment, local government finance. Married with two children.

Address: Whitesides, Pilgrims Way East, Otford, Sevenoaks, Kent TN14 5QN. Tel: 3743.

HOWELL, PAUL
UK, Norfolk, ED (C)

Mr Paul Howell is a farmer. B 1951; ed Greshams School, Holt, and St Edmund Hall, Oxford (BA agriculture and economics); political action officer, University Conservative Association. Desk officer for agriculture, Europe, and prices and consumer affairs at Conservative Research Department, 1973–75; political adviser to Minister of Agriculture to February 1974, and then to shadow Minister of Agriculture and shadow Minister for Prices and Consumer Affairs.

Address: Mansion House, Bond Street, Hingham (Norwich) Norfolk NR9 4HA. Tel: Attlebourgh 850275.

HUME, JOHN
UK, N Ireland, Soc (SDLP)

Mr John Hume was Northern Ireland's Minister for Commerce in 1974. Elected treasurer of Socialist Group at European Parliament, in July 1979. B 1937. MP for Foyle, Northern Ireland Parliament, 1969–73; SDLP member for Londonderry, NI Assembly, 1973–75, and NI Constitutional Convention, 1975–76. Deputy leader of the SDLP. Married with five children.

Address: 6 West End Park, Londonderry, N. Ireland.

HUTTON, ALASDAIR
UK, South of Scotland, ED (C)

Mr Alasdair Hutton has since 1964 been a British Broadcasting Corporation announcer; previously newspaper reporter. Chairman, Glasgow Kelvingrove Conservative Association. B 1940; ed Dollar Academy, Scotland, Brisbane State High School and Melbourne University. Special interests: defence, anti-terrorism and broadcasting. Married with one child.

Address: 14 Hamilton Drive, Glasgow G12 8DR, Scotland. Tel: 041-334 7775.

IPPOLITO, FELICE
Italy, Comm (PCI)

Sgr Felice Ippolito is Professor of Geology at the University of Rome; editor of several scientific magazines. Vice-chairman, Committee of the Geological and Mining Sciences, National Research Centre. Member, Upper Council on Mining and of Technical Committee on Hydrocarbons, Ministry of Industry. B November, 1919; degree in civil engineering.

Address: C.E.E.P.-Via del Tritone 46, 00187 Roma. Tel: 6781713.

IRMER, ULRICH
Germany, LD (FDP)

Herr Ulrich Irmer, barrister, has had his practice in Munich since 1973. Member of FDP since 1961; member of FDP Bavarian Executive Committe, being their spokesman on Europe. B January, 1939; graduated from Michigan High School.

Addresses: Kaufingerstrasse 25, 800 München 2. Tel: (089) 223387. Konradstrasse 10, 8000 München 40. Tel: (089) 3401630.

JACKSON, CHRISTOPHER
UK, East Kent, ED (C)

Mr Christopher Jackson is Director of Corporate Development, Spillers Ltd. Conservative parliamentary candidate at East Ham South, 1970, and Northampton, North, February 1974. B May 1935; ed Rye Grammar School; Kingswood School, Bath; Magdalen College, Oxford; Frankfurt University; London University. Special interests: economic affairs, trade and industry, including agriculture, and foreign affairs (EEC). Married with two children.

Addresses: Medlars, Oak Hill Road, Sevenoaks, Kent. Old Change House, 4–6 Cannon Street, London EC4.

JACKSON, ROBERT
UK, Upper Thames, ED (C)

Mr Robert Jackson served in the private office of Sir Christopher Soames, then Vice President of the EEC Commission with responsibility for external affairs, from 1974–76; Chef de Cabinet to the chairman of EEC's Economic and Social Committee, then Mr Basil de Ferranti, 1976–78. B 1946; ed Falcon College, Bulawayo and St Edmund Hall, Oxford (President of Oxford Union, 1967). Member, Oxford City Council, 1969–71. Contested Manchester Central, October 1974 general election. Was personal assistant to Mr William Whitelaw, chairman of the Conservative Party in 1974. Married.

Address: 37 Stockwell Park Crescent, London SW9. Tel: 01-737 4831.

JAKOBSEN, ERHARD
Denmark, ED (CD)

Mr Erhard Jakobsen, aged 62, chairman of the Centre Democrats Party, and an MP in Denmark as well. Member of the controlling body for Danish State Radio; former mayor of Gladsaxe. A leading defender of the EEC in Denmark. Originally was a Social Democrat, but broke away in 1973 to form the new party. Chairman, European Movement in Denmark, 1964–73. Member of the Council of Europe, and of the European Parliament since Denmark joined the EEC in 1973; only Danish politician with such long continuous membership of the EP.

Address: Søvej 27, 2880 Bagsvaerd.
Tel: 98 52 40

JANSSEN VAN RAAY, JAMES
Netherlands, EPP (CDA)

Mr James Janssen van Raay, barrister and solicitor, is chairman of Het Westen CHU election association, Rotterdam; national secretary of the CHU, and vice-chairman of the Christen Democratisch Appèl (CDA). B June, 1932; studies law at Leiden.

Addresses: PO Box 21150, 3001 AD Rotterdam: Mecklenburglaan 14, 3062 BJ Rotterdam.
Tel: 010-330244 and 010-146857.

JAQUET, GÉRARD
France, Soc (PS)

M Gérard Jaquet was elected a Vice-President of the European Parliament in July, 1979. Former minister and deputy. Member of Conseil d'Etat and of Comité Directeur of the Socialist Party. B January, 1916.

Address: 2, rue Armand Moissant, 75015 Paris.
Tel: 320 60 95.

JOHNSON, STANLEY
UK, Wight and Hampshire East, ED (C)

Mr Stanley Johnson has been head of the Environmental Pollution Division of the EEC Commission. B August 1940; ed Sherborne School and Exeter College, Oxford, and Columbia University, New York. Author of various publications and novels. Has a 500 acre family farm on Exmoor. Special interests: economics, environment, overseas aid.

Addresses: c/o Gickel, 51 Blomfield Road, London W9. Tel: 01-289 1898. West Nethercote, Winsford, Minehead, Somerset. Tel: Exford 325.

JONKER, SJOUKE
Netherlands, EPP (CDA)

Mr Sjouke Jonker is a member of the Economic and Social Committee of the European Communities, the executive of ARP (Anti-Revolutionary Party), and the general executive of the Christen Democratisch Appèl. Former Chef de Cabinet to Mr Mansholt, when President and Vice-President of the Commission; left the Commission as honorary Director-General. Formerly head of the agricultural information division in the EEC Commission. B September, 1924. As a journalist became parliamentary editor of *Rotterdammerbladen* and assistant editor of *Nederlandse Gedachten.*

Addresses: Dahlialaan 36, 1900 Jezus Eik (Belgie). Tel: 02-6571907. Aardbeistraat 26, 's-Gravenhage.Tel: 070-230879.

JOSSELIN, CHARLES
France, Soc (PS)

M Charles Josselin, engineer-economist, is Mayor of Pleslin-Trigavou. B March, 1938. Graduate in public law and political science. Chairman, Council of Côtes du Nord; deputy (1973–78).

Address: Préfecture des Côtes du Nord, 22000 Saint Brieuc. Tel: (96) 61 19 50.

JURGENS, HEINRICH
Germany, LD (FDP)

Herr Heinrich Jurgens, a farmer, is chairman of the Lower Saxony FDP Association. In 1967 became Burgomaster of Schaforden. B July, 1934. Married with two children.

Address: Oeftinghausen 3, 2831 Ehrenburg (Nds). Tel: 042 75/371.

KATZER, JOHANN
Germany, EPP (CDU)

Herr Johann Katzer was elected a Vice-President of the European Parliament in July, 1979. Deputy chairman, Christlich-Demokratische Union (CDU); deputy chairman of the CDU/CSU group in Bundestag of which he has been a member since 1977. President, European Union of Christian Democratic Workers, since 1977. From 1960, member of CDU Bundestag executive; 1965-69 Federal Minister for employment and social affairs. Chairman, Jakob-Kaiser Foundation. B January, 1919. Married with one child.

Address: Kastanienallee 7, 5000 Köln, 51. Tel: 38 3770.

KAVANAGH, LIAM
Ireland, Soc (Lab)

Mr Liam Kavanagh has been a member of the European Parliament since 1973, serving on the Committees on Social Affairs, Employment and Education, on Regional Policy, Regional Planning and Transport. Elected for Wicklow in 1969. B February 1935; ed De La Salle School, Wicklow; University College, Dublin. Labour opposition spokesman on fisheries, 1969-72, and on transport and power, 1972-73. Member, Dáil and Seanad Joint Committee on the Secondary Legislation of the European Communities, 1973-77; Wicklow County Council, since 1974 (vice-chairman 1976-77); Wicklow Urban District Council since 1974 (chairman 1974–75). Married with one son.

Address: Mount Carmel, Convent Road, Wicklow. Tel: (0404) 2582.

KELLETT-BOWMAN, EDWARD
UK, Lancashire East, ED (C)

Mr Edward Kellett-Bowman is a business consultant. Contested Pontefract in the 1959 general election. B February 1931; ed Reed's School, Surrey; Slough College of Technology and Cranfield Institute of Technology. Husband of Mrs Elaine Kellett-Bowman, MEP for Cumbria and MP for Lancaster. They have four step-children. Former chairman, London area Young Conservatives; former member of National Executive Committee and of Local Government National Advisory Committee. Served on five local authorities in London, 1957-74. Member, British Institute of Management.

Addresses: Park Farm, Gressenhall, Dereham, Norfolk NR19 2QL. 33d Curzon Street, London W1Y 7AE. Tel: 01-499 7248.

KELLETT-BOWMAN, MRS ELAINE
UK, Cumbria, ED (C)

Mrs Elaine Kellett-Bowman, a barrister (Middle Temple, 1964), farmer and social worker, has been a member of the European Parliament since 1975 serving on the Regional Policy Committee and the Social Affairs, Employment and Education Committee. Conservative MP for Lancaster since 1970. B July 1924; ed Queen Mary's School, Lytham; The Mount, York, and St Anne's College, Oxford. Alderman, Borough of Camden, 1968-71. Member, Press Council, 1964-68. Wife of Mr Edward Kellett-Bowman, MEP for Lancashire, East.

Addresses: House of Commons, Westminster, London. 42 School House Lane, Halton, Lancaster. 33d Curzon Street, London W1Y 7AE. Tel: 01-499 7248.

KEY, BRIAN
UK South Yorkshire, Soc (Lab and Co-op)

Mr Brian Key, a local government officer. B September 1947; ed Wath Comprehensive School and Liverpool University. B.A. (Hons). Member, Barnsley Metropolitan Borough Council since 1973. Sponsored by the Co-operative Party. Nalgo — past branch secretary. Chairman, Dearne Valley Constituency Labour Party. Special interests: local government and regionalism; energy, co-operative issues. Married.

Address: 57 Bly Road, Darfield, Barnsley S73 9DW, Yorkshire. Tel: 0226 753741.

KIRK, KENT
Denmark, ED (KF)

Mr Kent Kirk, aged 30, fishing skipper, chairman of the Esbjerg Fishing Association and member of the board of Denmark's Deep Sea Fishing Federation. A surprise candidate on the Conservative Party list, winning his place because of a strong personal following. Outspoken in his views about European cooperation, and often extremely critical of the EEC fisheries policy. Adviser to his party on fishery policy.

Address: Bellisvaenget 33, 6700 Esbjerg.

KLEPSCH, EGON
Germany, EPP (CDU)

Mr Egon Klepsch was elected chairman of the European People's Party Group (formerly Christian Democratic Group) of the European Parliament in July 1979. Vice-President of the EPP; chairman of Christian Democratic group in European Parliament, 1977-79; CDU member of Bundestag from 1965. B January, 1930; Doctor of Philosophy. Former lecturer on international politics. President, European Union of Young Christian Democrats, 1964-70; from 1976 chairman of CDU/CSU Bundestag working party on European policy. Married with six children.

Address: Lüderitzstrasse 41, 5400 Koblenz-Pfaffendorf. Tel: 753 42.

KLINKENBORG, JAN
Germany, Soc (SPD)

Herr Jan Klinkenborg is Mayor of Emden. Member, SPD Council and SPD Bureau of Weser-Ems. B September, 1935.

Address: Uphuser Strasse 9a, 2970 Emden (Nds.). Tel: 24009.

KÖHLER, HERBERT
Germany, EPP (CDU)

Herr Herbert Köhler has been a member of the Bundestag since 1972; treasurer, Rhineland CDU; member, North Rhine-Westphalia CDU executive; chairman, executive, Rhineland CDU Economic Union. Businessman. Member, Advisory Committee, European Coal and Steel Community, 1960-72. Co-founder, European Confederation of Iron and Steel industries (EUROFER), Luxembourg, and member of administrative board. Member, board of directors and executive committee, International Iron and Steel Institute; chairman, economic and financial policy committee, Düsseldorf chamber of trade and industry. B December, 1919. Married.

Address: Wildunger Strasse 6, 4100 Duisburg 25 (Huckingen).

KROUWEL-VLAM, MRS JOHANNA
Netherlands, Soc (PvdA)

Mrs Johanna Krouwel-Vlam has been a member of the European Parliament since 1977; former member of Dutch Parliament. B June, 1928.

Address: Bronkhorststraat 28, MK 7555 Hengelo. Tel: 05400-19307.

KÜHN, HEINZ
Germany, Soc (SPD)

Herr Heinz Kühn, a journalist, is a former Prime Minister of Nordrhein-Westfalen. Member of the Landtag and of SPD Bureau. B February, 1912.

Address: Roteichenweg 5, 5000 Koln 80. Tel: 688338.

LABBE, CLAUDE
France, DEP (DIFE)

M Claude Labbe is French Deputy for Hauts-de-Seine. President of the Rassemblement pour la Republique (RPR) group in the national assembly. Political adviser to RPR. Aeronautics inspector. B January, 1920; graduate in literature.

Address: 126, rue de l'Université, 75007 Paris. Tel: 2976063.

LALOR, PATRICK J.
Ireland, DEP (F-Fáil)

Mr Patrick J. Lalor became a vice-chairman of the DEP group at the European Parliament, in July 1979. Appointed Parliamentary Secretary to the Taoiseach and to the Minister for Defence and Government Chief Whip in July 1977. B July 1926; ed Knockbeg College, Co. Carlow. Formerly a general merchant. Elected to the Dail, for Laois-Offaly, in 1961 and at all elections since. Minister for Industry and Commerce, 1970-73; Minister for Posts and Telegraphs, 1969-70; Parliamentary Secretary to the Minister for Posts and Telegraphs and to the Minister for Transport and Power, 1966-69; Parliamentary Secretary to the Minister for Agriculture and Fisheries, 1965-66. Opposition chief whip, 1973-77.

Address: Upper Main St, Abbeyleix, Co. Laois.

LANGE, ERWIN
Germany, Soc (SPD)

Herr Erwin Lange, a compositor, is a member of the Bundestag. He was a member of the Committee on Budgets in the outgoing nominated European Parliament and is chairman of the committee in the new Parliament. B May, 1914.

Address: Am Buchenhain 8, 4300 Essen 16.

LANGES, HORST
Germany, EPP (CDU)

Herr Horst Langes, former headmaster, was first elected to the Rhineland Palatinate "Land" Assembly in 1967. Now Secretary of State to the Rhineland-Palatinate Ministry of Culture, Education and Religious Affairs. Member, Trier municipal council, since 1960, and of the Trier executive and the federal committee of CDU. B December, 1928. Married with five children.

Address: Bonhoefferstrasse 32, 5500 Trier. Tel: 31659.

LECANUET, JEAN
France, EPP (UFE)

M Jean Lecanuet is President of l'Union pour la démocratie française (UDF) and of the Centre des Démocrates Sociaux (CDS). Senator; chairman of the Foreign Affairs Committee of the Senate; Mayor of Rouen and President of the Conseil Général of the Seine-Maritime department. B March, 1920; graduate in literature and agrégé in philosophy.

Addresses: 282 Bd Saint-Germain, 75007 Paris: 41 rue Thiers, 76041 Rouen.

LEGA, SILVIO
Italy, EPP (DC)

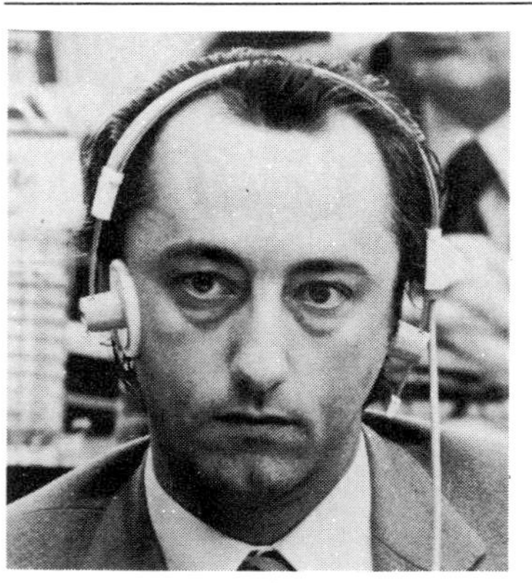

Sgr Silvio Lega, a businessman and doctor in jurisprudence, was provincial secretary of Turin DC, 1975-79. Elected provincial delegate of the Turin Young Christian-Democrats. B February, 1945. Single. Member of the Italian Sports Centre (Athletics); during his university studies he was in charge of the centre's regional mountain sports. Italian pole-vault champion, 1961.

Address: Via Gianfrancesco Re 15, 10146 Torino. Tel: 790246.

LEMMER, GERD
Germany, EPP (CDU)

Herr Gerd Lemmer was State Secretary to the Federal Ministry for Refugees and War Victims, and later in the Federal Ministry for Posts and Telecommunications, 1967-69. From 1969, executive with the Buckau R. Wolf AG Grevenbroich machine factory. Member, Remscheid municipal authority, 1952-1975; North Rhine-Westphalia "Land" assembly, 1958-75. North Rhine-Westphalia "Land" minister for federal affairs, 1962-66. Married with two children. B September 1925.

Address: Hindemithstrasse 28, 5630 Remscheid. Tel: (02191) 72316.

LENZ, FRAU MARLENE
Germany, EPP (CDU)

Frau Marlene Lenze has been a vice-President of the European Women's Union since 1977; executive member, 1975-77. Member, federal executive, CDU Women's Union. Translator. B July 1932; ed University of Heidelburg. General Secretary, European Women's Union 1967-71; adviser to external relations office, CDU federal headquarters, 1972-75. From 1976, rapporteur to the Bundestag's committee of enquiry on women and society.

Address: Friedrich-Ebert-Strasse 66, 5300 Bonn 2-Bad Godesberg. Tel: 363368.

LEONARDI, SILVIO
Italy, Comm (PCI)

Sgr Silvio Leonardi, a member of the European Parliament since 1976, has been an Italian MP since 1963. Former member of the Parliamentary Committee on the Budget and State Economic Participation (twice) and the Committee on the Budget and Planning. Author of *CEE-COMECON: due sistemi a confronto.* B July, 1914; degree in engineering.

Address: Corso Porta Ticinese 24, 20123 Milano. Tel: 8396228.

LEROUX, MME SYLVIE
France, Comm (PCF)

Mme Sylvie Leroux is a researcher in marine biology. B October, 1946.

Address: Mairie de Brest, 29200 Brest.
Tel: 80 80 55.

LEZZI, PIETRO
Italy, Soc (PSI)

Sgr Pietro Lezzi was elected a vice-chairman of the Socialist Group at the European Parliament in July, 1979. Member of EP since 1976. Former solicitor. Became Italian MP in 1963. Member of party since 1946; Party Provincial Secretary, 1957; member, Central Committee; in charge of committee on Southern Italy, 1959–61, and co-leader of the Central Section of Organisation. Town councillor, Castellammare di Stabia, 1954; Town councillor of Naples, 1960 and 1962. Has served as Secretary of Committee on the Budget and of the Committee on Foreign Affairs and as member of the Committee on the Budget and State Economic Participation. B December, 1922.

Address: Discesa Gaiola 8, 80123 Napoli.
Tel: 7691995.

LIGIOS, GIOSUÈ
Italy, EPP (DC)

Sgr Giosuè Ligios, member of the European Parliament since 1972 and vice-chairman of the Committee on Agriculture until June 1979. Member, Italian Senate, since 1972 and for three years previously was regional councillor, Sardinia. Member, DC regional committee for Sardinia. President of the provincial government of Nuoro, 1964-69. B December, 1928.

Address: Via Goberti 11, 08100 Nuoro.
Tel: 0784/31534.

LIMA, SALVATORE
Italy, EPP (DC)

Sgr Salvatore Lima, deputy director, Bank of Sicily and a law graduate, has been a member of the Italian Chamber of Deputies since 1968. Several times Under-secretary of State for Finance and for the Budget; more recently, member of Defence Committee. Mayor of Palermo for more than seven years. Commissioner Extraordinary of Sicilian Agrarian Reform Office, 1962-63. Secretary, Palermo Province DC party, 1961-68. Vice-chairman, Bank of Sicily. B January, 1928.

Address: Via Danae 19, Palermo (Valdesi). Tel: 454561.

LINDE, ERDMANN
Germany, Soc (SPD)

Herr Erdmann Linde, mechanical engineer, is Head of Department in a Volkshochschule. Member of the WDR Broadcasting Council. B February, 1943.

Address: Harpener Hellweg 301, 4630 Bochum — Harpen. Tel: (0234) 234625.

LINKOHR, ROLF
Germany, Soc (SPD)

Herr Rolf Linkohr, physicist, is local chairman of the Stuttgart SPD. B April, 1941.

Address: Asangstrasse 219a, 7000 Stuttgart 61.

LIZIN-VANDERSPEETEN, MRS ANNE-MARIE
Belgium, Soc (PSB)

Mrs Anne-Marie Lizin-Vanderspeeten, a graduate in economic science, is a Counsellor in the Cabinet of the Belgian Minister for Foreign Affairs. B January 1949. Local councillor; member, Socialist Party committee on women.

Address: 6, Chaussée d'Andenne, 5202 Huy. Tel: 085-230864.

LODERER, EUGEN
Germany, Soc (SPD)

Herr Eugen Loderer, a wire metal worker, is President of the Metalworkers' Union. B May, 1920.

Address: Am Niddatal 27, 6000 Frankfurt am Main 90. Tel: (0611) 763666.

LOMAS, ALFRED
UK, London, North-East, Soc (Lab)

Mr Alfred Lomas, secretary of the London Co-operative Political Committee and member, London regional executive of Labour Party. Former railway signalman. B April 1929. Councillor at Stockport, 1962-65. Special interests: international affairs, EEC, co-operative development.

Address: 23 Hatcliffe Close, London SE3. Tel: 01-852 5433.

LOO, CHARLES-EMILE
France, Soc (PS)

M Charles-Emile Loo, a typographer, is director of a workers' cooperative. Member, Socialist Party executive. B March, 1922.

Address: Socoma — 1, rue Forbin, 13003 Marseille. Tel: 959107.

LOUWES, HENDRIK
Netherlands, LD (VVD)

Mr Hendrik Louwes is a farmer. Member of the First Chamber and First Vice-President of his party's group. B February, 1921; ed Royal High School, Groningen; Wageningen Agricultural College and University of Illinois.

Address: Westpolder 22, 9975 WJ Ulrum. Tel: 05956-1504.

LÜCKER, HANS AUGUST
Germany, EPP (CSU)

Herr Hans August Lücker, member of the European Parliament since 1958; chairman of the Christian-Democratic Group, 1969-75; Vice-President, European Parliament, 1975-79. Director, Bavarian "Land" Chamber of Agriculture and Deputy General Secretary of Bavarian Farmers' Association, from 1947. Trustee, Ifo Institute for Economic Research, Munich, since 1949. Chairman, Institute for Structure Research, Frankfurt University. Member, CSU economic advisory council, since 1947. Member, Parliamentary Assembly of Council of Europe and WEU until 1961. B February, 1915. Married with three children.

Address: Uber der Klause 4, 8000 Munchen 90. Tel: 647098.

LUSTER, RUDOLF
Germany, EPP (CDU)

Herr Rudolf Luster has been a member of the Bundestag since 1976 and of the European Parliament since 1978. Barrister since 1963; notary since 1970. Member, board of trustees of Gesellschaft für Zukunftsfragen. Member, CDU since 1945. For many years member, CDU executive. "Land" of Berlin and district chairman in Berlin–Steglitz; member, Federal Party Tribunal of CDU, since 1973. 1950–1951 Berlin City councillor; 1967–1976, member of Berlin Parliament.

Address: Nassauische Strasse 15, 1000 Berlin 31 (Wilmersdorf). Tel: (030) 8615913.

LYNGE, FINN
Denmark, Greenland, Soc (Siumut)

Mr Finn Lynge, aged 46, director of the Greenland radio service, a former Catholic priest. Brilliant linguist, speaking eight languages, and a formidable debater on cultural topics. He was educated as a Catholic priest and was an assistant parish priest in the USA. In 1965 he became a parish priest in Godthaab, Greenland. He was relieved of this post when he got married.

Address: Østerbro 32 B, 3900 Godthaab, Greenland. Tel: 22673.

MACARIO, LUIGI
Italy, EPP (DC)

Sgr Luigi Macario is a trade union official; Vice-President of the European Trade Unions Confederation and of the International Confederation of Free Trade Unions. Leading official FIM-CISL (Metal Workers' Union) between 1962 and 1970; assistant Secretary General CISL, 1973-77; Secretary General, 1977-79. Member, National Economic and Employment Council (CNEL). B September, 1920.

Address: Via Latina, 18, 00179 Roma. Tel: 7580392.

MAFFRE-BAUGE, EMMANUEL
France, Comm (PCF)

M Emmanuel Maffre-Bauge, a wine grower, is former President of the Federation nationale des oriducteurs de vin de table. B December, 1921.

Address: Route de Gignac, Belarga, 34230 Paulhan. Tel: 980058.

MAHER, THOMAS
Ireland, LD (Ind)

Mr Thomas Maher, a farmer, was President, Irish Farmers' Association, 1967-76. B 1922; ed in Cashel. Member Economic and Social Committee of the EEC, 1973-78; President, Irish Agricultural Organization Society, and of the General Committee for Agricultural Co-operation in the EEC (COJECA). Married with three children.

Address: Castlemoyle, Boherlahen, Cashel, Co. Tipperary. Tel: Boherlahen 106.

MAIJ-WEGGEN, MRS JOHANNA
Netherlands, EPP (CDA)

Mrs Johanna Maij-Weggen, a nursing teacher, has held various posts in the ARP (Anti-Revolutionary Party) and CDA; was a member of the organization committee and the ARVC/CDA Women's Advisory Group and of the executive of the Dutch Women's Council. Member, Dutch Government delegation to 32nd UN General Assembly, New York, 1977. B December, 1943; attended the AZVU nurses school, Amstelveen, and studied social pedagogy at Amsterdam Municipal University.

Address: Pieter Bedijnstraat 38, 2202 VK Noordwijk aan Zee. Tel: 01719-10471.

MAJONICA, ERNST
Germany, EPP (CDU)

Herr Ernst Majonica is Vice-President of the German Council of the European Movement; President, 1966-76. B October, 1920. From 1950-55, Federal chairman of the "Junge Union Deutschlands"; 1950-57, member, CDU federal executive; 1950-72, member of the Bundestag; 1953-69, member of the CDU/CSU Bundestag political group executive; 1959-69, chairman of the CDU/CSU working party on external policy; 1953-72, member of the Bundestag external affairs committee. Married.

Address: Herzog-Johann-Strasse 5, 4770 Soest. Tel: 3741.

MALANGRÉ, KURT
Germany, EPP (CDU)

Herr Kurt Malangré has been chairman of the Aachen regional council since 1976. Burgomaster of Aachen, 1971-73, and chief burgomaster since 1973. Joined Aachen municipal assembly in 1969, becoming political group chairman, 1970. Lawyer in Aachen. B September 1934; studied law and political science in Bonn and Cologne. Widower with three children.

Address: Knöpgerweg 25, 5100 Aachen. Tel: 72517.

MARCHAIS, GEORGES
France, Comm (PCF)

M Georges Marchais is Secretary-General of the French Communist Party. Former metal worker. Deputy for Val-de-Marne. B June, 1921.

Addresses: Comité Central du PCF, 2 Place de Colonel Fabien, 75940 Paris Cedex 19. Tel: 238 66 55. Rue Guy Mocquet, 94000 Champigny sur Marne.

MARSHALL, JOHN
UK, London North, ED (C)

Mr John Marshall is a stockbroker; previously university lecturer in economics. B 1940; ed Glasgow Academy and St Andrew's University. Contested Dundee East in 1964 and 1966 general elections and East Lewisham in February 1974. Member, Aberdeen Town Council, 1968-70; Ealing Borough Council, since 1971. Has written for academic publications, "Aims of Industry" and various newspapers, and has appeared on television. Married.

Address: 59 Queen Anne's Grove, London, W5. Tel: 01-567 9220.

MARTIN, MAURICE
France, Comm (PCF)

M Maurice Martin is a member of the Central Committee of the French Communist Party. B April, 1927.

Address: Mairie de Carcassonne, 11000 Carcassonne.

MARTIN, MME SIMONE
France, LD (UFE)

Mme Simone Martin was President of CDJA (Young Farmers Departmental Centre) of the Haute-Marne, 1972-74; vice-chairman of the CNJA (Young Farmers National Centre), 1974-78. Secretary-general of a Chamber of Agriculture. Chairman of EDE (Departmental stock farming board) and member of the Economic and Social Committee of Champagne Ardenne. B April, 1943. Married with three children.

Address: Thonnance les Moulins, 52230 Poissons. Tel: 95 52 90.

MARTINET, GILLES
France, Soc (PS)

M Gilles Martinet is a journalist. B August, 1916. Graduate in literature and in history. Former MP; member, executive of French Socialist Party.

Address: 82, Bd Flandrin, 75116 Paris.
Tel: 72752 54.

MAUROY, PIERRE
France, Soc (PS)

M Pierre Mauroy is a member of the executive bureau of the Socialist Party. Deputy for the Nord. Mayor of Lille. Teacher. B July, 1928.

Address: Hôtel de Ville, 59000 Lille.

McCARTIN, JOHN
Ireland, EPP (F-Gael)

Mr John Joe McCartin, farmer and company director, has been a senator, Agricultural Panel, since 1973, and Leas-Cathaoirleach since 1977; member, Committee of Selection, 1973-77. B April 1939; ed St Patrick's College, Cavan. Member, Leitrim County Council, since 1967; Leitrim County Committee of Agriculture, since 1967; General Council of Committees of Agriculture, since 1967 (chairman, 1970-72); North-Western Health Board, since 1971; Irish Farmers' Association since 1965. Macra na Feirme national dairy stock judging champion, 1962.

Address: Mullyaster, Newtongore, Co. Leitrim.
Tel: (049) 34539.

MEGAHY, THOMAS
UK, South West Yorkshire, Soc (Lab)

Mr Thomas Megahy, a senior lecturer in further education. B July, 1929; ed Ruskin College, Oxford, and Huddersfield Technical Teachers Training College. B.Sc.(Economics), Dip. Econ and political science, Diploma in Further Education. Member, Mirfield Urban District Council, 1963-74; Kirklees Metropolitan District Council, 1973-78. Former member, Yorkshire and Humberside Regional and Economic Planning Council. Special interests: local government finance, education, EEC. Married with three sons.

Address: 6 Lady Heton Grove, Mirfield, West Yorkshire WF14 9DY. Tel: 0924 492680.

MERTENS, MEINOLF
Germany, EPP (CDU)

Herr Meinolf Mertens, farmer, is a member of the Westphalia-Lippe "Land" chamber of commerce. B June, 1923; passed master's examination in agriculture. From 1956, member of the district council (deputy district administrator); from 1966 member of the North Rhine-Westphalia "Land" Assembly. Married with four children.

Address: Bönkhausen 3, 5768 Sundern 6.

MESSMER, PIERRE
France, DEP (DIFE)

M Pierre Messmer was Prime Minister of France, 1972-74. Deputy for the Moselle; Mayor of Sarrebourg. B March, 1916; degree in oriental languages, Doctor of Law.

Address: Rue Erckmann Chatrian, 57400 Sarrebourg. Tel: 031658. 1 Rue Général Delanne, 92200 Nevilly sur Seine. Tel: 551 30 75.

MICHEL, VICTOR
Belgium, EPP (PSC)

Mr Victor Michel has been President of the Christian Workers' Movement, since 1973. B September, 1915; studied classics; industrial and commercial school; Higher Institute for Christian Social Action. Member, governing board, Catholic University of Louvain; chairman, consultative committee on regional planning; president, Cooperatives Chrétiennes (Christian cooperative movement); member, Conseil Supérieur de la Famille (High Council for Family Affairs); president, Semaines Sociales Wallonnes (Walloon social weeks). Married with five children.

Address: 14 rue de la Marjolaine, 1120 Bruxelles. Tel: (02) 216 47 36.

MODIANO, MARCELLO
Italy, EPP (DC)

Sgr Marcello Modiano is Chairman of the Chamber of Commerce of Trieste; National President, Small Industries Association; President, International Federation of Small and Medium-sized Businesses. Member, board of the Autonomous Organisation of the Port of Trieste; board of directors of the Bank of Friuli; chairman, committee for maritime and port problems of the Italian Union of Chambers of Commerce. B April, 1914; degree in jurisprudence.

Address: Via Milano 4, 34132 Trieste. Tel: (040) 30047.

MØLLER, PØUL
Denmark, ED (KF)

Mr Pøul Møller was elected a Vice-President of the European Parliament in July, 1979. Elected Danish MP in 1950; retired in 1971 because of illness. For many years he played a leading part in the affairs of the Danish Conservative Party and was Finance Minister, 1968-71. Since then he has been a senior editor on *Berlingske Tidende,* and chairman of Dansk Arbejde, a trade promotion organisation. A vice-chairman of European Democrat Group in the European Parliament, from July 1979.

Address: Carl Baggers Allé 6, 2920 Charlottenlund. Tel: (01) 632441.

MOORHOUSE, JAMES
UK, London South, ED (C)

Mr James Moorhouse is group environmental affairs adviser to the main board of Rio Tinto Zinc Corporation; previously with Shell. Contested St Pancras North in the general elections of 1966 and 1970. B 1924; ed St Paul's School and London University. Chartered engineer. Specialised knowledge of environmental affairs including pollution; industry and technology especially energy, oil and gas, nuclear power; civil aviation; foreign affairs. Member, General Council and General Purposes CCommittee, Conservative Group for Europe.

Address: Hill House, 64 Honor Oak Road, Forest Hill, London SE23 3SH. Tel: 01-930 2399 (Office) and 01-699 8806 (home).

MOREAU, JACQUES
France, Soc (PS)

M Jacques Moreau is a trade union official (CFDT). B 1933.

Address: 5, allée de Tourvoie, 94260 Fresnes. Tel: 237 22 97.

MOREAU, MME LOUISE
France, EPP (UFE)

Mme Louise Moreau is a member of the executive of the Centre des démocrates-sociaux (CDS), having previously been Vice-President of the Democratic Centre and the first President of the Association of Democratic Women. Deputy, in French Parliament for Alpes-maritimes since 1978, being the only CDS deputy in the Mediterranean regions. Mayoress of Mandelieu-La Napoule since 1973. B January, 1921; studied medicine. Company director. Active in the Resistance and won the Medal of the Resistance and the Rosette of Officer of the Légion d'honneur.

Address: 747a, Avenue des Pins, 06210 Mandelieu-La Napoule. Tel: (93) 479587.

MORELAND, ROBERT
UK, Staffordshire East, ED (C)

Mr Robert Moreland is a management consultant. He contested Pontypool in the October, 1974, general election. B 1941; ed Dean Close School, Cheltenham; Nottingham University, and Institute of World Affairs, Connecticut; post-graduate degree in management science, Warwick University. Former Assistant Budget Director, New Brunswick, Canada. Was a member of the Council of the Conservative Group for Europe.

Addresses: 7 Vauxhall Walk, London SE11: 17 Barnwood Road, Gloucester.

MOTCHANE, DIDIER
France, Soc (PS)

M Didier Motchane is a civil servant. B 1931. Member, executive, French Socialist Party.

Address: 6, rue Verneuil, 75007 Paris.

MÜLLER-HERMANN, ERNST
Germany, EPP (CDU)

Herr Ernst Müller-Hermann has been chairman and spokesman for the Central Association of the Motor Vehicle Trade, Bonn, since 1971. Member of the Bundestag since 1952, and of the European Parliament, 1958-65, and since 1977. Chairman, CDU/CSU Bundestag party working group on economic and nutritional affairs; member, CDU's economic systems and economic policy commission of the Business Council, and of CDU Federal working party on foreign policy. B September, 1915; awarded doctorate in political science. Member, Bremen Parliament, 1946-52. Married with three children.

Address: Rilkeweg 40, 2800 Bremen-Oberneuland. Tel: (0421) 25 94 17.

MUNTINGH, HEMMO
Netherlands, Soc (PvdA)

Mr Hemmo Muntingh is chairman of the Fondation Européenne pour L'Environnement; secretary of Landelijke Vereniging tot Behoud van de Waddenzee. B December, 1938; studied through Free University of Amsterdam.

Address: Westerweg 11, 9079 PD St. Jacobi-Parochie. Tel: 05189-673.

NARDUCCI, ANGELO
Italy, EPP (DC)

Sgr Angelo Narducci, a journalist and teacher at the Department of Social Communications at the Catholic University. Editor of the Catholic daily *Avvenire* since 1969; assistant editor, 1968-69. Assistant editor, *Gazzetta del Popolo,* 1966-68; editor, head of department and editor in chief of *Il Popolo,* 1958-66. Married with two children. B August, 1930.

Address: Via Feltre 7, 20134 Milano. Tel: 2151788.

NICHOLSON, SIR DAVID
UK, London Central, ED (C)

Sir David Nicholson is chairman of Rothmans International Ltd, and BTR Ltd, and a director of other companies. First chairman (1971-75) of British Airways. B September 1922; ed Haileybury and Imperial College, London University. Member, CBI Europe committee; chairman, CBI Environment Committee; member, UK Committee of Insead. Married with three children.

Addresses: 15 Hill Street, London, W1X 7FB. Howicks, Dunsfold, Surrey. Tel: 048-649 296. 10 Fordie House, Sloane Street, London SW1. Tel: 01-235 0053.

NIELSEN, JØRGEN
Denmark, LD (V)

Mr Jørgen Brøndlund Nielsen, secondary school teacher. Member of Parliament for the Liberal Party (Venstre) since 1971 and of the nominated European Parliament. Member, Danish delegation to the United Nations, 1972-73. In the European Parliament, he has specialised in farming, environmental and regional problems, serving on the agriculture and budgets committees. Married.

Address: Aggersborg, 9670 Løgstør. Tel: 08-22 10 60.

NIELSON, MRS TOVE
Denmark, LD (V)

Mrs Tove Nielsen became a vice-chairman of the Liberal and Democratic Group at the European Parliament, in July, 1979. Was Minister of Education, 1973-75; now consultant to the Danish Employers' Association. She has held a variety of posts within the Liberal Party (Venstre) and, as a teacher, she is familiar with educational problems and their political background. A member of the Danish Parliament (Folketing) from 1972-73, and again from 1975-77. President, Nordic Council for Adult Education, since 1975. B April, 1941.

Address: Kokkedalsvej 5 B, 2970 Hørsholm.

NORD, HANS
Netherlands, LD (VVD)

Mr Hans Nord was Secretary-General of the European Parliament, 1962-79. Elected treasurer, Liberal and Democratic Group of the European Parliament, July 1979. Member of the VVD's Foreign Affairs Committee. B October 1919; graduated in law at Leiden University.

Address: 15, rue Conrad 1, Luxembourg. Tel: 440283.

NORDLOHNE, FRANZ-JOSEF
Germany, EPP (CDU)

Herr Franz-Josef Nordlohne has been a member of the Bundestag since 1972. Former town council administrator. B March, 1939. Since 1970 active on the CDU National Committee on social policy; since 1973 on the CDU National Committee on structural policy; since 1972, member, Federal Party committee; member, Social Affairs Committees, since 1963. Married with one child.

Address: Josefstrasse 24, 2842 Lohne. Tel: (04442) 3444.

NORMANTON, TOM
UK, Cheshire East, ED (C)

Mr Tom Normanton is an industrialist and director of both public and private companies in engineering and textiles. Member, European Parliament, since 1973 serving on Economic and Monetary Committee and Energy and Research Committee. Conservative MP for Cheadle since 1970; contested Rochdale, 1964 and 1959. Council member, CBI. B March 1917; ed Manchester Grammar School, Manchester University and Manchester College of Technology. Past president, British Textile Employers' Association; vice-president, International Textile Federation. Member, Textile Industrial Training Board, 1967-70 and, since 1968, of Central Training Council.

Address: Bollin Court, Macclesfield Road, Wilmslow, Cheshire SK9 2AP. Tel: 24 930. 6 Paultons St., Chelsea, London SW3 5DP. Tel: 01-352 6842.

NOTENBOOM, HARRY
Netherlands, EPP (CDA)

Mr Harry Notenboom has been a member of the European Parliament since 1971, having served as vice-chairman of the Christian-Democratic Group. Member, Dutch Second Chamber, from 1963. Has also been Deputy Secretary, Dutch Catholic Middle Classes Association, and Director, Limburg Catholic Middle Classes Association. B August, 1926; studied at Tilburg Economic Institute.

Address: Postbus 347, Venlo. Tel: (077) 19668.

NOTHOMB, CHARLES-FERDINAND
Belgium, EPP (PSC)

Mr Charles-Ferdinand Nothomb became national president of the Christian Social Party for the third time in 1979, previously being president in 1972 and 1976-77; member, political bureau, EPP. President, Belgian Chamber of Deputies, 1979; member of Belgian Parliament for the Arlon-Marche-Bastogne district since 1968. Member, Council of Europe and parliamentary assembly of WEU, 1968-73. B May, 1936; doctor of law, degree in economics. Secretary and then chargé de mission in private office of Minister of French Culture, Brussels, 1966-68. Professor of comparative politics, ICHEC (Catholic Institute of Advanced Commercial Studies), Brussels.

Address: Palais de la Nation, 10 rue de la Loi, 1000 Bruxelles. Tel: 512 98 00.

NYBORG, KAI
Denmark, DEP (FRP)

Mr Kai Nyborg is a dealer in toys. Member of the Danish Parlliment since 1973, for the Progress Party formed in 1972 in protest against high taxation. He trained for a career in trade or insurance. For many years, chairman of the Danish toy dealers' federation. Member of the European Parliament since 1973; a vice-chairman of the European Progressive Democrat group from July 1979. B April, 1922.

Address: Kretavej 5, 4800 Nykøbing F. Tel: 03-85 70 03.

O'CONNELL, DR JOHN
Ireland, Soc (Lab)

Dr John F. O'Connell, medical practitioner, is editor of the *Irish Medical Times*. Deputy since 1965 representing Dublin South-West until 1977 and Dublin Ballyfermot since. B January 1930; ed St Vincent's, Glasnevin, Dublin; Royal College of Surgeons, Dublin. Labour opposition spokesman on social welfare, 1969-72, and on health, 1972-73. Alderman, Dublin City Council, since 1974. Member, Eastern Health Board, since 1971; Eastern Regional Development Organisation, since 1971; Board of St. James' Hospital, since 1972; Jervis Street Hospital Board, since 1974; Irish TGWU since 1969; Irish Medical Association since 1954; Irish Medical Union since 1963; NUJ since 1975.
Address: 64 Inchicore Road, Dublin 8. Tel: 754751.

O'DONNELL, THOMAS
Ireland, EPP (F-Gael)

Mr Thomas O'Donnell was Minister for the Gaeltacht, 1973-77; Deputy for Limerick East since 1961. B August 1926; ed Crescent College, Limerick; Salesian College, Pallaskenry, Co. Limerick; University College, Dublin. Fine Gael opposition frontbench spokesman on transport and power, 1969-73. Member, Dáil and Seanad Joint Library Committee, 1961-69; Special Committee on Company Law, 1962; Mid-Western Regional Tourism Organisation, 1968-73; Muintir na Tire, 1951-61. He served as Chairman, Dromin Guild and member, Limerick Federation, 1955-58; Editor of the monthly journal *Landmark*, 1958-61.

Address: 37 Thomas Street, Limerick.

OEHLER, JEAN
France, Soc (PS)

M Jean Oehler, a builder's merchant, is a member of the Comité Directeur of the French Socialist Party. Local councillor.

Address: 28, rue Virgile, 67200 Strasbourg.
Tel: (88) 30 51 31.

O'HAGAN, LORD
UK, Devon, ED (C)

Lord O'Hagan was an Independent member of the European Parliament from 1973 to 1975, serving on its social affairs committee. Front bench spokesman in the House of Lords for the Conservatives since 1977 on the EEC, transport and environment. B 1945; ed Eton and New College, Oxford. Married with one daughter.

Address: Sutton Court, Stowey, Pensford, Bristol, Avon BS18 4DN.

O'LEARY, MICHAEL
Ireland, Soc (Lab)

Mr Michael O'Leary was Minister for Labour, 1973-77; President of the EEC Council of Social Affairs Ministers, 1975, and President of the annual conference of the International Labour Organization, 1976. Deputy Leader of the Labour Party. Deputy for Dublin North-Central since 1965. B May 1936; ed Presentation College, Cork; University College, Cork; Columbia University, New York. Labour opposition spokesman on foreign affairs, 1965-69, on labour, 1966-69, on industry and commerce, 1969-72, and on education, 1972-73. Founder member, Ireland Council of Labour. President, European Regional Conference of the International Labour Organisation, 1974.

Address: 47 Wellington Rd, Ballsbridge, Dublin 4.

OLESEN, KJELD
Denmark, Soc (S)

Mr Kjeld Olesen, deputy chairman of the Social Democratic Party in Denmark since 1973 and first on the party's list. Became secretary to the Lord Mayor of Copenhagen. In 1956, joined the SDP as a full-time official; in 1966, became member of the Danish Parliment; Defence Minister, 1971-73; Minister for Public Works, 1977-78. B July, 1932.

Address: Vamdrupvej 54, 2610 Rødovre.
Tel: (01) 70 94 64.

ORLANDI, FLAVIO
Italy, Soc (PSDI)

Sgr Flavio Orlandi, former national secretary of the PSDI, became an Italian MP in 1958. Journalist; Editor of *La Giustizia.* Member of several parliamentary committees including Public Works, Education, the Budget and Foreign Affairs. Secretary of the committee supervising the radio/TV corporation; Vice-Chairman of the committee of inquiry into the limits imposed on competition. Chairman, Committee on the Budget and State Economic Participation. B April, 1921; degree in political science.

Address: Via Livio Tempesta 22, 00151 Roma.
Tel: 06/5346683.

PAISLEY, THE REV IAN
UK, Northern Ireland, Ind (Dem U)

The Rev Ian Paisley, leader of the Ulster Democratic Unionist Party, has represented North Antrim at Westminster since 1970. Minister of Religion; Moderator of the Free Presbyterian Church. Founded Protestant Unionist Party and sat as Protestant Unionist MP from 1970-74. B April, 1926; ed Model School, Ballymena, and Ballymena Technical College, South Wales Bible Colleges, and Reformed Presbyterian Theological College, Belfast. Ordained 1946. Won Bannside in 1970 and was MP in Stormont until 1972. Democratic Unionist MP for North Antrim in N.I. Assembly, 1973-75, and UUUC member in the N.I. Constitutional Convention, 1975-76.

Address: The Parsonage, 17 Cyprus Avenue, Belfast BT5 5NT, N Ireland. Tel: 655694.

PAJETTA, GIANCARLO
Italy, Comm (PCI)

Sgr Giancarlo Pajetta, a journalist, has been an Italian MP since 1946. In 1925 joined the Communist Student Group. Called to Paris by the Party leadership in 1931, he directed the Communist Youth Federation which he represented at the IV National Congress. Became editor of *L'Unità* in 1945. Regional Secretary for Lombardy until 1948. Member of party leadership and the Political Office. Former member and three times vice-chairman, Parliamentary Committee on Foreign Affairs. B June, 1911.

Address: Via delle Botteghe Oscure 4, 00186 Roma.

PANNELLA, MARCO
Italy, TCDG (PR)

Sgr Marco Pannella was elected to the Italian Parliament in 1976; chairman, parliamentary group of Partito Radicale. Journalist. One of party's founders. Chairman, League of Conscientious Objectors, since 1973. Founded "Socialist Movement for Civil Rights and Liberties. May 13th League". Using unorthodox methods such as hunger strikes, has helped pass bills on divorce, conscientious objection, vote for 18-year-olds, etc. Promoted referendum on abortion. Member, committee for general guidance and supervision of the broadcasting services. B May, 1930; degree in jurisprudence.

Address: Via Collalto Sabino 40, 00199 Roma.

PAPAPIETRO, GIOVANNI
Italy, Comm (PCI)

Sgr Giovanni Papapietro was a member of the Party's Federal Committee, 1956–64, and in charge of the Cultural Committee. Secretary, Communist Federation of Bari, since 1964. Elected to the Central Committee and Central Control Committee at the XII Congress. Chief of the Communist Group at the Regional Council of Puglia since 1970. B January, 1931.

Address: Via Trevisana 66/a, 70123 Bari.

PATTERSON, BEN
UK, West Kent, ED (C)

Mr Ben Patterson was Deputy Head of the London office of the European Parliament. Former research assistant to the Director of the Conservative Political Centre. Contested Wrexham, 1970 general election. B 1939; ed Westminster School and Trinity College, Cambridge. Special interests: European affairs, economic affairs, housing and problems of immigrants. Married with two children.

Address: Birchenholt, Wellingtonia Avenue, Crowthorne, Berkshire RG11 6AF: 11 Buckingham Street, Strand, London WC2N 6DF. Tel: 01-839 1340.

PEARCE, ANDREW
UK, Cheshire West, ED (C)

Mr Andrew Pearce has been an official in the Customs Department of the European Communities Commission in Brussels since 1974. Founder and chairman, British Conservative Association in Belgium; deputy chairman, European Conservative Forum. Parliamentary candidate at general election in 1970 and a by-election in 1969. B 1937; ed Rydal School, Colwyn Bay, and Durham University. Married with three children.

Address: 663 Chester Road, Great Sutton, South Wirral L66 2LN. Tel: 051-339 2696.

PEDINI, MARIO
Italy, EPP (DC)

Sgr Mario Pedini, a university lecturer, was a member of the European Parliament, 1959-69. Several times Under-Secretary to the Prime Minister of Italy. Under-Secretary for foreign affairs; minister for relations with Parliament, for cultural assets and environment; for education; and for scientific research. Executive secretary and provincial political secretary of DC. B December, 1918.

Address: Via Festo Aveino 214, 00130 Roma. Tel: 34 55 202.

PELIKAN, JIRI
Italy, Soc (PSI)

Sgr Jiri Pelikan was born in Czechoslovakia in February, 1923. Journalist. Former Director of Radio Prague. Along with Dubcek, he was one of the promoters of the '68 "Spring". Refugee, but has now become a naturalized Italian.

Address: Via della Rotonda 36, 00186 Roma. Tel: 65 42 228.

PENDERS, JOHANNES
Netherlands, EPP (CDA)

Mr Johannes Penders is a member of the staff of the Scientific Council for Government Policy; has worked at the Ministry of Foreign Affairs and was Permanent Secretary of the KVP, Second Chamber Parliamentary Party. Member, European Movement. Serves on executive of the Foundation for Social Services in Leidschendam, Wassenaar and Voorschoten, and on executive of Universitas-Foundation for Cooperation between Catholic universities in the Netherlands and Indonesia. B April, 1939.

Address: Voorburgseweg 11, Leidschendam. Tel: (70) 27 86 91.

PERCHERON, DANIEL
France, Soc (PS)

M Daniel Percheron is a teacher. Regional councillor for Nord Pas de Calais; member, executive, French Socialist Party. B 1942.

Address: Lycée Diderot, Avenue Montaigne, 62220 Carvin. Tel: (16-20) 37 01 73.

PETERS, JOHANNES WILHELM
Germany, Soc (SPD)

Herr Johannes Wilhelm Peters, a miner, is secretary with responsibility for training in the Mine and Energy Workers' Union. B December, 1927.

Address: Senftenbergstrasse 16, 4600 Dortmund 14 (Scharnhorst).

PETRONIO, FRANCESCO
Italy, Ind (MSI-DN)

Sgr Francesco Petronio was elected an Italian MP in 1972. Journalist; editor of the magazine *L'Italiano;* contributor to *Il Secolo d'Italia* and several magazines. Former National President of FUAN and National Vice-Secretary of the party's youth movement. Councillor of Trieste in 1958; Rome, 1960–65; and of Milan. Member of party's central committee. B December, 1931.

Address: Via Felice Casati 20, 20124 Milano. Tel: 222 876.

PFENNIG, GERO
Germany, EPP (CDU)

Herr Gero Pfennig has been a member of the Bundestag and the Council of Europe since 1977. Read law at the Free University of Berlin and the University of Freiburg. Doctorate in Law. Assistant in Faculty 09 (jurisprudence) at the Free University of Berlin, 1968–73; assistant professor since 1973. Member of CDU since 1964; from 1971 to 1975 district councillor, Berlin-Zehlendorf; April-November 1975, member Berlin Parliament. B February, 1945. Married.

Address: Waldsaugerpfad 6, 1000 Berlin 38.
Tel: 803 6416.

PFLIMLIN, PIERRE
France, EPP (UFE)

M Pierre Pflmlin was elected a Vice-President of the European Parliament in July, 1979. Mayor of Strasbourg, one of the meeting places of the European Parliament, for the past 20 years. Prime Minister of France, May 12 to June 1, 1958, and occupied many posts as a minister. Former member, Consultative Assembly of the Council of Europe, of which he was President, 1963–65. Deputy for Bas-Rhin. B February, 1907; doctor of law. President of MRP, 1956–59.

Address: 9, rue Brûlée, 67000 Strasbourg.
Tel: 32 43 40.

PICCOLI, FLAMINIO
Italy, EPP (DC)

Sgr Flaminio Piccoli, journalist, has been editor of *L'Adige* for over 25 years. Chairman, Italian Catholic Press Association, and Secretary General, International Federation of Catholic Journalists. Elected political secretary, DC party, 1969. Member of Parliament from 1958. Minister of State Participation in two governments. Chairman, DC parliamentary group. B December, 1915; graduate in modern languages and literature.

Address: Via Massimi 45, 00136 Roma.

PININFARINA, SERGIO
Italy, LD (PLI)

Sgr Sergio Pininfarina is a member of the board of directors of Ferrari and of the committee of the General Confederation of Italian Industry. Since 1966, chairman of Pininfarina; also chairman, Union of Industrialists of Turin. B September, 1926; qualified in mechanical engineering at Turin Polytechnic Institute and studied in England and United States. In 1955 began the design and construction of a new factory in the Grugliasco district which went into operation in 1958.

Address: Piazza Duca d'Aosta 18, 10129 Torino. Tel: 70 32 32.

PINTAT, JEAN-FRANÇOIS
France, LD (UFE)

M Jean-François Pintat was elected a vice-chairman of the Liberal and Democratic Group of the European Parliament in July, 1979, having been chairman in the outgoing nominated Parliament. Engineer. Senator for Gironde; Mayor of Soulac-sur-mer. National secretary, Republican Party; vice-chairman, national movement of French local representatives. Chairman, Senate Energy Group, National Water Council, and Petroleum Board. B July, 1923. Married with one child.

Address: Villa Symphonie l'Amélie, 33780 Soulac-sur-mer.

PIQUET, RENÉ
France, Comm (PCF)

M René Piquet, metal worker, is secretary of the Central Committee of the French Communist Party. B October, 1932.

Address: Comité Central du PCF, 2, Place du Colobel Fabien, 75940 Paris Cedex 19. Tel: 238 66 55.

PLUMB, SIR HENRY
UK, Cotswold, ED (C)

Sir Henry Plumb, the new chairman of the European Parliament's Committee on Agriculture, was President of the National Farmers' Union, 1970–79; chairman, British Agricultural Council, since 1975. Became member, Council of NFU, 1959; Vice-President, 1964 and 1965; Deputy President, 1966–69. B March, 1925; ed King Edward VI School, Nuneaton. Past president, Comité des Organisations Professionels Agricoles de la CEE (COPA). Vice-President, International Federation of Agricultural Producers; member, Council of Management, Centre for European Agricultural Studies; European Liaison Group for Agriculture; Council of Animal Health Trust.

Address: Southfields Farm, Coleshill, Birmingham B46 3EJ. Tel: 0675-63133. Flat 10, 4-7 Clonie House, Knightsbridge, London. Tel: 01-584 9093.

POIRIER, MME HENRIETTE
France, Comm (PCF)

Mme Henriette Poirier, a teacher, is a member of the Central Committee of the French Communist Party. B October, 1936.

Address: Fédération du PCF, 15/17 rue Furtado, 33000 Bordeaux. Tel: 91 45 06.

PONCELET, CHRISTIAN
France, DEP (DIFE)

M Christian Poncelet, civil servant and former minister. Senator for Vosges. B March, 1928; graduate of national professional school.

Address: 17 rue des Etats Unis, 88200 Remiremont (Vosges). Tel: 620400.

PONIATOWSKI, MICHEL
France, LD (UFE)

M Michel Poniatowski is honorary President of the Republican Party (PR). Assistant Director in the cabinet of M Pierre Pflimlin, 1957; Director in the cabinet of M Valery Giscard d'Estaing, 1962; Deputy for Val d'Oise, 1967–73; Secretaire Général, Federation Nationale des Republicains Independants. Mayor of Isle Adam (Val d'Oise). Minister of Public Health and Social Security, 1973–74; Minister of State, Ministry of Interior Affairs, 1974–77; President, Federation Nationale des Republicains Independants, 1975; Roving ambassador, personal representative of the President of the Republic, 1977. B May, 1922. Licencié in law.

Address: 22, Bd Jean Mermoz, 92200 Neuilly. Tel: 745 4530.

PÖTTERING, HANS-GERT
Germany, EPP (CDU)

Herr Hans-Gert Pöttering, a lawyer, has been on the staff of the CDU/CSU Bundestag group since 1976; personal adviser to the deputy group chairman, Dr Burkhard Ritz. B September, 1945. District chairman, Osnabrück "Land" "Junge Union" 1974–76. Since 1974, chairman of the Bersenbrück municipal CDU and member, Osnabrück "Land" CDU district executive. Since 1976, member Osnabrück-Emsland CDU executive; and "Junge Union" Lower Saxony "Land" executive. Married with one child.

Addresses: Richard-Wagner-Strasse 15, 5300 Bonn 1. Tel: (02221) 658984. Dombogen 3, 4558 Bersenbrück. Tel: (05439) 1581.

PRAG, DEREK
UK, Hertfordshire, ED (C)

Mr Derek Prag was a European Commission civil servant until June 1973; now an independent consultant on Common Market affairs and an economic journalist. B 1923; ed Emmanuel College, Cambridge. Chairman, London Europe Society; member, executive committee and national council of European Movement. Married with three children.

Address: 27 Longton Avenue, Upper Sydenham, London SE26 6RE. Tel: 01-778 5605 and 01-659 1787.

PRANCHERE, PIERRE
France, Comm (PCF)

M Pierre Pranchere, a farmer, is a member of the Central Committee of the French Communist Party. B July, 1927.

Address: CES, Boulevard Georges Clemenceau, 19012 Tulle. Tel: 26 49 99.

PRICE, PETER
UK, Lancashire West, ED (C)

Mr Peter Price, a solicitor, is vice-chairman of the Conservative Political Centre's national advisory committee; member, National Union executive committee. B 1942; ed Worcester Royal Grammar School; Southampton University; and College of Law, Guildford. Chairman, Cardiff branch of European Movement, since 1975, and of Welsh committee, European Movement, 1973–75. Contested Caerphilly in 1970 general election, Aberdare 1964 and 1966.

Address: 37 Heol-St Denys, Lisvane, Cardiff CF4 5RU. Tel: 0222-761792 (home), 0443-404344 and 0443-402982 (office).

PROUT, CHRISTOPHER
UK, Salop and Stafford, ED (C)

Mr Christopher Prout, a barrister (Middle Temple), has been lecturer in law at the University of Sussex; he also practices privately. Deputy chairman, Brighton Pavilion Conservative Association. B 1942; ed Sevenoaks School, Manchester University, and Queens College, Oxford. Has published and advised on matters concerning trade and financial relationships between the EEC and Eastern Europe and the EEC and the Third World.

Addresses: c/o 54 Broad Street, Ludlow, Salop SY8 1BR. Tel: 0584-2187. Congreve Manor, Penkridge, Staffordshire. Tel: 078571-2802.

PROVAN, JAMES
UK, North East Scotland, ED (C)

Mr James Provan, farmer and regional councillor. Past council member, Scottish National Farmers' Union and its legal committee; president, Fife and Kinross area NFU. Member, Tay River Purification Board. B December, 1936; ed Oundle and Royal Agricultural College, Cirencester. Married with three children.

Address: Wallacetown, Bridge of Earn, Perth, Scotland.

PRUVOT, MME MARIE-JANE
France, LD (UFE)

Mme Marie-Jane Pruvot, headmistress of a primary school, has been active for some years in "Perspectives et réalités" clubs, being a member of the national bureau. Chairman, Federation Departmentale of Yvelines. B December, 1922. Married with three children.

Address: La Brocéliande — Parc, Briançon, 78570 Andresy. Tel: 974 83 72.

PULETTI, RUGGERO
Italy, Soc (PSDI)

Sgr Ruggero Puletti is lecturer in the History of Literature at the University of Perugia. Director of *Umanità,* official organ of the PSDI. B March, 1924; degree in arts.

Address: Via Savonarola 63, 06100 Perugia. Tel: 30 123.

PÜRSTEN, ALBERT
Germany, EPP (CDU)

Herr Albert Pürsten is chairman of the East-Westphalian-Lippe CDU; member, Westdeutscher Rundfunk radio board. Teacher. B February, 1923. Member, North Rhine-Westphalia "Land" Assembly, deputy CDSU group chairman since 1966. Founder, Lübbecke district "Junge Union" 1952, and district chairman, 1954; deputy chairman, Westphalia-Lippe "Junge Union", 1956–62. Member, CDU "Land" executive from 1961; deputy CDU "Land" chairman from 1970; chairman of the Westphalia-Lippe CDU protestant workers' circle 1961–1978; chairman of the Westphalia-Lippe CDU sports council 1958–1976. Married with four children.

Address: Lessingstrasse 4, 4992 Espelkamp.

PURVIS, JOHN
UK, Mid-Scotland and Fife, ED (C)

Mr John Purvis is an adviser to Scottish companies and English and American financial institutions on banking, money markets, foreign exchange, trade development and corporate planning. Director and secretary, Brigton Farms Ltd. B 1938; ed Trinity College, Glenalmond and St Andrews University. Member, taxation committee, Scottish Landowners' Federation. Married with three children.

Address: Gilmerton House, St Andrews, Fife, Scotland KY16 8NB. Tel: St Andrews 0334-73275 (home) and 0334-75830 (office).

QUIN, MISS JOYCE
UK, South Tyne and Wear, Soc (Lab)

Miss Joyce Quin, a university lecturer and member of the Association of University Teachers. B November, 1944; ed Whitley Bay Grammar School, Newcastle University and London School of Economics. BA (French), MSc (International Relations). Formerly a researcher for the Labour Party's International Department; member, Durham Constituency Labour Party; chairman, Elvet branch. Special interests: European and international politics.

Address: 16 Hazeldene, Whitley Bay, Tyne and Wear NE25 9AL. Tel: Whitley Bay 0632-521537.

RABBETHGE, FRAU RENATE-CHARLOTTE
Germany, EPP (CDU)

Frau Renate-Charlotte Rabbethge, a district chairman of the "Europa Union" formerly worked as foreign correspondent and interpreter with the Zeiss firm (Göttingen). In 1978, elected to executive, Lower Saxony CDU Women's Union, the Lower Saxony "Land" Association's advisory committee on the family, the executive of Einbeck CDU, became European affairs spokesman of Lower Saxony CDU Women's Union, member of CDU federal committee on women in the Middle Classes, and the agricultural committee, European Women's Union. B October, 1930. Married with two children.

Address: Haus Borntal, 3352 Einbeck.

RADOUX, LUCIEN
Belgium, Soc (PSB)

Mr Lucien Radoux, Director of the European Foundation for International Exchanges, was a member of the nominated European Parliament. Senator for Brussels. B July, 1921.

Address: 60c, avenue de la Toison d'Or (Boite 6), 1060 Bruxelles.
Tel: (02) 539 1960 and (02) 513 38 00.

REMILLY, EUGÈNE
France, DEP (DIFE)

M Eugène Remilly was elected treasurer of the European Progressive Democrat Group in July, 1979. President of French confederation of tobacconists and Vice-President of the European tobacconists' confederation.
B February, 1925.

Address: 92, rue Saint Lazare, 75008 Paris.
Tel: 522 94 66.

REY, JEAN
Belgium, LD (PRL)

Mr Jean Rey was President of the EEC Commission, 1967–70, being a member from 1958. Honorary President, Arbitration Court of International Chamber of Commerce, and of International European Movement. President, Paul-Henri Spaak Foundation. Doctor of law, honorary advocate, company director and former minister, having been Minister for Reconstruction, 1949–50, and Minister for Economic Affairs, 1954–58. Was Deputy for Liège. B July, 1902. Married with four children.

Address: 16, rue Hovade, 4040 Tilff. Tel: 041/88 11 31.

RHYS WILLIAMS, SIR BRANDON
UK, London South-East, ED (C)

Sir Brandon Rhys Williams has been a member of the European Parliament since 1973; delegate to Council of Europe, 1970–72. A consultant with Management Selection Ltd, 1963–71. Formerly with ICI Ltd. Conservative MP for Kensington, South, 1968–74, and for Kensington since 1974; contested Pontypridd, 1959, and Ebbw Vale in 1960 by-election and 1964. B November, 1927; ed Eton and Bolton Technical College on a special industrial course. Married with three children.

Addresses: Miskin Manor, Pontyclun: 32 Rawlings Street, London SW3.

RINSCHE, GÜNTER
Germany, EPP (CDU)

Herr Günter Rinsche, an economist, was a member of the Bundestag, 1965–72. Member, North Rhine-Westphalia "Land" assembly since 1975, being CDU group spokesman on economic affairs. Chief burgomaster of Hamm from 1964. B July, 1930. Member, North Rhine-Westphalia "Europa Union" "Land" executive and of German Council of European Movement. Chairman, planning committee, Institute for International Şolidarity; executive member, Konrad Adenauer Foundation. President, North Rhine-Westphalia convention of municipal authorities; deputy "Land" chairman, Westphalia-Lippe savings bank and giro association. Married with two children.

Address: Feldgarten 15, 4700 Hamm 1. Tel: 02381-52330.

RIPA DI MEANA, CARLO
Italy, Soc (PSI)

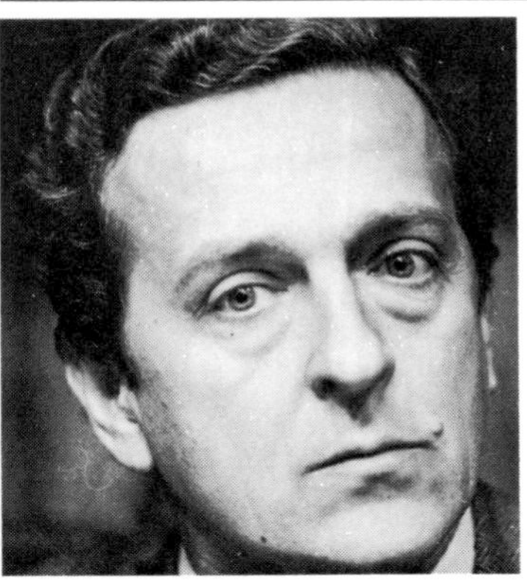

Sgr Carlo Ripa di Meana, a journalist, was President of the Biennial International Exhibition of Modern Art in Venice for five years. Leader of the International Section of the Italian Socialist Party. B August, 1929; degree in political science.

Address: Dorsoduro 73, 30123 Venezia

ROBERTS, MRS ANN CLWYD
UK, Mid and West Wales, Soc (Lab)

Mrs Ann Clwyd Roberts, broadcaster and journalist, is vice-chairman of the Arts Council of Wales and a member of the Arts Council of Great Britain. B 1944; ed Holywell Grammar School, Queen's School, Chester, and University College, Bangor. Was Labour candidate at Denbigh in 1970 general election and at Gloucester in October, 1974. Specially interested in the National Health Service and was a member of the Royal Commission on the National Health Service which reported in 1979. Community health councillor. Member, National Union of Journalists. Married.

Address: 1 Lon Werdd, St Fagon's, Cardiff, South Glamorgan, Wales. Tel: 0222-593492.

ROGERS, ALLAN
UK, South East Wales, Soc (Lab)

Mr Allan Rogers, was elected a Vice-President of the European Parliament, in July, 1979. Secretary/whip of the UK Labour Party group of members in the European Parliament. A district secretary of the Workers' Educational Association; former professional geologist. B October 1932; ed Swansea University. BSc, geology. Fellow of the Royal Geographical Society. Member, Gelligaer Urban District Council, 1967–77; Glamorgan County Council, 1970–74, and Mid Glamorgan County Council since 1974. Chairman, Polytechnic of Wales. TGWU. Married with three daughters and one son.

Address: 14 Dilwyn Avenue, Hengoed, Mid Glamorgan, South Wales CF8 7AG. Tel: Hengoed (0443) 812395.

ROMUALDI, PINO
Italy, Ind (MSI-DN)

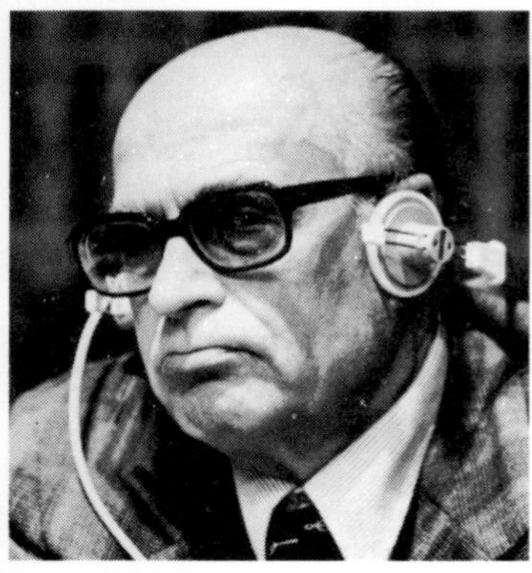

Sgr Pino Romualdi has been a member of the Italian Parliament since 1953. General Vice-Secretary, MSI-Destra Nazionale. Editor of *Il Popolo Italiano* until 1957. Twice member of the Parliamentary Committee on Industry and Commerce; member of Defence Committee in 1976. B July, 1913; degree in political science.

Address: Via Tacito 41, 00193 Roma.

ROMAGNOLI CARETTONI, SIGNORA TULLIA
Italy, Comm (PCI)

Signora Tullia Romagnoli Carettoni was elected an Italian Senator in 1963; twice Vice-Chairman of the Senate. Former member of European Parliament. Teacher and author. Member, Socialist Party's Central Committee, 1957–66. Town councillor of Cassano Spinola. A founder, Movement for Autonomous Socialists, 1966; thereafter, Secretary, Parliamentary Group, "Independents of the Left". Former member, Parliamentary Committees on Education and the Fine Arts, Foreign Affairs, and Industry and Commerce. Vice-chairman, Italian Advisory Committee for Human Rights; chairman, Germany/Italy Association and Parliamentary Italy/Vietnam Group. B December, 1918; arts degree.
Address: Via Boncompagni 16, 00187 Roma.
Tel: 48 53 81.

ROSSI, ANDRÉ
France, LD (UFE)

M André Rossi, a former vice-president and member of the nominated European Parliament, is Deputy for Aisne and Mayor of Château-Thierry. Secretary of State, Ministry of Information, then Minister of Foreign Trade, 1974–78. County councillor for canton of Châtillon-sur-Marne. Head of French delegation to UN Economic and Social Council. B May, 1921.

Address: 35a Quai de Grenelle, 75015 Paris.

ROUDY, MME YVETTE
France, Soc (PS)

Mme Yvette Roudy is a journalist. Member, executive, French Socialist Party. B 1929.

Address: 162 Bd Montparnasse, 75014 Paris. Tel: 354 42 01.

RUFFOLO, GIORGIO
Italy, Soc (PSI)

Sgr Giorgio Ruffolo, an economist, is the author of numerous publications and essays. President of Finanziaria Meridionale. B August, 1926. Member, Central Committee of Italian Socialist Party.

Address: Piazza della Libertà 20, 00192 Roma. Tel: 35 99 444.

RUMOR, MARIANO
Italy, EPP (DC)

Sgr Mariano Rumor was Prime Minister of Italy, 1968–70 and 1973–74. Chairman, Christian Democratic World Union, since 1974; President, European Union of Christian Democrats since 1974. Elected deputy at the constituent assembly and member of the Chamber of Deputies since 1948 and of Senate since 1979. Several times Under-Secretary for Agriculture, then Minister; several times Minister of the Interior. Deputy national secretary DC party, 1950–51 and 1954–58; political secretary, 1963–64 and 1967. B June, 1915. Arts graduate; professor.

Address: Via Kenia 58, 00144 Roma. Tel: 06-59 19 427.

RYAN, RICHIE
Ireland, EPP (F-Gael)

Mr Richie Ryan was President of the EEC Council of Finance and Economic Ministers, January to June, 1975, being the Republic of Ireland's Minister for Finance, 1973–77, and Minister for the Public Service, 1973–77. Lawyer. B November, 1929. Chairman, International Monetary Fund and World Bank 1977; Governor, European Investment Bank and International Monetary Fund and World Bank Group, 1973–77. Won Dublin South-West in July 1959 and represented the constituency until 1969. Following the revision of the constituency, he won a seat in 1969 and 1973 in Dublin South-Central. Member, European Parliament, 1973; Assembly of the Council of Europe, 1968–73; Dublin City Council, 1960–73.

Address: St Mary's, 127 Templelogue Road, Terenure, Dublin 6.

SABLÉ, VICTOR
France, LD (UFE)

Mr Victor Sablé became a member of the High Court of Justice in 1978; Secretary of the Bureau of the National Assembly, 1967. Elected Deputy for the 3rd Division of Martinique, 1958, and was re-elected in 1962, 1967, 1968, 1973 and 1978. Commonwealth Senator, 1960. B November 1911; Doctorate in Law from the Law Faculty in Paris. Member, Conseil General du Marin, Martinique, 1945; member, Council of the Republic, 1946; chairman, Franc Area Banana Growers Interprofessional Committee, 1956. Married with one child.

Address: 140 Avenue Victor Hugo, 75116 Paris. Tel: 727 85 17.

SALISCH, FRAU HEINKE
Germany, Soc (SPD)

Frau Heinke Salisch is an interpreter. B August, 1941.

Address: Kopernikusstrasse 22, 7500 Karlsruhe. Tel: 0721-571603 and 0721-572057.

SALZER, BERNHARD
Germany, EPP (CDU)

Herr Bernhard Salzer, consultant civil engineer, is a member of the CDU executive for the "Land" of Hesse; deputy chairman, CDU Federal Committee on Cultural and Educational Policy. B September, 1940. Mayor of Marburg since 1976. CDU group chairman, Darmstadt City Council, 1968–76; member of the Landtag, 1970–76, and CDU spokesman on cultural and educational policy, 1972–76. Married with two children.

Address: Dieburger Strasse 240, 6100 Darmstadt. Tel: 66151/714240.

SARRE, GEORGES
France, Soc (PS)

M Georges Sarre is President of the Socialist group on Paris Council. Inspector of Post Office. B 1935.

Address: 22, rue Edouard Lockroy, 75011 Paris. Tel: 700 43 90.

SASSANO, MARIO
Italy, EPP (DC)

Sgr Mario Sassano is an electrical engineer. ENEL (state owned electricity industry) executive. Has been a member of research committees appointed by DC party and helped to draft technical bills. Married with four children. B October, 1923.

Address: Viale le XXI Aprile 5, 00162 Roma. Tel: 831 29 94.

SCHALL, WOLFGANG
Germany, EPP (CDU)

Herr Wolfgang Schall served in the Army from 1936 until he retired at his own request for political work with the CDU in 1971. From 1945–55 he was a prisoner of war in Russia. From 1959–61 and 1965–68 he commanded Panzer Grenadier Brigades; from 1968–71 on Army Staff, Federal Defence Ministry. Chairman, CDU Böblingen district association; member, CDU North-Württemburg executive. B March, 1916. Married with two children.

Address: Waldweg 53, 7772 Uhldingen 2.
Tel: (07556) 8390.

SCHIELER, RUDOLF
Germany, Soc (SPD)

Herr Rudolf Schieler, a barrister, is a former Minister of Justice. Member of Baden-Wurttemberg Landtag; deputy chairman of the SPD in the Landtag. B May, 1928.

Address: Stephenaienstrasse 21, 7800 Freiburg.

SCHINZEL, DIETER
Germany, Soc (SPD)

Herr Dieter Schinzel, a physicist, is head of a social organization. B November, 1942.

Address: Melatenerstrasse 89a, 5100 Aachen.
Tel: 84874.

SCHLEICHER, FRAU URSULA
Germany, EPP (CSU)

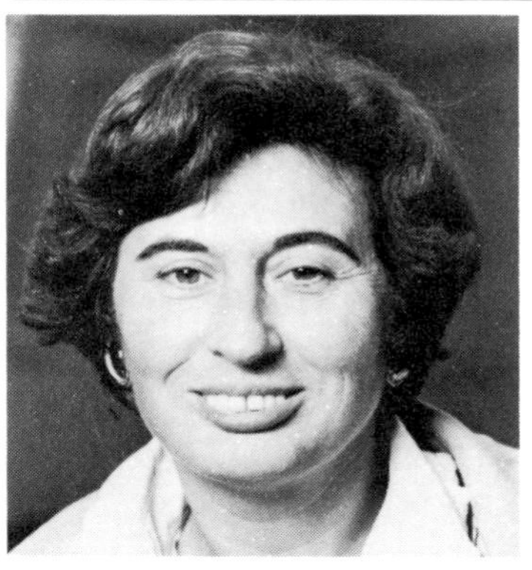

Frau Ursula Schleicher has been a member of the Bundestag since 1972; chairman, Bundestag committee on problems of women and society, and deputy chairman, committee on youth, family and health problems, since 1976. Committee member, CSU group in Bundestag and of CDU-CSU parliamentary group. CSU adviser on women's rights, 1965–75. Praesidium member, German Council for the European Movement, since 1974; deputy federal chairman, German Catholic Workers' Movement, and chairman, CSU Women's Organisation for Lower Franconia, since 1975; member, Social Affairs Committee of European Union of Women, since 1976. B May, 1933.

Address: Backoffenstrasse 6, 8750 Aschaffenburg. Tel: (06021) 27594.

SCHMID, GERHARD
Germany, Soc (SPD)

Herr Gerhard Schmid is a member of the Niederbayern-Oberpfalz SPD district executive. Chemist; research fellow. B May, 1946.

Address: Innere Passauer Strasse 55, 8440 Straubing. Tel: (09421) 6527.

SCHMITT, HEINZ
Germany, Soc (SPD)

Herr Heinz Schmitt is a member of the Regional Council of the Lutheran Church in Westphalia; member, Bielefeld Town Council. Plumber and fitter; union secretary. B August 1920.

Address: Südheide 27, 4800 Bielefeld 14. Tel: 17 33 11 and 40 11 68.

SCHNITKER, PAUL
Germany, EPP (CDU)

Herr Paul Schnitker, master painter, has been, from 1968, president of the Münster chamber of handicrafts; from 1972, president of the central association of German handicrafts and the German Assembly of Craftsmen and the Federal Union of Professional Association; from 1974, president of the International Federation of Handicrafts and from 1979 chairman of the joint committee of Deutsche Gewerbliche Wirtschaft (German trade and industry). B January, 1927. Married with four children.

Address: Hammer Strasse 36, 4400 Munster. Tel: (0251) 43093.

SCHÖN, KARL
Germany, Soc (SPD)

Herr Karl Schön is Mayor of Bendorf. Chairman, Koblenz local SPD. Stone cutter; member of the building workers' trade union. B July, 1923.

Address: Danngasse 3, 5413 Bendorf 1/Rhein. Tel: (02622) 2021.

SCHON, KONRAD
Germany, EPP (CDU)

Herr Konrad Schon is Professor of Political Science and Political Education, Saarland Teacher Training College. CDU political group chairman, Saarland "Land" Assembly, 1972; Minister of Finance, 1974; re-elected to "Land" Assembly, 1975; European affairs spokesman to Saarland "Land" government, 1976. B May, 1930. Married.

Address: Am alten Forsthaus 19, 6670 St Ingbert —Rohrbach. Tel: (06894) 5591.

SCHWARTZENBERG, ROGER-GÉRARD
France, Soc (PS)

M Roger-Gérard Schwartzenberg is Vice-President of Mouvement des radicaux de gauche (MRG). Agrégé in public law and political science; professor of law and political science. B April, 1943.

Address: 3, rue de Rivoli, 75004 Paris. Tel: 272 78 94.

SCHWENCKE, OLAF
Germany, Soc (SPD)

Herr Olaf Schwencke is a member of the Bundestag and of the Parliamentary Assembly of the Council of Europe. Chairman, Council of Europe's Committee for Architectural Heritage. B January, 1936. Theologian; tutor.

Address: Wilhelmstrasse 17, 3070 Nienburg (Weser). Tel: (05021) 13636.

SCIASCIA, LEONARDO
Italy, TCDG (PR)

Sgr Leonardo Sciascia is a member of the Italian Parliament. B January, 1921. Writer; particularly interested in problems concerning the Sicilian Mafia. In 1975 he stood as an "independent" on the Communist list at the administrative elections. He resigned from the European Parliament in September, 1979.

Address: Viale Scaduto 10/B, 90144 Palermo.

SCOTT-HOPKINS, JAMES
UK, Hereford and Worcester, ED (C)

Mr James Scott-Hopkins is leader of the European Democrat Group, formerly the European Conservative Group. Member, European Parliament, since 1973; deputy leader, Conservative Group, 1974, and a Vice-President of the Parliament, 1976–79. Conservative MP for West Derbyshire, 1967–79, and for North Cornwall, 1959–66; Parliamentary Secretary, Ministry of Agriculture, Fisheries and Food, 1962–64. Farmer and marketing consultant. An Opposition spokesman for agriculture, 1964–66, and on Europe, 1974–79. B November, 1921; ed Eton and New College, Oxford, and Emmanuel College, Cambridge.

Address: European Democrat Group, St Stephen's House, Victoria Embankment, London. 602 Nelson House, Dolphin Sq, London. Tel: 01-828 6682.

SCRIVENER, MME CHRISTIANE
France, LD (UFE)

Mme Christiane Scrivener became Secretary of State to the Minister for Economy and Finance (consumption) in 1976 and Deputy Secretary-General of the Republican Party in 1978. B September, 1925; ed Paris University (law and arts), Springfield University, Massachusetts (linguistics) and Harvard Business School. Creation and general direction of Association for the Organization of Short Training Periods in France (ACTIM), 1958, and of the Association for the Organization of Technical Cooperation Missions (ASMIC) in 1961; creation of Industrial and Economic Technical Cooperation Agency (ACTIM), 1968, becoming Director-General of ACTIM in 1976. Married with one child.

Address: 21, Avenue Robert Schuman, 92100 Boulogne-sur-Seine. Tel: 8254411.

SEAL, BARRY
UK, West Yorkshire, Soc (Lab)

Mr Barry Seal, principal lecturer at a polytechnic. B October, 1937; ed Heath Grammar School, Halifax; Bradford University, and European Business School. Diploma in Chemical Engineering; MSc, PhD, CEng. Member, Institute of Chemical Engineers and the British Institute of Management. Member, Bradford City Council, 1971–74; Bradford Metropolitan District Council (leader of Labour group) since 1974. Labour parliamentary candidate at Harrogate in October, 1974 election. Member, National Association of Teachers in Further and Higher Education. Special interests: European development, education, management and finance. Married with one daughter and one son.

Address: 5 Paddock Close, Wyke, Bradford, Yorkshire. Tel: 0274 671888.

SEEFELD, HORST
Germany, Soc (SPD)

Herr Horst Seefeld was a member of the bureau of the Socialist Group in the outgoing European Parliament. Member of the Bundestag. President of the German Council of the European Movement. Press officer. B November, 1930.

Address: Im Brettspiel 53, 7518 Bretten.
Tel: (07252) 1903.

SEELER, HANS-JOACHIM
Germany, Soc (SPD)

Herr Hans-Joachim Seeler is a member of the Hamburg SPD executive and of the Hamburg Parliament. Lawyer; former Senator. B August, 1930. Chairman, Wandsbek SPD.

Address: Sonnentauweg 3, 2000 Hamburg 71.
Tel: (040) 6414199.

SEGRE, SERGIO
Italy, Comm (PCI)

Sgr Sergio Segre became an Italian MP in 1972. Journalist; member of editorial staff of *L'Unità* since 1945: head of foreign services, special correspondent in Berlin and Bonn (1952-57), and co-director (1969-70). Editorial Secretary of *Rinascita,* 1958-61; Deputy Editor of *Stasera.* Member of Party's Central Committee and in charge of the Foreign Affairs Section since 1970. Twice member of Parliamentary Committee on Foreign Affairs. B September, 1926.

Address: Via dei Giornalisti 64, Roma.
Tel: 3454079.

SEIBEL-EMMERLING, FRAU LIESELOTTE
Germany, Soc (SPD)

Frau Lieselotte Seibel-Emmerling, a teacher, is a member of the Bavarian Landtag. B February, 1932.

Address: Virchowstrasse 15a, 8500 Nürnberg. Tel: (0911) 564467.

SEITLINGER, JEAN
France, EPP (UFE)

M Jean Seitlinger, a lawyer, began his political life side by side with Robert Schuman, in his native Moselle region. Elected to French Parliament, together with the founder of the European Coal and Steel Community, in 1956; re-elected in Sarreguemines in 1958, defeated in 1962 but elected again in 1973 and in 1978. Former Secretary-General, European Christian Democratic Union; now holds same post in the European People's Party. National adviser to the CDS on foreign policy. B November, 1924.

Address: 19, rue de l'Eglise, 57200 Sarreguemines. Tel: 87-98220.

SELIGMAN, MADRON
UK, Sussex West, ED (C)

Mr Madron Seligman has, since 1972, been marketing director of the APV group which has 60 companies worldwide. B 1918; ed Harrow and Balliol College, Oxford (President of the Union). Special interests: international affairs, industrial and employment matters, small businesses and trade. Married with four children.

Addresses: PO Box No 4, Crawley, W. Sussex RH10 2QB. Tel: 37457 or 27777. Micklepage House, Nuthurst, near Horsham, Sussex. Tel: Lower Beeding (040376) 259.

SHERLOCK, DR ALEXANDER
UK, Essex South West, ED (C)

Dr Alexander Sherlock is a qualified medical practitioner and a barrister. Member, Suffolk County Council since 1973. B 1922; ed Magdalen College School, Oxford; Stowmarket Grammar School and London Hospital Medical School. Special interests: safety and health in industry; transport, manufacture and use of hazardous substances and appropriate associated legislation; control of environmental pollution. Married with children and grandchildren.

Address: 58 Orwell Road, Felixstowe, Suffolk IP11 7PS. Tel: 4503.

SIEGLERSCHMIDT, HELLMUT
Germany, Soc (SPD)

Herr Hellmut Sieglerschmidt was a member of the nominated European Parliament. Member of the Bundestag; former Senate councillor. Member, Synod of Lutheran Church of Germany. Journalist. B October, 1917.

Address: Nibelungenstrasse 5a, 1000 Berlin 39. Tel: (036) 8136886.

SIMMONDS, RICHARD
UK, Midlands West, ED (C)

Mr Richard Simmonds is a farmer and estate business consultant, previously a surveyor. B 1944; ed Trinity College, Glenalmond and studied politics and economics in Hamburg and marketing in EEC. Researched speeches and reports for Conservative front bench spokesmen on taxation, juvenile crime and European affairs. Former area Young Conservative chairman. Founding vice-chairman, Young European Democrats; council member, Conservative Group for Europe. Married with three children.

Addresses: Woodlands Farm, Cookham Dean, Maidenhead, Berkshire SL6 9PJ. Tel: Marlow 4293 (office). Dyers, Cookham Dean, Maidenhead, Berkshire. Tel: Marlow 3269.

SIMONNET, MAURICE-RENÉ
France, EPP (UFE)

M Maurice-René Simonnet, Professor of European law in the Faculty of Law at Lyons, is a former Secretary-General of the Catholic Association of French Youth, a graduate from the School of Political Sciences, and a qualified lawyer. Elected to the French Parliament after the liberation; he remained there until 1962, serving as Secretary of State from 1957–58. In 1962, he was elected chairman, Foreign Affairs Committee, National Assembly. Secretary-General of the MRP, 1955–62. B October, 1919.

Address: CDS – 205, Bd Saint-Germain, 75007 Paris. Tel: 16(1) 544 72 50.

SIMPSON, ANTHONY
UK, Northamptonshire, ED (C)

Mr Anthony Simpson, a barrister, has worked in the legal service of the European Commission in Brussels since 1975. Contested Leicester, West, in both 1974 general elections. B October, 1935; ed Rugby and Magdalene College, Cambridge. In Brussels he has been chairman of the European Democrat Forum, and a member of the committee of the British Conservative Association in Belgium. Member, Oadby Urban District Council, 1968–71. Special interests: defence, and Community law, legal affairs, transport and environmental matters.

Addresses: Avenue Michel-Ange 57, 1040 Brussels: Bassets, Great Glen, Leicestershire.

SKOVMAND, SVEN
Denmark, TCDG (Folkebevaegelsen)

Mr Sven Skovmand, editor, is a joint chairman of the new European Parliament group for Technical Coordination and Defence of Independents. Member of Danish Parliament, 1968–73 as a Radical Liberal and is still on the list of that party's candidates in Aarhus. He has been connected with the commercial section of the movement against the Common Market since it was formed in April 1972. Author of a number of school and reference books. B September, 1936.

Address: Ravnsmosevej 2, Hedegard, 8584 Tranehuse.

SPAAK, MRS ANTOINETTE
Belgium, Ind (FDF-RW)

Mrs Antoinette Spaak, a deputy for Brussels, is President of the Front Démocratique des Francophones (FDF). B June, 1928; graduate in philosophy and letters.

Address: 11, avenue Maurice, 1050 Bruxelles. Tel: (02) 648 03 62.

SPAUTZ, JEAN
Luxembourg, EPP (CSV)

Mr Jean Spautz is a deputy and president of the confederation of christian associations in Luxembourg. B 1931. Has served as a coopted member of the consultative assembly of the Council of Europe in Strasbourg.

Address: 12, rue Pierre Dupong, Schifflange. Tel: 48 97 97 (bureau), 54 82 42 (private).

SPENCER, TOM
UK, Derbyshire, ED (C)

Mr Tom Spencer has been with J. Walter Thompson since January 1976. Assistant to director of Britain in Europe Campaign, 1975; member, Council of European Movement, 1968–75; vice-president, Young European Federalists, 1972–75. B 1948; ed Nautical College, Pangbourne and Southampton University, where he was chairman of the university Conservative Association. Ex-chairman, New Forest Young Conservatives.

Addresses: Heath House, 13 Goulton Road, Goulton, Clapton, London E5 8HA. Tel: 01-985 5839. The Edge, Eyam, nr Bakewell, Derbyshire.

SPICER, JAMES
UK, Wessex, ED (C)

Mr James Spicer, whip to the European Democrat Group, has been a member of the European Parliament since 1975 acting as the link between the Conservative Whips Office at the Commons and the Conservative members in the European Parliament. MP for Dorset, West, since February 1974; company director and farmer. Member, House of Commons Select Committee on European Secondary Legislation, 1974–75. Chairman, Conservative Group for Europe, 1975–78; Vice-President of the group since 1978. Contested Southampton, Itchen, in a by-election in 1971. Special interests: agriculture, defence and foreign affairs. B 1925; ed Latymer Upper School. Served in Regular Army, 1943–57. Married with two children.

Address: Whatley, Beaminster, Dorset.
Tel: 0308 862337.

SPINELLI, ALTIERI
Italy, Comm (Ind Sin)

Sgr Altieri Spinelli was a member of the EEC Commission, 1970-76, being responsible for industrial policy; member of outgoing nominated European Parliament and an Italian MP since 1976. Freelance journalist and author. Founded the European Federalist Movement, 1943. Founder and director (1967-70) of the Institute of International Affairs. Counsellor for European problems in the Nenni ministry. Former member of the Parliamentary Committee on Foreign Affairs; chairman, parliamentary group. B August, 1907.

Address: Clivo Rutario 5, 00152 Roma.
Tel: 06 5896 343.

SQUARCIALUPI, SIGNORA VERA
Italy, Comm (PCI)

Signora Vera Squarcialupi was elected an Italian Senator in 1976 as an independent on the Communist list. Member of the outgoing nominated European Parliament since 1976. After lengthy experience as a television journalist, particularly in the news department and on programmes concerned with women, she became member of the editorial staff of the television and radio news for regional and national transmission. Member, Parliamentary Committee on Public Health. B August, 1928; arts degree.

Address: Via Losanna 16, 20154 Milano.
Tel: 3458781.

STEWART-CLARK, SIR JOHN
UK, Sussex East, ED (C)

Sir John Stewart-Clark has been managing director of Pye of Cambridge Ltd since 1975. Elected treasurer of the European Democratic Group at the European Parliament, July 1979. B September, 1929; ed Eton; Balliol College, Oxford; Harvard Business School. With J and P Coats Ltd, 1952–69; managing director, J and P Coats, Pakistan, Ltd, 1961–67; J. A. Carp's Garenfabrieken, Holland, 1967–69; Phillips Electrical Ltd, London, 1971–75. Member, Royal Company of Archers, Queen's Bodyguard for Scotland. Contested Aberdeen, North, 1959 general election. Married with five children.

Address: Holmsley House, Holtye Common, near Cowden, Kent. Tel: 034286-541.

SUTRA DE GERMA, GEORGES
France, Soc (PS)

M Georges Sutra de Germa is a winegrower. B 1930. Municipal councillor; member, National Agricultural Commission.

Address: Campagne Montplèsy, 34120 Pezenas. Tel: 98 12 77.

TAYLOR, JOHN DAVID
UK, Northern Ireland, ED (Off UU)

Mr John David Taylor was Northern Ireland's Minister of State for Home Affairs, 1970–72, and Parliamentary Secretary at that department, 1969–70. MP for South Tyrone 1965. Member, NI Assembly, 1973–75, and NI Constitutional Convention, 1975–76. Partner of G D Taylor and Associates, architects and civil engineers, since 1966. Privy councillor (N Ireland). B December, 1937. Married with one child.

Address: Mullinure, Armagh BT61 9EL, N Ireland, UK. Tel: Armagh 0861-522409.

TAYLOR, JOHN MARK
UK, Midlands East, ED (C)

Mr John Mark Taylor is senior partner Taylor Allsopp and Co and a director of small companies concerned with fuels, transport and chemicals. Contested Dudley East in both general elections in 1974. B August, 1941; ed Bromsgrove School and College of Law; studied civil engineering at Birmingham University before qualifying as a lawyer. Leader, West Midlands Metropolitan County Council, since 1977, being chairman of its policy committee. Member, West Midlands Economic Planning Council, West Midlands Planning Authorities Conference. Deputy chairman, Association of Metropolitan Authorities.

Address: 19 Emscote Green, Solihull, West Midlands, B91 1TB. Tel: 021 704 9212. 211 St Bernards Road, Solihull.

TINDEMANS, LEO
Belgium, EPP (CVP)

Mr Leo Tindemans was Prime Minister of Belgium, 1974–78. Chairman of European People's Party and vice-chairman, European Union of Christian Democrats (EUCD); chairman, Christelijke Volkspartij (CVP). B April, 1922. Married with four children. National secretary, Christian People's Party, 1958–65; Burgomaster of Edegem, 1965–76; Secretary-General, EUCD, 1965–73; Minister for Inter-Community Relations, 1968–72; Minister of Agriculture and for Small Firms and Traders, 1972–73, then deputy Prime Minister and Minister for the Budget, 1973–74.

Address: Jan Verbertlei 24, 2520 Edegem.

TOLMAN, TEUN
Netherlands, EPP (CDA)

Mr Teun Tolman, member of the Second Chamber since 1963, and of the European Parliament since 1978, is a farm manager and an administrator of agricultural organizations and polder boards. B September 1924. Former vice-chairman, European Young Farmers, and chairman, Christian Youth Association in Friesland. Vice-chairman, Dutch CHJO; alderman and member of the provincial executive.

Address: Hoofdweg 45b, 8474 CA Oldeholtpade, p Wolvega. Tel: 05610-2463.

TRAVAGLINI, GIOVANNI
Italy, EPP (DC)

Sgr Giovanni Travaglini, a civil engineer, has been Professor at the Faculty of Sciences, Bari University, since 1953. Head of Civil Engineer's Department in Brindisi, Matera and Naples, 1953–65; Superintendent of Construction for Calabria and Campania, 1965–71. Director-General, Upper Council of Public Works. Chairman, Save Venice Committee, and of committee set up to restore the Tower of Pisa. Chairman, National Commission for the Construction of Large Dams, and of the National Seismic Services Scientific Commission. B October, 1924.

Address: Via Tasso 480, 80127 Napoli. Tel: 081-650313.

TUCKMAN, FREDERICK
UK, Leicester, ED (C)

Mr Frederick Tuckman is managing director of a consultancy firm in Germany specialising in human resources and chairman, partner and member, respectively, of similar firms in Finland, the United States and London. Since 1970 has spent much time on the continent of Europe in this job. Secretary, Bow Group, 1958–59, and Council member, 1955–63; chairman, Greater London area, Conservative Political Centre, 1968–69. Contested Coventry North in 1970 general election. B June 1922; ed London University. Married with three children.

Addresses: 6 Cumberland Road, London SW13 9LY – "Bassetts", 3 The Nook, Great Glen, Leicestershire.

TURNER, AMÉDÉE
UK, Suffolk, ED (C)

Mr Amédée Turner, QC, patent barrister and author. Called to the Bar (Inner Temple) 1954; practised patent bar, 1955–57; Associate, Kenyon and Kenyon, patent attorneys, New York, 1957–60; returned to London practice, 1960. Contested Norwich North in the general elections of 1964, 1966 and 1970. B March 1929; ed Temple Grove, Heron's Ghyll, Sussex; Dauntsey School, Wiltshire; Christ Church, Oxford. Chairman, Conservative Party Foreign Affairs Forum.

Addresses: 1 Essex Court, Temple, London EC4 9AR. Tel: 353-8507. The Barn, Westleton, Saxmundham, Suffolk. Tel: Westleton 235.

TYRRELL, ALAN
UK, London East, ED (C)

Mr Alan Tyrrell, QC, has a specialised knowledge of industrial relations. Called to Bar, 1956; Recorder of Crown Courts since 1972; QC, 1976. B 1933; ed Bridport Grammar School and London School of Economics. Candidate, Paddington Borough Council, 1958; South Lewisham 1961. Married with two children.

Address: 15 Willifield Way, London NW11.
Tel: 01-455 5798.

VAN AERSSEN, JOCHEN
Germany, EPP (CDU)

Herr Jochen van Aerssen has been a member of the Bundestag since 1976 and of the European Parliament since 1977. B April, 1941; studied at universities of Bonn, Cologne and Freiburg. Appointed Doctor of Law 1970. From 1971, lawyer and independent consultant to Düsseldorf Chamber of Trade and Industry. Member of CDU since 1964; member, Rhineland CDU "Land" executive, Kleve CDU district executive, and North Rhine-Westphalia "Land" Assembly (since 1970). From 1978, president of the North Rhine-Westphalia "Europa Union"; chairman, German-Netherlands committee on cultural and educational policy for North Rhine-Westphalia.

Address: Elfgenweg 33, 4000 Düsseldorf 11.
Tel: (0211) 594188.

VAN DEN HEUVEL-DE-BLANK, MRS IEN
Netherlands, Soc (PvdA)

Mrs Ien van den Heuvel-de Blank was elected a vice-chairman of the Socialist Group in the European Parliament in July, 1979. Former member of the Dutch Parliament and PvdA chairman; former chairman of PvdA women's organization. B August, 1927.

Address: Engelberg 8, 3956 VL Leersum.
Tel: 03434-1376.

VAN DER GUN, FRANS
Netherlands, EPP (CDA)

Mr Frans van der Gun has had long service with the Catholic Trades Union Movement. Member of the Second Chamber. Member of the European Parliament since 1971; was chairman of the Committee on Social Affairs, Employment and Education. Was Secretary of the Catholic Housing Institute, the Dutch National Catholic Trades Union Federation, the Labour Foundation and the Socio-Economic Council. Former member, Hagestein Municipal Council. B November, 1918.

Address: Prof Hugo de Vrieslaan 53, Utrecht. Tel: (030) 71 10 33.

VANDERPOORTEN, HERMAN
Belgium, LD (PVV-ELD)

Mr Herman Vanderpoorten is Senator for Mechelen-Turnhout. Lawyer. B August, 1922. Provincial councillor for Liberal Party, 1949; chairman, Flemish Liberal Association, 1957–72, except for period 1966–69. Minister of Home Affairs, 1966–68; Minister of Justice, 1973–77; joint vice-chairman, PVV, 1972–73; vice-chairman, Cultural Council, 1972; vice-chairman, Belgian Council, European Movement, 1979. Married with three children.

Address: Antwerpsesteenweg 2, 2500 Lier. Tel: 031/80 08 54.

VANDEWIELE, MARCEL
Belgium, EPP (CVP-EVP)

Mr Marcel Vandewiele was elected a Vice-President of the European Parliament in July, 1979. Senator for the Bruges district since 1968; State Secretary for Planning and Housing in 1973. Member, European Parliament, since 1972. B July, 1920. Became national secretary, Young Catholic Workers, 1939. Elected by CVP Congress in 1957 to be member of the national committee and bureau of CVP; Secretary-General, Belgian General Christian Workers' Federation, 1958. Member,. board of the company Brugse Zeevaartinrichtingen; chairman, Zon en Zee Centre for Social Tourism, Westende. Married with five children.

Address: Witte Molenstraat 108, 8200 Brugge – St. Michiels. Tel: (050) 31 83 03.

VAN MIERT, KAREL
Belgium, Soc (BSP)

Mr Karel van Miert is vice-chairman of the Federation of Socialist Parties of the European Communities and chairman of BSP (Belgische Socialistische Partij) Flemish Socialists. B January, 1942; diplomatic sciences; post-graduate studies in European affairs.

Addresses: Merelstraat 7, 3070 Everberg. Keizerslaan 13, 1000 Brussels. Tel: 02/513 82 70.

VAN MINNEN, JOHAN
Netherlands, Soc (PvdA)

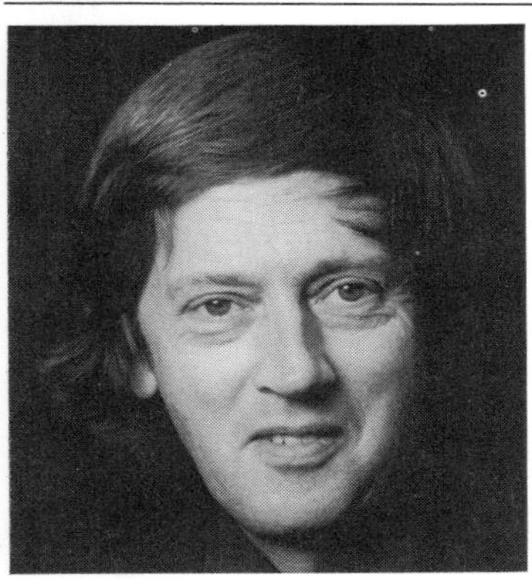

Mr Johan van Minnen, a journalist, is a former ombudsman of the Ombudsman Foundation (VARA television). B October, 1932.

Address: Straatweg 224, 3621 BZ Breukelen. Tel: 03462-3443.

VANNECK, SIR PETER
UK, Cleveland, ED (C)

Sir Peter Vanneck, a member of the London Stock Exchange, was Lord Mayor of London, 1977–78 and Sheriff to the City of London, 1974–75. Royal Navy and Fleet Air Arm service 1939–49, followed by service with the Royal Auxiliary Air Force. Inspector RAuxAF, 1963–73; Hon Inspector-General since 1974. ADC to the Queen, 1963–73; Gentleman Usher to the Queen from 1967. B January, 1922; ed Geelong Grammar School; Stowe; Trinity College, Cambridge; Harvard. Past Master, Guild of Air Pilots and Air Navigators; special trustee, St Bartholomew's Hospital, since 1974; trustee, RAF Museum, since 1976.
Addresses: Rowe and Pitman, City Gate House, 39–45 Finsbury Sq, London EC2. Tel: 01-606 1066. 9 Pensioners Court, Charterhouse, London EC1. Tel: 01-250 0555.

VAYSSADE, MME MARIE-CLAUDE
France, Soc (PS)

Mme Marie-Claude Vayssade is leader of a workers' education centre. B 1936.

Address: 78, rue du Maréchal Oudinot, 54000 Nancy. Tel: 555 035.

VEIL, MME SIMONE
France, LD (UFE)

Mme Simone Veil was elected President of the European Parliament in July 1979. She was appointed Minister of Public Health by President Giscard d'Estaing in May 1974, and became Minister of Public Health and Family Affairs in April 1978, resigning in June 1979. B July 1927; qualified in law at the Institut d'Etudes Politiques in Paris and admitted to the bar in 1956. Joined prisons service, Ministry of Justice, 1957, specialising in probation and rehabilitation. Appointed Secretary-General of the Conseil Supérieur de la Magistrature (Supreme Council of the Judiciary), in 1970.

Address: 11 Place Vauban, 75007 Paris. Tel: 551 09 68. 32 rue de Babylone, 75007 Paris. Tel: 556 88 06.

VERGEER, WILLEM
Netherlands, EPP (CDA)

Mr Willem Vergeer has been a member of the First Chamber since 1961 and of the European Parliament since 1978; became a vice-chairman of the EPP Group of the Parliament in July 1979. National chairman of the KVP (Catholic Popular Party); member, executive of CDA. Leader of the Dutch CD delegation in the European Parliament until June 1979. B March, 1926. President of a Technicians' Federation; chairman, Utrecht central office of Dutch Catholic Trades Union Federation, the advisory council of the Netherlands Federation of Trades Unions, the Christian National TU Federation, and the Dutch Catholic TU Federation.

Address: Rubicondreef 34, 3561 Utrecht. Tel: 030-61 44 11 or 08866-2366.

VERGES, PAUL
france, Comm (PCF)

M Paul Verges, journalist, is Secretary-General of the Communist Party of Réunion. B March, 1925.

Address: 87 rue Pasteur, 97400 St Denis de la Réunion (Ile de la Réunion).

VERHAEGEN, JORIS
Belgium, EPP (CVP-EVP)

Mr Joris Verhaegen has been Burgomaster of Hulshout, since 1953; chairman of the board, Kempem Inter-municipal Development Society, since 1963; member of the Senate, since 1968; and, since 1977, member of the Directorate Committee of the Society for Regional Development (GOM) and of the European Parliament. B May, 1921. Worked successively in the Federation of Christian Unions (ACV) of Malines and Turnhout, in the Christian Union of Metal Workers, and in the Cabinet of Mr De Saeger, Minister of Public Works.

Address: Booischotseweg 11, 3160 Hulshout. Tel: 015-222339.

VERNIMMEN, WILLY
Belgium, Soc (BSP)

Mr Willy Vernimmen is Senator for Oudenaarde-Ronse/Aalst. Former trade union secretary. B December, 1930. Alderman at Gramont.

Address: Kasteelstraat 20, 9500 Geraardsbergen. Tel: 054-413228.

VERONESI, PROTOGENE
Italy, Comm (PCI)

Sgr Protogene Veronesi became an Italian Senator in 1972. Physics lecturer. Director, Bologna section, National Institute of Nuclear Physics. Joined the PCI in 1945. Bologna town councillor; chairman, Bologna's gas and water board; Bologna provincial councillor. Member, Parliamentary Committee on Education and the Fine Arts; Vice-chairman, Parliamentary Committee which supervises CNEN (National Committee for Nuclear Energy); Secretary, Special Committee on ecological problems; Vice-chairman, Committee on Industry and Commerce. B February, 1920.

Address: Via Mascarella 77, 40126 Bologna. Tel: (051) 22 51 67.

VERROKEN, JOANNES
Belgium, EPP (CVP-EVP)

Mr Joannes Verroken nas been a member of the Belgian Parliament for the Christian People's Party (CVP) for the district of Oudenaarde since 1950. First Vice-President of the Chamber, chairman of the Committee on Public Health, the Family and the Environment, member of the Benelux Interparliamentary Consultative Council. B January, 1917; licentiate in philosophy and Letters; qualified secondary school teacher (advanced level).

Address: Edelareberg 8, 9700 Oudenaarde.

VETTER, HEINZ OSKAR
Germany, Soc (SPD)

Herr Heinz Oskar Vetter, a fitter, is President of the German trade union federation. Vice-chairman and former chairman, International Confederation of Free Trade Unions (ICFTU).

Address: von-Behring-Strasse 2, 4330 Mulheim a.d. Ruhr. Tel: (0208) 36620.

VISENTINI, BRUNO
Italy, LD (PRI)

Sgr Bruno Visentini was a member of the Italian Parliament, 1972–76; Minister of Finance, 1974–76; Senator, 1976; and in March 1979 became Minister of the Budget. B August, 1918; lawyer. Lecturer in commercial law at Rome University and then in 1948 became member, board of directors of IRI (Institute for Industrial Reconstruction). Chairman of IRI, 1950–72, and chairman of Olivetti, Ivrea, from 1964. Married.

Address: Piazza di Spagna 15, 00187 Roma. Tel: 67 89 788 or 67 94 651.

VON ALEMANN, FRAU MECHTHILD
Germany, LD (FDP)

Frau Mechthild von Alemann, librarian, has been a member of North Rhine-Westphalian Parliament since 1975. Member, executive committee, Federation of European Liberals and Democrats (ELD/LDE). Responsible for European affairs in North Rhine-Westphalian FDP. B January, 1937.

Address: Friedrich-von-Spee-Strasse 3, 4000 Düsseldorf 31. Tel: 0211/400257.

VON BISMARCK, PHILIPP
Germany, EPP (CDU)

Herr Philipp von Bismarck has been a member of the Bundestag since 1969, and of the European Parliament since 1978. Member, CDU national executive; Lower Saxony CDU Executive. Treasurer, Lower Saxony CDU; chairman, CDU Economic Council. Member, board of CDU/CSU Protestant Affairs Working Group, and of the board of the Hermann Ehlers Foundation, Kiel. B August, 1913. Between 1967 and 1971 was President of Hanover Chamber of Industry and Commerce, also chairman, Lower Saxony Association of Chambers of Commerce and member, board of the Conference of German Trade and Industry. Married with six children.

Address: Ortsteil Schweimke Nr 18, 3122 Obernholz.

VONDELING, ANNE
Netherlands, Soc (PvdA)

Mr Anne Vondeling was elected a Vice-President o the European Parliament in July, 1979. Former member of the Dutch Parliament; President of Chamber, 1972–79. Former chairman of Dutch labour party. B March, 1916.

Mr Vondeling was killed in a road accident on November 21, 1979.

Address: Nijlansdijk 73, 426 Leeuwarden. Tel: 05100-33216.

VON DER VRING, THOMAS
Germany, Soc (SPD)

Herr Thomas von der Vring is a university lecturer former Rector of University of Bremen. B. May, 1937.

Address: Meissener Strasse 7, 2800 Bremen. Tel: 0421-351557.

VON HASSEL, KAI-UWE
Germany, EPP (CDU)

Herr Kai-Uwe von Hassel was Federal minister for defence, 1963–66; Federal minister for refugees and war victims, 1966–69; and President of the German Bundestag, 1969–72. Bundestag member, 1953–54, and since 1965; President of the Bundersrat, 1955–56. President of the European Union of Christian Democrats (EUCD); President of WEU; Vice-President of the EPP and of World Union of Christian Democrats; chairman, Hermann Ehlers Foundation. Prime Minister of Schleswig-Holsteign "Land" government, 1954–63. B April 1913. Married with two children.

Addresses: Bundeshaus, 5300 Bonn 12. Tel: 1655774. Fordestrasse 11, 2392 Glucksburg (Ostsee). Tel: (04631) 2517.

VON WOGAU, KARL
Germany, EPP (CDU)

Herr Karl von Wogau, commercial lawyer. Political activities in the "Junge Union" and CDU since 1964; member, CDU "Land" committee on economic and social policy and of the district and federal executive of the CDU/CSU Middle Classes Association. Has worked for Europa Union since 1971. B July, 1941. Married.

Address: Bertholdstrasse 4, 7844 Neuenburg/ Breisgau. Tel: (07631) 72867.

WAGNER, MANFRED
Germany, Soc (SPD)

Herr Manfred Wagner, businessman, is President of the Saar Trade Union Federation and of the Inter-Regional Council of Trade Unions of the Saar, Lorraine and Luxembourg. Member of the Saarland Landtag; deputy chairman of the political group. Member of the Economic and Structural Advisory Council to the Prime Minister of the Saarland. Vice-chairman, Sarrebruck SPD. B January, 1934.

Address: Finkenweg 30, 6604 Saarbrucken-Brebach-Fechingen. Tel: 06892/2786 (private), 0681/46611 (bureau).

WALTER, GERD
Germany, Soc (SPD)

Herr Gerd Walter, a further education lecturer, is deputy chairman of Schleswig-Holstein SPD. B April, 1949; graduate in political science.

Address: Morier Strasse 45, 2400 Lubeck 1. Tel: 49 44 07.

WALZ, FRAU HANNA
Germany, EPP (CDU)

Frau Hanna Walz has been a member of the European Parliament since 1973, being Chairman of the Committee on Energy and Research until June 1979. Member of Bundestag since 1969. Lawyer. Deputy chairman, Hesse CDU, since 1967; member of assembly of Council of Europe and of WEU, 1970–73. Member, executive, Hesse CDU political group in the Landtag, 1962–69. B November, 1918. Married with three children.

Address: Magdeburger Strasse 72, 6400 Fulda. Tel: 0661-75291.

WARNER, SIR FREDERICK
UK, Somerset, ED (C)

Sir Frederick Warner spent 29 years in the Diplomatic Service, his final appointment before retirement being Ambassador to Japan, 1972–75. Now chairman and director of companies and farmer. B May, 1918; ed Wixenford; RNC Dartmouth; Magdalen College, Oxford. Head of South-East Asia Department, Foreign Office, 1960; Imperial Defence College, 1964; Ambassador to Laos, 1965–67; Minister, Nato, 1968; Under Secretary, Foreign and Commonwealth Office, 1969; Ambassador and Permanent UK Representative to UN, 1969–72.

Address: Laverstock, Bridport, Dorset. Tel: Broadwindsor 543.

WAWRZIK, KURT
Germany, EPP (CDU)

Herr Kurt Wawrzik has been a member of the Bundestag since 1969, and of the European Parliament since 1977. Member, European Union. Treasurer, Deutsche Welthungerhilfe (German World Famine Relief), since 1977. Moulder. Member, works council, Daimler-Benz, 1951–75; Mannheim Town Council, 1965–69. Held honorary offices in metal industry trade union. Member of board of AOK Mannheim. B February, 1929. Married with two children.

Address: Am Wildpark 9, 6800 Mannheim 31. Tel: (0621) 72 16 00.

WEBER, FRAU BEATE
Germany, Soc (SPD)

Frau Beate Weber, a teacher, is deputy chairman of the SPD executive. Member, Heidelburg municipal council. B December, 1943.

Address: Sickingenstrasse 1, 6900 Heidelberg. Tel: 06221-33626.

WEISS, MME LOUISE
France, DEP (DIFE)

Mme Louise Weiss, as the oldest member, presided at the opening session of the new Parliament for the election of the President. B January 1893. Agrégée at university. Journalist, special report writer, film producer and explorer. Member, French committee of Unesco.

Address: 15 avenue du Président Wilson, 75116 Paris. Tel: 723 50 65.

WELSH, MICHAEL
UK, Lancashire Central, ED (C)

Mr Michael Welsh is director of market development with Levi Strauss and Co Europe SA having been with the company since 1969. General manager, Channel Road Services Ltd, 1966–69. B 1942; ed Betteshanger School, Deal; Dover College and Lincoln College, Oxford. Vice-chairman, British Conservative Association in Belgium. A former Conservative branch officer in Putney and Chelmsford. Married with two children.

Address: Clos des Chênes 68, 1170 Bruxelles.

WETTIG, KLAUS
Germany, Soc (SPD)

Herr Klaus Wettig is a research worker. B August, 1940. Member, SPD Bureau, Hanover, and of party committee for Lower Saxony.

Address: Rohnsterrassen 6, 3400 Göttingen. Tel: (0551) 58150.

WIECZOREK-ZEUL, FRAU HEIDEMARIE
Germany, Soc (SPD)

Frau Heidemarie Wieczorek-Zeul, a teacher, is a member of the South Hesse SPD executive and the SPD national executive. Former chairman, Young Socialists. Chairman, European Liaison Office, International Youth Organizations. B November, 1942.

Address: Michelstädter Strasse 1, 6090 Rüsselsheim. Tel: (06142) 32868.

WOLTJER, EISSO P.
Netherlands, Soc (PvdA)

Mr Eisso P. Woltjer is a member of the teaching staff at Deventer Agricultural College. B January, 1942; studied at Wageningen Agricultural College.

Address: Berqkwartier 10, 5801 PS Venray. Tel: 04780-84324.

WURTZ, FRANCIS
France, Comm (PCF)

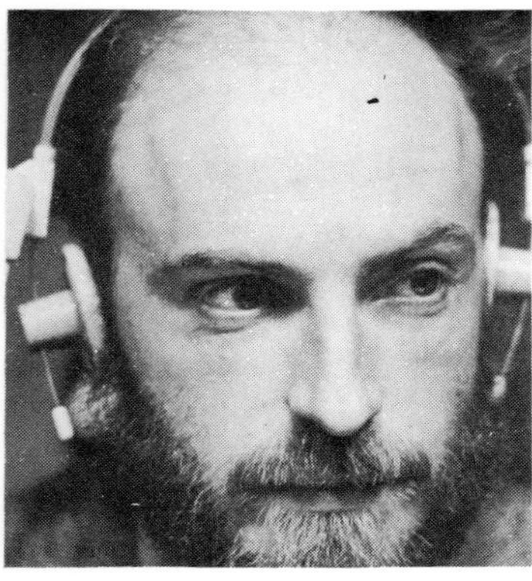

M Francis Wurtz is a teacher. Member of Central Committee of the French Communist Party. B January, 1948.

Address: Comité Central du PCF, 2 Place du Colonel Fabien, 75940 Paris Cedex 19. Tel: 238 66 55.

ZACCAGNINI, BENIGNO
Italy, EPP (DC)

Sgr Benigno Zaccagnini, surgeon specialising in pediatrics, was elected deputy at the constituent Assembly in 1946 and a member of Chamber of Deputies in 1948. Political secretary (former chairman) Party National Council; chairman, Owner-Farmers Federation of the province of Ravenna. Former Under-Secretary of State for Labour and Social Security, and subsequently Minister of Labour, and Minister of Public Works. Chairman, Christian-Democratic Parliamentary Group; has been Deputy Speaker of the Chamber of Deputies.

Address: Via di Roma 30, 48100 Ravenna. Tel: 27222.

ZAGARI, MARIO
Italy, Soc (PSI)

Sgr Mario Zagari was elected a Vice-President of the European Parliament, in July 1979; a Vice-President of the former nominated Parliament. Unsuccessfully contested Presidency in July 1979. B September, 1913; lawyer and journalist. Chairman, Committee on European Law, Milan Centre for Social Studies and Social Protection, and President, Institute for the Promotion of European Studies in the Developing Countries (ISEPS). Director of the periodical *Sinistra europea* (European left) since 1953. Has held office in several Italian governments, being Under Secretary of State at the Foreign Ministry, Minister for Foreign Trade, and Minister for Justice.

Address: Piazzo Augusto Imperatore 32, 00186 Roma. Tel: 67 80 898.

ZECCHINO, ORTENSIO
Italy, EPP (DC)

Sgr Ortensio Zecchino, a doctor in jurisprudence, is Professor of Law and of criminal procedure at the University of Urbino. Member, Campania Regional Council, since 1970, and a member of his party's executive for the Campania region. Town councillor and alderman 1946–69. Former member, general council of the Institute for External Trade. In 1975, he became his party's secretary for the province of Avellino. B April 1943. Married with three children.

Address: Via d'Afflitto 70, 83031 Ariano Irpino (Avellino). Tel: 871171.

ZU SAYN WITTGENSTEIN BERLEBURG, PRINCE CASIMIR
Germany, EPP (CDU)

Prince Casimir zu Sayn Wittgenstein Berleburg is chairman of Hesse CDU economic committee. President of Steuben-Schurz-Gesellschaft and member, board of Atlantik-Brucke, both registered associations. B January, 1917. From 1939–49, executive director of Alsen'sche Portland Cement Fabriken KG, Hamburg; 1949–51, managing director of Alwitt Trading Ltd, London; 1951–54, on board of Sachtleben AG, Cologne; 1954–61, on the board of Metallgesellschaft AG, Frankfurt/Main, and, since 1961, its deputy chairman. Married with four children.

Addresses: Leerbachstrasse 21, 6000 Frankfurt am Main. Metallgesellschaft AG, Reuterweg 14, 600 Frankfurt am Main.
Tel: (0611) 1592583.

ROBERTS, MISS SHELAGH — **UK by-election**
UK, London South-West, ED (C) — **September, 1979**

Miss Shelagh Roberts, whose election for this seat was ruled invalid because of her membership of the Occupational Pensions Board, from which she then resigned, won the seat again at the by-election held in September, 1979. Chairman, National Union of Conservative and Unionist Associations, 1976–77, and of Conservative Party Women's National Advisory Committee. Industrial relations consultant. Member, Greater London Council, since 1970; chairman, Planning and Transportation Committee of Association of Metropolitan Authorities. Member, Port of London Authority. B 1924; ed St Wyburn School, Birkdale.

Address: 23 Dovehouse Street, London SW3 6JY

How EEC money was spent on direct elections

The holding of direct elections to the European Parliament was a constitutional innovation without parallel. Other international organizations, including the Commonwealth, Nato and the Council of Europe, have regular meetings, some formal, others more informal, of parliamentarians. Only the European Community gives its parliamentary body even a minor decision-making role, and only in the Community is this body now directly elected by the electorate of the member countries. Direct elections therefore represented a major experiment to incorporate some of the concepts of parliamentary government into an international organization whose main decision-making process relies essentially, in the Council of Ministers, on traditional inter-governmental diplomatic negotiations.

In 1977 the European Parliament and the European Commission agreed that the novel aspect of the elections and the generally low public understanding of how laws and other decisions were made at Community level required an information programme in the period leading up to the elections. Accordingly, some £13·8 million was voted in the 1978 and 1979 budgets of the European Parliament to this end and another £3·6 million for the Commission. Of the Parliament's total, £8·34 million was allocated to the political groups and the other £5·46 million was largely allocated to a neutral multi-media information campaign to be carried out jointly with the Commission. Of the total funds for neutral information £1·1 million was allocated to the United Kingdom, representing approximately 2½ pence per voter.

The joint Parliamentary-Commission body set up to control this programme, comprising three parliamentarians and two commissioners, decided that advertising agencies and other firms should be called in to execute the programmes. Tenders on the same basis were put out in all the Nine and contracts awarded on the basis of the proposals made. In the United Kingdom the principal contract was awarded to Lintas: London, the advertising agency subsidiary of the Anglo-Dutch group Unilever, while other contracts were awarded to Northern Displays International for the organization of touring exhibitions and to R. L. Polk (Great Britain) for print handling and distribution.

In most of the Nine, membership of the Community is not a matter of significant political controversy. However, in both the United Kingdom and Denmark, it was clear that "neutral" information had to be interpreted very strictly. Hence the emotive style of the French slogan "Europe is hope" and the Italian "Italy needs Europe; Europe needs Italy", was considered to be inappropriate. Moreover, research showed that the degree of understanding of the British electorate of how the Community works was so low that basic information about the Community and the Parliament was required before the electorate could be expected to vote. It was in the last resort the responsibility of the political parties and candidates to persuade the voters to go to the polls.

Accordingly, the British information programme, through exhibitions, pamphlets, films and other visual aids and, finally, advertising, stressed that a new form of franchise was available to the electorate and that they should exercise that right on June 7. "Have your say on June 7. Use your Eurovote" was the basic slogan adopted.

Nonetheless, various political circumstances and anxieties, notably on the part of the then (Labour) Government, dogged the British programme. Uncertainty when the General Election would be held and the wish to avoid clashing with it meant that the main thrust of the programme was aimed at April, when extensive advertising was scheduled in the press, the most flexible medium in terms of timing.

Before April, a start was made with touring exhibitions visiting towns in different parts of the country and a substantial demand was building up for publications and audio-visual material. However the General Election was called at the end of March for May 3 and, in accordance with a request made earlier by the British Government, all active operations were suspended, including the cancellation of 191 site bookings for the exhibitions.

Following the United Kingdom General Election on May 3 the programme was reactivated to a limited extent for a 2½ week period with the advertising ending on May 27. By polling day some 10 million items of literature had been distributed and, particularly through television, the audio-visual material had reached a wide audience.

So far as public knowledge was concerned, there was a steady rise throughout the period of the programme. In the autumn of 1978 only 52 per cent of a sample of electors had even heard of the European Parliament and only 30 per cent knew that elections were to take place at all. NOP monitors carried out later for the Parliament and Commission inicated that by mid-April the figures had risen to 64 per cent and 50 per cent. After the advertising began on May 10 there was a further substantial increase on May 17-22, with 76 per cent aware of the existence of the Parliament and 71 per cent aware that elections were to take place.

However, the proportion of the electorate which stated a certain intention to vote remained low, averaging 27 per cent during April and reaching only 32 per cent on May 17-22. It was during this latter period that the political parties opened their electoral campaigns, such as they were. The plethora of polling in early 1979 (Welsh and Scottish referendums, general, local and parish council elections) and the financial and political exhaustion of the parties after the General election largely explained why the "will certainly vote" figure of May 17-22 — 2½ to 3 weeks before polling day — was so accurate compared with the actual turnout on June 7.

Usually, pollsters calculate that half of the "will probably vote" respondents will turn out on polling day. By this token, between the last NOP monitor and June 7 another 14 per cent of the electorate should have been persuaded to vote, making a turnout of 46 per cent.

In short, knowledge that an event was to take place was insufficient motivation for two voters out of three; the majority were not persuaded by the political parties that it was in their interests to vote on June 7. Indeed, on the Labour side, when so few political activists were themselves prepared to go out campaigning, canvassing or knocking up, that is not surprising. The Conservatives, meanwhile, were apparently content that this should be so, for an active and controversial campaign could only have benefited the Labour and Liberal parties.

In the 1978 and 1979 (calendar year) budgets of the European Parliament and Commission appropriations were voted for "information about direct elections". The sums concerned, in approximate sterling equivalents to the European units of account,* (EUAs) were for the whole Community:

	European Parliament	*European Commission*
1978	£6,400,000	£3,300,000
1979	£7,400,000	£330,000
TOTALS	£13,800,000	£3,630,000

In both years the European Parliament appropriations were split between its Directorate General for Information and Public Relations and the Parliament's six political groups, as follows:

	E.P. Information	*Political Groups*
1978	£3,100,000	£3,300,000
1979	£2,360,000	£5,040,000
TOTALS	£5,460,000	£8,340,000

Over the two years, therefore, the following sums were allocated:

Political Groups	*E.P. Information*	*Commission*
£8,340,000	£5,460,000	£3,630,000

Most of the Parliament's information funds and the Commission's funds were allocated to a joint multi-media information programme. The allocation to the United Kingdom for this purpose was £1,113,000.

* The equivalent is approximate because 1) different EUAs were used for the 1978 and 1979 Community budgets; 2) The EUA/£ parity fluctuates.

The political groups' funds were allocated in accordance with the number of members they had in the nominated Parliament and the number of languages they used.

The distribution of funds to the groups was:

	1978	*1979*	*TOTAL*
Socialists	£1,000,000	£1,490,000	£2,490,000
Christian Democrats	£810,000	£1,200,000	£2,010,000
Liberals & Democrats	£560,000	£890,000	£1,450,000
European Progressive Democrats	£330,000	£500,000	£830,000
Communists	£330,000	£500,000	£830,000
European Conservatives	£270,000	£460,000	£730,000
Independents	£15,000	£15,000	£30,000

Decisions about the distribution of the political groups' funds to their constituent national parties and other expenditures were decided by the groups individually.

For comparative purposes, U.K. Government expenditure (or equivalent services) on elections is approximately as follows:

a) Annual renewal of electoral register	£12 million
b) Administration of polling	£5 m
c) Cost of free distribution of candidates' electoral addresses	£5 m
d) Estimated value of party political broadcasts on radio and television	£10 m

British state aid to political parties represented in the House of Commons is of the order of £350,000 per annum.

Four powers available

Parliament's advisory and supervisory role

European Parliament or European Assembly? In British politics the choice of title tends to be a litmus-paper test of a politician's attitude towards the institution itself. The British Labour Party, for example, deferring to those of its members who question membership of the European Community or who resent the European Parliament as a threat to Westminster sovereignty, consistently refers to a European Assembly, with an undisguised intention of downgrading whatever happens in the two hemicycles in Strasbourg and Luxembourg.

The fact is that on March 30, 1962, what the Treaty of Rome itself calls an Assembly passed a resolution to take the name of the European Parliament. It was a natural thing for a group of members of parliament from the Six original Parliaments of the European Economic Community to do; they saw the hemicycles of Strasbourg and Luxembourg as an extension of their parliamentary duties.

What, anyhow, is in a name? The origins of the Assembly or Parliament are clear. Under the Treaty of Paris, 1951, a Common Assembly was created as one of the institutions of the European Coal and Steel Community; and the ECSC led on, under the Treaty of Rome, to the European Economic Community providing for an Assembly "which shall consist of representatives of the peoples of the States brought together in the Community", exercising the advisory and supervisory powers conferred upon it by the Treaty.

The European Parliamentary Assembly came into being on March 19, 1958, and provided the democratic element to complement the EEC Council of Ministers, the EEC Commission in Brussels, and the European Court of Justice in Luxembourg. In general, it may be said that the Commission proposes, the Council of Ministers disposes, and the Court of Justice ensures that Community law is obeyed. What, then, is the role of the Assembly or Parliament?

It is advisory and supervisory, or, as British critics put it, merely consultative. It does not form or dismiss a government, as the House of Commons at Westminster may. But, then, nor does Congress in Washington.

The European Parliament itself lists four powers:

(1) The right to be consulted about Community legislation and to influence the shape it takes.

(2) The right to question Commission and Council and thereby prompt the disclosure of information.

(3) The power to dismiss the European Commission by passing a motion of censure; and

(4) The power to amend and pass or reject the Community's budget.

There is no proposal that after the direct elections of June 7–10, 1979, the powers of the European Parliament should be increased beyond the provisions of the basic Treaty of Rome. It has become a vested interest for some politicians, not only in the United Kingdom, to emphasize the limits on the European Parliament's powers and to ensure that the limits are observed for fear of the growth of a Frankenstein monster.

Winston Churchill had a word, or rather a few words, for it. Looking at the future of free Europe, he once said that he preferred democracy to grow as a plant rather than to be designed as a blueprint. Mr Ronald Hayward, general secretary of the British Labour Party and an anti-Market man, said much the same thing when he visited the European Parliament in 1978: "I believe when you elect a body – a committee, council, or Parliament – there is bound to be, over a passage of time, more power requested by that elected body, and eventually they get it. You cannot dismiss an elected body. Direct elections are, in my view, the first step along the road to a federal European Parliament which will, in due course, ask for and receive more powers than it has at the moment."

It is certainly misleading to say that the European Parliament's existing powers are no more than advisory or supervisory. Specifically, it has the power to dismiss the entire Commission, an ultimate deterrent once unsuccessfully invoked by the British and Danish

Conservatives, although they recognised that the right to appoint or reappoint Commissioners lay with the Council of Ministers and, therefore, the Governments of the Nine.

It may reject or alter the non-obligatory part of the Community budget, or about 30 per cent. of total spending, and in December 1977 and 1978 took a stand on its parliamentary powers. Increasingly the European Parliament has used its right to question the Council of Ministers and the members of the Commission, and to hold public investigations by its committees, on the model of American Senate inquiries. The seeds of parliamentary growth have been sown, although only an optimist would delude himself that the Churchillian plant will bear early fruit. European idealists hope that a European Parliament elected rather than nominated will, as Mr Hayward feared, demand room to grow.

In a sense, the fact that there have been direct elections at all provides an example of the Parliament's authority, if not power, so long as it works within the Rome Treaty. The first proposal from the Parliament for the fulfilment of the Treaty obligation to have direct elections, instead of nomination, was blocked for nearly a decade by the French. To vindicate the provisions of the Rome Treaty, the European Parliament in 1969–70 threatened to arraign the Council of Ministers (that is, the ministerial representatives of the Governments of the Six) before the European Court of Justice. Only then did the Council of Ministers begin to move towards direct elections, reluctantly and sluggishly.

The original date was set for direct elections in 1978. In the event, there was a further year's delay – and the United Kingdom Government under Mr Callaghan was by no means the last government of the Nine to pass the necessary domestic legislation.

It is often said alike by friends and critics that the European Parliament will never, or at any rate in the foreseeable future, develop beyond the role it has been set in the Rome Treaty. Certainly, Governments in the United Kingdom, France, and Denmark have insisted that there shall be no increase in the European Parliament's powers beyond the provisions of the Treaty without agreement by national parliaments. Nevertheless, the Rome Treaty has not proved to be strict Biblical writ.

For example, the most important *strategic* body in the Community today is the European Council, or the triennial meeting of heads of government, which finds no place in the foundation Treaty.

Secondly, the Luxembourg agreement, 1966, on unanimity voting in the Council of Ministers directly breaches the Treaty.

Thirdly, the Council of Ministers has extended the budgetary powers of the nominated European Parliament, and at the Paris summit, 1974, extended the Parliament's legislative competence.

To look at the European Parliament through eyes trained at Westminster is not the best way, perhaps, to judge its powers or influence. The Parliament has a continental, not a Westminster, history and procedure. It can bring the Council of Ministers and the Commission before the European Court of Justice if either fails to observe the Rome Treaty; it can be petitioned by private citizens; and it can embarrass the Council and the Commission (although so far it has tended to be coy) by opening its committee meetings and inquiries to the public and thereby create and motivate public opinion.

Friends of Europeanist ideals hope that the 1979 direct elections will bring a stronger democratic dynamism into the European Parliament. Several lines of democratic development have already been discussed. Parliament could insist that all Commission proposals should go straight on to the Council of Ministers after Parliament has approved or amended them, and that if Parliament rejects Commission proposals that should be an end to them. At present legislation is returned from Parliament to Commission, which may refuse to accept amendments.

The Parliament could also insist on the right, as European Conservatives once attempted, to dismiss Commissioners singly rather than en bloc, thereby breaking the control of national governments, through the Council of Ministers, over the Commission. Parliament could also fight for the power to reject parts of the Community budget: it already has the power to reject the budget as a whole and to scrutinize all items of income and expenditure. On the principle of denial of Supply until grievances are redressed, it could also make approval of the budget dependent on satisfaction from the Council of Ministers and the Commission.

Such possibilities lie in the future, perhaps the remote future. For the present, the European Parliament is moving on from a nominated or delegated Parliament, a reflection of party strengths in national assemblies, to a directly elected Parliament whose members will have a direct answerability to constituents.

The nominated European Parliament, which met for the last time in May, consisted of 198 members from the Nine and met in chambers at Strasbourg and Luxembourg, the locations agreed by the founding Six. Membership was made up as follows: 36 from the Houses of Parliament at Westminster (26 from the House of Commons and 10 from the House of Lords); 10 from the Dail and Seanad in Dublin; 14 from the Chamber of Representatives and Senate in Brussels; 10 from the Folketing in Denmark; 36 from the National Assembly and Senate in Paris; 36 from the Bundestag in Bonn; 36 from the Chamber of Deputies and Senate in Rome; six from the Chamber of Deputies in Luxembourg; and 14 from the States General in The Hague.

There is no sign over the entrances to the chambers in Strasbourg and Luxembourg saying: "Abandon nationality all ye who enter here", but that is in theory what happens. In the outgoing Parliament, as in the new, MEPs became members of transnational groups; the Socialist Group, with 66 members from nine Community countries; the Christian-Democrat Group, 53 members from seven countries; the Liberal and Democrat Group, 23 members from eight countries; the European Progressive Democrat Group, 18 members from three countries; the European Conservative Group, 18 members from Britain and Denmark; and the Communist and Allies Group, 18 members from three countries. There were three independent members, including Mrs Winifred Ewing, who sat for the Scottish National Party. Because members were nominated by national parliaments, delegations altered if there was a national general election.

The new Parliament, which met for the first time in the Palais de l'Europe at Strasbourg on July 17, has 410 members, all of whom were directly elected by ballot between June 7–10. Membership is apportioned among the Nine as follows:

United Kingdom, France, Italy, and West Germany, 81 members each; Netherlands, 25; Belgium, 24; Denmark 16; Republic of Ireland, 15; and Luxembourg, six.

Only Britain (England, Scotland, and Wales) used the first-past-the-post system of election, apart from the Danish constituency of Greenland returning one member; and the West German MEPs from West Berlin were, in effect, nominated, under the quadripartite peace treaty. Northern Ireland, returning three MEPs, used the single transferable vote as one constituency.

Landmarks of the European Community

1946 Winston Churchill's Zurich speech urging Franco-German reconciliation within "a kind of United States of Europe".

1947 American aid for European recovery proposed by US General Marshall. Welcomed by Ernest Bevin, UK Foreign Secretary.
Benelux created: economic union of Belgium, Luxembourg, and the Netherlands.

1949 Statute of the Council of Europe signed.

1950 Robert Schuman proposes placing French and German coal and steel under a common authority.

1951 Treaty setting up the European Coal and Steel Community signed in Paris.

1952 ECSC authority starts work in Luxembourg under Jean Monnet, first president.

1955 Messina conference: Foreign Ministers of the Six propose further steps towards full European integration.

1957 Rome Treaties setting up the Common Market and Euratom signed.

1958 Rome Treaties come into force, and the Common Market and Euratom are set up.

1961 The Six issue Bonn Declaration aimed at political union.
The United Kingdom and Denmark request membership negotiations; Ireland applies for EEC membership. Negotiations with UK open at Brussels in November, and in December three neutral countries (Austria, Sweden, and Switzerland) apply to associate with the Common Market.

1962 In March the UK applies for membership of the ECSC and Euratom. In July the first regulations fulfilling the common agricultural policy come into effect.

1963 President de Gaulle on January 14 says that Britain is not ready for EEC membership, and on January 29 British negotiations with the Six are broken off, a week after the Franco-German Treaty of Cooperation is signed in Paris.

1965 Common Market Commission proposes that from July 1, 1967, all Community countries' import duties and levies be paid into Community budget and that the powers of the European Assembly be increased.
On July 1 the Council of Ministers fails to reach agreement by fixed date on financing the CAP, and French boycott of Community institutions begins a crisis lasting seven months.

1966 Foreign Ministers of the Six agree to resume full Community activity.
Agreed that on July 1, 1968, the Community's customs union and common farm policy should be completed.

1967 Council of Ministers agrees to introduce a uniform system of value-added tax.
The United Kingdom, Denmark, and Ireland formally apply for membership of the Community on May 10–11.
On November 27 General de Gaulle, at a Press conference, objects to UK entry, and on December 19 the Council reached deadlock on UK and other membership applications. Harold Wilson leaves the UK application "on the table" and thereby does not withdraw it.

1968 Customs union completed and a common external tariff operates around the Common Market.
In July single market introduced for dairy and beef products, and the last discriminations between workers of member states were removed.

1969 Commission urges Six to coordinate economic and monetary policies more closely, and advocates system to help member countries in balance-of-payments difficulties.
At the end of April Georges Pompidou succeeded President de Gaulle, who resigned. On October 1 the Commission reaffirmed that applications for membership of the Community be opened as soon as possible. On October 21 Willy Brandt became German Chancellor, and on December 1–2 Six Heads of Government, at The Hague, agreed to enlarge and strengthen the Community.
At a long Council sitting December 19–22 permanent arrangements were agreed to finance the CAP, providing the Community with its own resources from 1978 and strengthening the European Assembly's budgetary powers.

1970 Labour Government in London published on February 10 a White Paper stating that long-term benefits of joining the Community were likely to outweigh the costs.
In June, the Six set 1980 as target date for monetary and economic union, and on June 19 Edward Heath succeeded Harold Wilson as Prime Minister. On June 30 membership negotiations were opened in Luxembourg between the Six, Britain, Denmark, Ireland, and Norway.

1971 Community's "own revenue" system began to operate on January 1; on February 1 the common fisheries policy took effect; and on February 9 the Six launched a 10-year plan for full economic and monetary union.
The terms of UK entry were set out in July in a White Paper, *The United Kingdom and the European Community.* At the party conferences that autumn Conservatives and Liberals gave overwhelming support to the outcome of the negotiation, but Labour's conference rejected the terms by a ratio of five to one.
The House of Commons, on October 28, voted by a majority of 112 votes in favour of a Government motion approving entry: 356 votes to 244, with 23 abstentions.

1972 Mr Heath as Prime Minister signed the Treaty of Accession to the EEC on January 22, and during the year the 11-clause European Communities Bill, which made the necessary changes in law consequent on entry, passed through both Houses of Parliament to Royal Assent.

1973 The UK, with Ireland and Denmark, entered the Communities on January 1, and later that month 18 Westminster MPs and Peers took their seat for the first time in the European Assembly at Strasbourg. Peter Kirk led the Conservative delegation, but the Labour Opposition did not take up its allocation of seats.

1974 After defeat in a general election on February 28, Edward Heath was succeeded as Prime Minister by Harold Wilson, and, with James Callaghan as Foreign Secretary, the new Labour Government began the "renegotiation" of the Conservative terms for entry.
Labour's 1974 manifesto offered the right of a consultative referendum to determine UK membership of the Community as a means of uniting a divided party.

1975 Labour's Referendum Bill was given a second reading in the House of Commons on April 10 by 312 votes to 248 and reached Royal Assent on May 8.
On June 5, 64.5 per cent. of the United Kingdom electorate voted in the first British national referendum: 17,378,581 (67.2 per cent.) votes were cast in favour of continued membership, and 8,470,073 (32.8 per cent.) against. Only the remote islands of the Shetlands and the Western Isles failed to produce a "yes" majority.
Labour MPs were nominated from Westminster to take their seats in the European Assembly for the first time.

1977 At Florence, in September, Mr Roy Jenkins, President of the Commission, revived the question of European economic and monetary union and gave an old Community objective a new importance.

1978 The European Parliament in December rejected the Community budget for 1979, under its Treaty powers, and refused to retreat. It would be April, 1979, before a budgetary compromise was reached conceding most of the increased spending outside the common agricultural policy that Parliament had demanded.

1979 The European Monetary System began to operate among the Eight, with the Labour Government in the United Kingdom deferring a decision. Later, in May during the direct elections campaign, the new Conservative Government, under Mrs Thatcher as Prime Minister, stated that "we shall look for ways in which Britain can take her rightful place within it" (EMS).
At Athens on May 28 the Nine agreed that Greece should become the tenth member from January 1, 1981. Negotiations with Portugal and Spain for a Community of Twelve continue.
Between June 7–10 the first direct elections took place for the European Parliament.
On July 17, the first meeting of the directly elected European Parliament was held in Strasbourg when Mme Simone Veil (France) was elected President.

Party Manifestos in Britain

Parties call for reform of agricultural policy

The manifestos on which the three main British parties fought the European campaign alike recognized the possibility of popular disillusionment about United Kingdom membership over the costs and benefits of United Kingdom membership of the Community, or else the fears of party leaders that Community membership had been suffering from a bad press. Conservative, Labour and Liberal platforms all included the plank of reforming the common agricultural policy. Yet the manifestos varied widely in Europeanist spirit and in commitment to membership.

Labour and Conservative leaders both produced 5,000-word documents, and the essential difference between them was that a mainly anti-membership committee of the National Executive Committee produced Labour policy, complete with a threat of possible withdrawal, and those who drafted the Conservative policy recognised that they could not dissociate themselves from the Heath Government's responsibility for carrying the United Kingdom into the European Community. Neither of the two big parties could align itself, in a manifesto, with any other party inside the Community. Whether for or against membership, they wanted to be seen as nationally independent, as fighting for the United Kingdom interest.

The Liberals, on the other hand, associated themselves with a long and turgid European manifesto published by the European Liberals and Democrats, and contented themselves with a cursory summary of its contents to make a carefully modulated nationalist point or two. Liberals, after all, claim that in the United Kingdom they win the largest Liberal vote in Europe, but it is in other Community countries that they get the taste of power, with two Liberal Presidents, three Prime Ministers and deputy Prime Ministers, and five Foreign Ministers. Hence the Liberal emphasis on the reform of the electoral system – for the Community in 1984, as well as in the United Kingdom's domestic politics.

Labour's manifesto came out in January, 1979, after heart-searching semantic debate on whether it should be called "Labour in Europe", "Labour for Europe", or "Labour and Europe". That was of a piece with events in the summer of 1978, when Mr Ian Mikardo, chairman of the NEC's international committee, as well as Mr Ron Hayward, the party's general secretary, had left other Community socialist party leaders in no doubt that the British Labour Party could not subscribe to a joint European socialist manifesto for the first direct elections. Consequently, the joint document for the only party that covers all the Nine had to be called a political declaration, couched in deliberately abstract language.

British Labour's European manifesto became the work of a liaison committee, with Mr Tony Benn, a leading critic of membership, as chairman. The Benn committee, in the name of the NEC, went ahead to draft a manifesto to which only five or six members of the then Labour Cabinet would have given wholehearted assent.

That gave rise to difficulty when the European campaign opened and the Labour manifesto had to be launched, or relaunched. The date chosen was May 24, three weeks after the domestic election in which Mrs Thatcher had supplanted Mr Callaghan as Prime Minister and formed a Conservative Government. At a meeting of the NEC, Mr Callaghan objected to being the wheelhorse that would be required to launch a manifesto out of line with the European strategy followed by the Government he had led. The compromise reached was that Mr Hayward, the general secretary, should preside over the press conference, Mr Callaghan should be the main speaker, and that the supporting cast should consist of three NEC anti-membership figures: Mr Benn, Mr Eric Heffer, and Mrs Barbara Castle, a retired Westminster MP but a candidate in the European elections.

Mr Callaghan, in and out of Government better known as an Atlanticist than an ardent Europeanist, as Foreign Secretary had "renegotiated" the Heath terms of United Kingdom entry to the Community in 1974, and unlike five or six members of his Cabinet had reconciled himself to the United Kingdom's destiny in Europe, though not uncritically when he struck a balance between the costs and the benefits. When he had to introduce and recommend a Labour European manifesto he thought crude and unreal, he brought all his political skill to bear to conceal any differences of opinion that would be counter-productive for Labour candidates at the polls on June 7.

For him the most dangerous words in the Benn committee's manifesto appeared in the penultimate paragraph: "We declare that if the fundamental reforms contained in this manifesto are not achieved within a reasonable period of time, then the Labour Party would have to consider very seriously whether continued EEC membership was in the best interests of the British people".

That followed a call for "a major revision of the Treaty of Rome"; "the creation of a wider but much looser grouping of European States"; the continuance of the European Assembly as a consultative body rather than "a real Parliament" and opposition to any extension of its powers; the restoring of Westminster powers over Community legislation; and the use of the Community to advance socialism.

Mr Callaghan, as the Labour renegotiator of the terms of United Kingdom accession to the Treaty of Rome, had reason to know that such electoral demands were inimical to membership and partnership with other socialist parties within the Community. And the day after launching the British manifesto he was due to visit Paris to join in an electoral "spring festival" with other Community socialist leaders.

Withdrawal from membership of the Community? Mr Callaghan blandly met the question as an irrelevance in the new circumstances after the United Kingdom domestic election. "I doubt," he said, "if this question is going to arise in the lifetime of the Assembly. There will be a Conservative Government (in the United Kingdom) and there will be no question of our being in the position (to withdraw) unless they collapse under the weight of their own follies. I do not think this question will arise during that period and when we get a new Labour Government it will be for us to consider what the position is. For the lifetime of this European Assembly the objectives are clear: reform the common agricultural policy, change the budgetary costs, and work together on technological change."

Mr Callaghan later added that the Labour manifesto was consistent "with a constructive but critical approach." He commented that "theologians" would be able to discuss semantics about the manifesto in the context of his renegotiation of terms, but "if you are trying to make differences between those of us on the platform, you will not succeed". Mr Callaghan's adroitness made sure that the theologians did not succeed, but he failed to remove journalistic doubts that the Labour leadership remained badly split.

During the Labour press conference Mr Callaghan showed that he placed little importance on Article 138 of the Rome Treaty, which calls on the Assembly to "draw up proposals for elections by direct universal suffrage in accordance with a uniform procedure in all Member States", or, indeed, on the assumptions of Liberals and the outgoing European Parliament that the next quinquennial direct elections will be on a uniform system.

At the Conservative press conference to launch the European manifesto, Mrs Thatcher at least agreed wholeheartedly with Mr Callaghan on that. "We are still free to fight the next election," she said, "on the basis agreed by the Council of Ministers. I think we have the best system (that is, first-past-the-post) in this country. You do not have to go to one system of PR."

The Conservative manifesto, published on May 18, was drafted in an entirely different tone from the Labour manifesto, although it repeated similar demands for reform of the CAP and budgetary justice. It opened with the statement that the new Conservative Government elected on May 3 stood "committed to the proposition that our future lies unequivocally within the European Community" and, maintaining the orientation throughout, vied with the Labour document in being constructive and critical, with the emphasis on constructiveness.

But both parties emphasized the severe limitations on the importance of the powers in the European Assembly where they were competing for seats. For Labour "the European Assembly does not have, and must not have, the right to override our own Parliament and decide matters of Government policy". For Conservatives, "We shall be electing a deliberative and advisory Parliament, not a government of legislature", and the European Parliament "already has the powers it needs and when directly elected there will be a growth in its political influence". At Westminster, neither the Government nor the alternative Government want the European Parliament to grow in ambition and become a rival.

In Mrs Thatcher's words, "we enter the elections as committed Europeans"; and she looked forward to the Conservatives being the largest group in the Parliament from any country in the Nine.

Conservatives will attempt to achieve Community reform and change not by confrontation but by partnership and reasoned argument. They accept that "the case for a common European market in agricultural produce remains strong" and that the cost to the British taxpayer of abandoning the common agricultural policy and going back to a system of deficiency payments across the board would be very heavy.

Yet Mrs Thatcher's Government would press for fundamental reforms of the CAP in the interests of efficient British farmers, consumers, and taxpayers; and (unlike Labour) it would "support a devaluation of the Green Pound within five years". There must be a freeze in common prices for products in structural surplus, though national governments wishing to help farmers should be allowed to do so as a social rather than an agricultural solution.

Whereas the Labour manifesto maintains "opposition to economic and monetary union", the Conservative document argues that "it obviously makes sense for the Member States to cooperate more closely in the economic sphere". Mrs Thatcher's Government regrets the Callaghan Government's decision, alone among the Nine, not to become a full member of the European Monetary System, and "we shall look for ways in which Britain can take her rightful place within it". On the Community budget, the Conservative line favours low public expenditure and reduced tax burdens, and there is a suggestion that increases in Community spending on funds other than the CAP should be counterbalanced by national cuts.

Conservative MPs in the new European Parliament are given the clearest guide to the party leadership's view of their role: "If the Parliament uses its existing powers effectively they are fully equal to the tasks before it, especially as the directly elected members will have more time to devote to European matters. We fully endorse the section in the Treaty that prevents the Parliament from adding to its powers unilaterally and we have no plans for their extension. The Parliament should be complementary to the national Parliaments, improving not usurping their existing democratic control of government and beureaucracy."

That language, that attitude towards the first directly European Parliament is not shared by the Liberals, either in Britain or in the eight countries of the Nine where they are a political force. (Only the Irish Republic is unrepresented in the Federation of Liberal and Democratic Parties of the EEC.)

"We are the only UK political party which is united and fully committed to the ideal of European unity," proclaims the British Liberal addendum to the joint manifesto, and it adds that the new European Parliament will be fully effective only if "the political forces in it work together across national lines". To that end, the Parliament must work for political integration to match the economic integration of the Community.

The Liberal record on Europeanism is more consistent, if not historically longer, than that of the Conservatives, and Mr Russell Johnston and Lord Gladwyn, who have sat in the European Parliament as Liberals, had none of the Conservative difficulty in joining an established group and none of the British Labour delegation's occasional discomforts in living as internationalist members of the Socialist group.

Yet Mr David Steel, the party leader, and all his rank and file know that the Liberal label within the Community covers a multitude of parties and beliefs that virtually spread across the whole spectrum of British national politics. Within the Community there are Right-wing Liberals, centrist Liberals, and Left-wing Liberals, and perhaps that explains why the liberal multi-national manifesto had to be a document proving by its extraordinary length that no point had been omitted or left unrefined.

Launching the manifesto at the National Liberal Club on May 16, Mr Steel, the British party leader, spoke of course with an optimism about the chances for European PR by 1984 that Mrs Thatcher and Mr Callaghan were soon to kill off. "The second round of (European) elections," he said, "is to be on an agreed system, and it is inconceivable that the other Eight will want to adopt the British system of first-past-the-post."

It is also now clear that it is inconceivable that Mrs Thatcher or Mr Callaghan will want to adopt any system except the British; and the crucial Article 138 of the Treaty of Rome states that the question shall be determined in the Council of Ministers "by means of a unanimous vote".

But if, as Sir Harold Wilson used to say, a week is a long time in politics five years before the next European direct elections is an age, and Mr Steel, with his huge unrewarded block of United Kingdom votes, may live in hope. At least, as he could claim on May 16, the Liberals are the only British party able to fight in Northern Ireland as well as England, Scotland, and Wales.

European People's Party

Together towards a Europe for free people

The European People's Party (Christian Democrat) electoral platform adopted unanimously by its Congress on February 22 and 23, 1979 in Brussels, was as follows:
We, the European People's Party, bringing together men, women and young people from all walks of life in the countries of the European Community.
Convinced that our national states are no longer in a position to overcome the challenges of our time by themselves.
Inspired by the will to build for people from all sections of the population a European Union with the ultimate political aim of a federation in which everyone will feel welcome.
Guided by the knowledge that the major problems of our present-day world can be resolved only with the aid of an intellectual and moral system of human coexistence, as there are no purely technical remedies for these problems.
Are resolved in this spirit and inspired by fundamental Christian values, to implement our Political Programme as a contribution towards the construction of a Europe in the service of mankind, a Europe that is tolerant and open to the world.

The Christian Democratic aim is therefore

A EUROPE FOUNDED ON FREEDOM AND SOLIDARITY

— that guarantees the inviolable dignity, freedom and responsibility of man – that recognises the intellectual and material effort necessary for his self-realisation as something which must not be superseded by an ideology of standardisation;
— that protects and promotes the family as the basic form of human coexistence, neither the State nor society being able to take the place of the parents in guiding the child towards maturity as a moral being;
— that seeks to provide social justice and help people to help themselves, particularly the weakest members of society: the handicapped, the elderly and the poor;
— that is as equally opposed to individualism without moral constraints as it is to inhumane collectivism.

Our aim is

A EUROPE FOUNDED ON RESPONSIBILITY

— that safeguards at all political and juridical levels the fulfilment of human rights and fundamental freedoms without which there is no just social order;
— that helps to develop the richness of European civilization which, in its diversity and unity, is a bond uniting our Europe of nations – an opportunity to construct a humane society and to counteract the danger of uniformity, aimlessness, materialism and ideological indoctrination;
— that is capable of safeguarding its own personality and self-determination in the spirit of international solidarity;
— that translates its intellectual and cultural vocation into responsibility for others, in particular for the peoples of the Third World, equal partnership with these peoples being an important precondition for justice and peace in the world;
— that strives for a more equitable and humane economic order and creates areas of solidarity between the industrialised and the developing countries, for which the Convention of Lomé can serve as a model;
— that draws up in equal partnership with the countries of the Third World a new strategy for development policy and growth;
— that accepts its moral and human responsibility towards the countries of Eastern Europe with which we have common historical bonds, and helps to overcome the division of Europe by peaceful means and to restore the right to self-determination of all European peoples.

Our aim is

A DEMOCRATIC EUROPE OPEN TO THE OUTSIDE WORLD

— that practises, as its form of government, pluralist democracy which conforms to our view of a modern society based on partnership. It consists of controlled power for a limited period and based on a constitution. The pluralist democracy demands respect for the rights of racial, ethnic, ideological and religious groups;

— that condemns and combats violence and terrorism as a means of solving social or political conflicts;

— that decentralises political power on the principle of "subsidiarity", in particular to the local authorities by reinforcing local self-administration, and to the regions by recognising and involving them;

— that is ready to admit as soon as possible Greece, Portugal and Spain as Member States, countries which belong to Europe by virtue of their cultural vocation and history, in order to consolidate our common democratic ideals;

— that, by directly electing the European Parliament, strengthens democratic control over Community institutions, fully assumes its necessary powers for the smooth working of the Community and duly improves the Community decision-making procedure, particularly in the Council of Ministers;

— that moves progressively towards "European Union" and from day to day increasingly speaks with one voice in order to make its contribution to freedom and solidarity, justice and peace throughout the world and, at the same time, supports its legitimate interests.

Our aim is

A EUROPE OF ECONOMIC AND SOCIAL PROGRESS AND FULL EMPLOYMENT

— that helps man to improve his living conditions with the aid of the effective system known as the social market economy. This system is based on the free responsibility and creative enterprise of the individual, the parties to collective agreements and the cooperation of the public authorities. This system promotes the progressive development of a human community based on partnership and solidarity towards shared responsibility, participation and joint ownership by employeees in national and multinational undertakings. The social market economy is better suited to the elimination of unemployment, poverty, hunger and distress than a central managed economy and is our alternative to inhuman class struggles. It remains the function of the public authorities to lay down the main economic and social guidelines:

— that, through the creation of a European monetary system can advance to Economic, Monetary and Social Union and, finally, to European Political Union;

— that, to this end, provides adequate funds by transfer of resources for a vigorous regional, structural and social policy and institutes an equally vigorous economic policy leading to the elimination of regional imbalances; this policy is aimed at reasonable stability, qualitative growth, protection of the environment and the consumer. It requires a binding common code of conduct for multinational undertakings;

that implements a forward-looking energy policy which reduces our dependence on imports; such a policy presupposes the provision of adequate funds for the development of indigenous and alternative energy sources. Particularly in the case of nuclear energy and its waste disposal all necessary safety measures and inspection arrangements must ensure protection of human life and the environment and takes measures to prevent the pollution of European waters;

— that adopts a European Charter of Employees' Rights and produces an increased humanization of the working environment. This improvement in working conditions should be set out sectorally in European collective agreements which could cover, among other matters, the organisation of working hours and an improved distribution of the work available. Equal pay for men and women must be achieved;

— that ensures equal rights and obligations for European migrant workers by eliminating all discrimination against them;

— that ensures that men and women agree on and observe their roles at home, at work and in society on an equal basis, and that gives them effective and equal access to all levels of education and of cultural, professional and political life;

— that gives young people better educational qualifications and career prospects for a future in which everyone will find a place in working life and society corresponding to his or her abilities and skills. This is to be encouraged by, for example, the harmonization of teaching and training curricula and the more widespread recognition of final diplomas and by promoting greater mobility among young workers and students;
— that with the aid of appropriate State provided family benefits ensures large families adequate incomes for the education and training of children as well as an appropriate standard of living;
— that affords appropriate protection for small and medium-sized undertakings, craftsmen and the middle classes, who base their life on self-reliance and readiness to take risks. By their enterprise they make an above-average contribution to economic progress and an effective social system;
— that encourages the modern family farm which has so far survived despite dynamic structural changes to the economy to guarantee secure food production, which will continue in the future to be indispensable to the general interest.

We endorse the objectives and basic principles of the common agricultural policy, as set out in the Treaty of Rome; we underline the need for a better balance between the northern and southern regions, elimination of undesirable trends and a structural policy taking account of the rural areas.

Our aim is

A EUROPE FOUNDED ON FREEDOM, SECURITY AND PEACE

— that is aware that its free social, economic and constitutional order can be expanded and improved only if it is ready and able to defend its freedom from internal and external threats;
— that ensures full implementation of the Helsinki Final Act as a possible way to lasting détente on the basis of mutual and balanced concessions (*). Berlin (West) remains the touchstone for genuine détente in Europe;
— that strives to obtain a mutual, balanced and monitored reduction of forces and armaments in Europe and in the world;
— that assumes its full responsibility in the Atlantic Alliance on which our security in this situation depends and which must be strong enough to discharge this task;
— that actively supports the observance of human rights and civil liberties throughout the world and opposes any form of despotism – because respect for the rights of other people means peace for everyone.

We Christian Democrats, guarantors of a unified and fraternal Europe, intend to complete the work of European unification that was begun by our great statesmen Robert Schuman, Alcide De Gasperi and Konrad Adenauer.

We call upon all political and social forces to cooperate with a dynamic political will.

There is only one common answer to the present crisis: more powers, more resources and more authority for Europe!

Direct elections will increase Parliament's democratic legitimacy and thus reinforce Europe's weight and influence.

We want the executive authority of the Community to be strengthened and the powers of the European Parliament extended by amendments to the Treaty.

We call upon all of the 180 million voters to cast their vote!

No great venture can succeed unless the people give it their free and full support –
This also applies to You:
Help us to build the future of Europe!

TOGETHER TOWARDS A EUROPE FOR FREE PEOPLE

(*) This section only applies to member-parties of the EPP from countries which are members of the North-Atlantic Alliance.

The Conservative Party

Conservative manifesto for Europe 1979

Since May 4, Britain has had a Conservative government – a government committed to the proposition that our future lies unequivocally within the European Community.

It is the aim of this new Government to work with our eight partners to build up the strength of the Community while obtaining a fairer deal for our own country than it has had under a Labour government. We believe our new Government can do this because it will have behind it not only the strength of a party that has always been loyal to the European ideal but those numerous voters in other parties who share the same commitment. We want not only a better deal for Britain but a better, stronger Europe for all Europeans.

In a few weeks' time, at the beginning of June, 180 million electors throughout the nine countries of the European Community will be able, for the first time, to vote for their own representatives in the European Assembly (usually known as the European Parliament). Since 1973 nine national governments have been working together in the Community. Now individual citizens have the opportunity to join in a common political enterprise to shape their future in *their* Community.

The decisions taken in Europe are important. They affect our trade, our economy, our industry, our agriculture, our regions and our jobs. The character of the Community depends on the attitudes, hopes, beliefs, ideals and efforts of those who help to build it.

The elected British members of the European Parliament will be acting on behalf of our interests when they discuss the major decisions taken at Community level.

The Parliament already has the powers it needs and when directly elected there will be a growth in its political influence. The first essential is to use these powers more effectively in establishing proper democratic control at every level of Community decision-making in the interests of ordinary people.

In this field the new Parliament will be working in partnership with Westminster. Conservatives here at home, in Government and Parliament, and in Europe will be part of the same team. We want to make a success of Britain's membership of the Community and to influence it in a Conservative, rather than a Socialist, direction. For this, a strong Conservative representation in the directly elected European Parliament is essential.

But these elections are not only important for us in Britain. The increasing political and commercial influence exercised by the Community in the world means that there will be interest in the results extending far beyond the frontiers of the Nine. The balance of political power in the Community – the largest trading bloc in the world – is of direct relevance to a whole range of questions upon which the prosperity, and with it the freedom, of the West depends.

The belief that the nations of Western Europe can solve their common problems more successfully if they work together led to the establishment of the European Community. The arguments for it are stronger now than ever before. In June we have the chance to strengthen this partnership.

However, we shall be electing a deliberative and advisory Parliament, not a government or legislature; and as a party we shall, of course, be in a minority in that Parliament. It would therefore be inappropriate to make promises which, acting on our own, we could not fulfil. So we shall use this opportunity to put forward our proposals on how the Community should be improved for the benefit of us all.

This manifesto sets out our practical approach.

Britain in the Community

For almost two decades Conservatives have believed that Britain's future is best assured as a member of a free, strong and democratic European Community. Harold Macmillan first applied for membership in 1961; Edward Heath then started the negotiations which culminated in entry in 1973; under Margaret Thatcher we took the lead in the referendum campaign in 1975 to win the vote for continued membership; and in 1978 Conservative votes in Parliament secured the passage of the Act implementing direct elections.

Recovering Our Influence

Our belief in Europe remains unshaken. Of course, there are some Community policies which we want to change because they do not at present suit Britain's – or Europe's – best interests. But it is as absurd for Britain to threaten to break up the Community simply because it dislikes some particular policy as it would have been to threaten to break up Britain because we disliked the policies of the Labour government. It is wrong to argue, as Labour do, that Europe has failed us. What happened under Labour was that our country was prevented from taking advantage of the opportunities which membership offers.

Labour's damaging economic policies blunted our competitive edge and made it more difficult for our companies to sell their goods in our partners' markets. What is more, the frequently obstructive and malevolent attitude of Labour Ministers weakened the Community as a whole and Britain's bargaining power within it.

By forfeiting the trust of our partners, Labour made it much more difficult to persuade them to agree to the reforms that are necessary in such important areas as the Common Agricultural Policy, the Community Budget and the Common Fisheries Policy.

Conservatives want Britain to recover her influence by demonstrating her commitment to the Community's true ideals and purposes. This will enable us to promote the interests of each and every part of the Kingdom – England, Scotland, Wales and Northern Ireland – and to play a leading and constructive role in the Community's efforts to tackle the many problems it faces.

We will do this by concentrating on four main objectives:

(1) To foster an outward-looking Community which could become one of the twin pillars of freedom and democracy in the world together with our friends in the USA.
(2) To encourage a common-sense natural development of the Community.
(3) To press for practical reforms in common policies so that they benefit *all* the nations of the Community, including Britain.
(4) To seek an effective role for the Parliament within its existing powers in ensuring the Community serves the *people* of Europe, not just governments or industry.

The change of attitude that we seek will be one of the main priorities of the Conservative Government. The return of a large majority of Conservatives to the European Parliament will show our partners that the British people have firmly rejected Labour's negative and damaging approach, and strengthen the mutual trust and understanding on which the Conservative Government will build.

A Community of Nations

There is nothing incompatible between taking this sort of positive approach to Community membership and safeguarding Britain's national identity. We see Europe growing into a close partnership of sovereign states which have developed the habit of working together through such institutions as are necessary for pursuing joint policies in a democratic way. But those customs, traditions, institutions, civil rights, liberties and laws on which our distinctive national identity depends will always remain a matter for Britain alone. It is precisely because we want Britain to prosper at home, and to fulfil her historic role of defending freedom in the world, that we seek to make a success of our partnership in Europe.

A Common-sense Community

Cooperation will grow naturally if the Community concentrates on practical possibilities for progress rather than trying to lay down grandiose plans. Common policies are far more likely to be acceptable – and far more likely to be accepted – when cooperation is seen to be natural and necessary to meet a common problem or need. So the Community should intervene only where the individual states are unable to achieve their objectives on their own or where a project is better undertaken on a Community basis. We should support sensible proposals by the Community where they replace and reduce, rather than extend or add to, the existing activities of the Member States.

A Community of Interests

The interests of Britain and the Community are usually close or even identical. Isolated from the rest of the Community, Britain would find it far more difficult to weather the storms of today's uncertain world: the threats to liberty and democracy; the menace posed by Soviet expansion in Africa and Asia; the impact on our oil supplies of events in the Middle East; the slump in steel and shipbuilding; the economic effects of unstable currencies; the growing protectionism in all five continents; and the emergence of industries producing cheaper goods in the less developed world. We share these problems with our European partners and we can overcome them more readily if we act with them.

A strong and prosperous Community is one of the best guarantees of a strong and prosperous Britain. Nevertheless, just as Britain cannot benefit if the Community is weak because we have failed to respond to the legitimate interests of our partners, equally the Community cannot be strong if Britain is weak because the Community has failed to protect our interests.

A Community of Opportunities

In Britain we are always at our best as one nation working together in a common enterprise. We must now grasp the opportunities available to us in the Community.

For our *country*, the European Community presents an opportunity to influence world events once again – by acting in consultation with all the most powerful nations in Western Europe.

For our *industry*, it offers a huge home market of 260 million people for the new advanced-technology industries in which we have the ideas and expertise to lead the world.

For our *people*, membership provides the opportunity to break down barriers and to help mould the character and destiny of the whole Community. And as these barriers are removed we are increasingly free to live, work and set up new industries and businesses throughout the nine partner nations.

Europe in the world

Enlarging the Community

In the Community, the nations of Europe are striving to provide a stronghold of freedom and democracy in the world. So we welcome the proposed membership of Greece, Portugal and Spain following their restoration of democratic institutions. The economic costs of their admission are outweighed by the political gains for Western democracy of a larger, stronger Europe.

Speaking with One Voice

Britain's history places her in a unique position to guide Europe away from a narrow inward-looking view and outwards to the wider world. We attach high importance to the development of the coordination of foreign policy within the Community. In a world dominated by the super-powers, Britain and the other Member States are best able to protect their international interests, and to contribute to world peace and stability, when they speak with one voice or at least in unison. By working with our partners, Britain's own position in the world can be strengthened and our objectives secured more readily.

In areas of common concern to all the members, such as the Eastern Mediterranean, the Middle East and Central and Southern Africa, the enormous economic influence of the Community can be given a political impact.

Britain's Links with the World

Cooperation within Europe must never be allowed to undermine the close bonds we have forged over many years with countries of the Commonwealth, such as Canada, Australia and New Zealand, and with the USA, to all of whom we are bound by ties of history, tradition, family and friendship and with whom we share a commitment to freedom, liberty and democracy. We must continue to develop this into a strong relationship with the whole Community. We are aware that Community policies often affect these countries and we shall work to safeguard their legitimate interests. In strengthening democracy and promoting trade in Europe we must not undermine them elsewhere.

Cooperation with Nato

The defence of Britain and the West is a matter for Nato. But while the roles of the EEC and Nato are different, they are also complementary. Without the economic security that membership of the Community provides, Britain cannot make her full and proper contribution to her partnership with other European states and the USA and Canada in the Alliance, which alone can provide the military security on which our political freedom and stability depend.

Although defence is not covered by the Treaties, it is important to improve the cooperation and consultation between the Community and Nato on matters of common concern. Much can be done by the Community to coordinate the armaments industry particularly in areas of high-cost technology.

The Community's Trade

Like Britain, the Community has to trade in the world to live; so it must direct the considerable influence it derives from its responsibility for over 40 per cent. of the free world's trade to promoting more liberal trade. We want to see the barriers overseas against Community exports scaled down, and an effective and speedy response to "dumping" in our home markets. We fully support the renegotiated Multi-Fibre Arrangement for textiles and will press for it to be monitored effectively and speedily. Stronger measures should be taken against heavily subsidised competition from the Soviet Union and other Comecon countries in rail and shipping rates and in road freight.

Sometimes in the past difficulties have arisen because the Community has taken decisions in matters of trade and finance without sufficient consideration of their political consequences for other countries, such as Turkey. We need better machinery for ensuring that commercial policy is properly coordinated with other aspects of foreign policy in the Community.

Helping the Developing World

Europe has a vital interest in helping to bring prosperity to the world's poorer nations which provide a growing market and supply many of the raw materials on which we depend. Britain's dual membership of the Commonwealth, which spans all five continents, and the Community places us in a unique position to bring together the developing nations and our European partners. We look forward to a successful completion of the renegotiation of the Lomé Convention, and would like to see a more coherent approach to areas like the Indian sub-continent and South-East Asia which fall outside its terms of reference. Member States should be persuaded to direct a growing proportion of their own aid through Community channels, but the Parliament should ensure that there is effective machinery for monitoring this expenditure.

Developing our Resources

In a world threatened in the future with shortages, the countries of Europe fortunately have great resources of food and energy. We must have sensible policies for their development.

Agriculture

The case for a common European market in agricultural produce remains strong. The cost to the British taxpayer of abandoning the Common Agricultural Policy (CAP) and going back to a system of deficiency payments across the board would be very heavy. A sensibly-administered CAP should provide the best way of ensuring a secure supply of food at stable prices. It is worth noting that Western Europe has been well fed during the last 20 years, while Eastern Europe has suffered frequent food shortages.

But in its present form, the CAP penalises many efficient farmers in Britain and elsewhere; forces consumers to pay unnecessarily high prices; and imposes a huge burden on the Community's taxpayers who have to pay for the storage and disposal of ever larger agricultural surpluses. We shall therefore press for a number of fundamental reforms.

We would support a devaluation of the Green Pound within five years to a point which would enable British producers to compete on level terms with those in the rest of the Community.

There must also be a freeze in common prices for products in structural surplus, including dairy products and cereals. This should be maintained until the surpluses are eliminated. A freeze will cause difficulties for small and relatively inefficient farmers in some of the other member countries. National governments wishing to help such farmers should be allowed to do so. This should be seen for what it is – a social rather than an agricultural problem – and the cost should not fall on the CAP.

As far as the disposal of existing surpluses is concerned, priority should be given to measures to increase consumption within the Community.

We are also opposed to the Commission's proposal for an increase in the co-responsibility tax on milk production, since this would unfairly penalise efficient British dairy farmers.

Although it is important for the Community to achieve a high degree of self-sufficiency in food, the CAP should be made sufficiently flexible for it to be possible to import more low-cost food. The Community should not seek to exclude high-quality Australian and New Zealand produce from our markets. The whole economy of New Zealand in particular relies heavily on exports to Britain; so we will strive within the

Community to obtain lasting arrangements to provide continuing access to our market and to avoid deals with other countries that could undermine her economy.

Fishing

Labour's failure to secure an agreement with the rest of the Community which acknowledged Britain's special position has created damaging uncertainty for our fishing industry. An acceptable Common Fisheries Policy must recognise both that the move to 200-mile limits since we joined the Community has changed the entire international situation and our own circumstances, and that our waters contain more fish than the rest of the Community put together.

There is a clear need for a comprehensive policy on conservation. This should include: a limit on the total allowable catch; a clear set of rules to control the amount of fishing and the methods used; recognition that the coastal states must have sole responsibility for control over their waters, since they alone have the knowledge and capability to enforce conservation rules; enforcement of rules against *all* fishermen; and measures to protect the rights of in-shore fishermen. We shall also press for an adequate exclusive zone; a further considerable area of preferential access; and a substantial British share of the total allowable catch, which recognises Britain's contribution in terms of waters.

The Conservative commitment to the Community's success means that we are much better placed than Labour to ensure – as we must – that the Commission and the other Member States take account of Britain's legitimate fishing interests.

Energy

Events in Iran have reminded us of Europe's vulnerability to an energy crisis. We strongly support the Commission in its efforts to reduce the Community's dependence on imported energy, by encouraging production, energy saving and research into new energy sources.

From next year Britain will be self-sufficient for a time in oil, as well as in coal and gas. This puts us in a different position from our partners who will continue to be substantial importers. Nonetheless, we cannot be indifferent to their energy problems since our own prosperity is linked with theirs. Moreover, we may have to become net oil importers ourselves within a decade.

One way to reduce the Community's vulnerability is to lessen its dependence on imported coal. So it was disappointing that Labour were unable to reach agreement with our partners about the measures designed to stimulate greater production and consumption of Community – including British – coal.

While Britain must retain the fullest control over her own energy policy, cooperation within the Community is clearly sensible in many areas of research and development, including the Community's important studies on nuclear safety and waste disposal. Future innovations will require huge amounts of capital; so we must avoid wasteful duplication of effort by working closely with our partners, as in the Community's joint research programme on nuclear fusion (JET), which is based in Britain.

Strengthening the European economy

Economic cooperation can never be a substitute for sensible economic policies at home. Labour's mismanagement of our national economy ensured that Britain fared far worse than most of her partners in the last five years. There can be no hope of national recovery until these policies are reversed.

But the national economies of the Nine are now very closely linked by ties of investment and trade. In addition, the post-1973 recession and inflation, and the emergence of low-cost competitors in newly industrialised countries in the Third World, have presented all the Community countries with common economic and industrial problems which they cannot hope to solve on their own.

Monetary Cooperation

For these reasons it obviously makes sense for the Member States to cooperate more closely in the economic sphere. That is why we regret the Labour government's decision – alone amongst the Nine – not to become a full member of the new European Monetary System. We support the objectives of the new system, which are currency stability in Europe and closer coordination of national economic policies, and we shall look for ways in which Britain can take her rightful place within it.

Opening up the Market

One of the keys to lasting prosperity throughout the Community is the creation of a genuinely common market in which goods, services and capital can move freely, and in which firms from different Member States can compete on an equal footing.

In an increasingly protectionist world Britain in particular stands to gain from progress in this direction, since we depend even more heavily than most of our partners on exports for a rising standard of living and full employment. Unemployment in Britain, which soared under Labour, would rise even higher if we were cut off from the Community. It has become our largest single market, taking nearly 40 per cent. of our exports and providing a stable free trade area as the basis on which our industry can compete worldwide.

The Community must open up the market, sweep away national restrictions on competition and fair trade, liberalise exchange controls, simplify customs procedures and break down protectionist barriers. This was enshrined in the Treaty of Rome, which was inspired by the ideals of free competition, a common market for trade and industry, higher living standards and free movement for our people.

Competition and Harmonisation

Free competition is the consumer's ally.

The Commission must make governments as well as companies abide by the rules of free and fair competition, for example in the advertisement and management of public sector contracts. We shall consider carefully the present scale, shape and pace of the programmes for harmonisation of technical standards for products and company law. Where national regulations which impose differing technical requirements and standards in each country are an obstacle to trade, we shall support speedy action by the Community to remove them.

For example, some industries (such as insurance, building societies, car components and equipment leasing) are anxious to promote constructive harmonisation to increase the opportunities open to them. Subject to our overall policy, for the consumer we want harmonisation that genuinely protects his interest. In road transport we want less frontier bureaucracy and an end to the complex system of permits and quotas for freight.

The overall benefits of this policy should be more vigorous competition, lower prices and wider choice for the consumer, and easier exporting for our manufacturers.

On the other hand, some proposals for harmonisation would simply impose extra costs and disruption on our industries without providing any compensating increase in trade. Harmonisation for its own sake is unnecessary, and we shall work to prevent it. Article 100 of the Treaty of Rome should be interpreted strictly and measures introduced only if they "*directly* affect the establishment or functioning of the Common Market". The Commission should be obliged to prove that there is a clear advantage to manufacturers and consumers in each case.

The general rules under which firms have to trade should be designed to create fair competition. Where Community rules are required for this they should be accepted; but where they are irrelevant, the Community should not interfere with national regulations.

Competition in Air Travel

The principles of competition which govern other industries in the Community should also be applied to air travel. More competition with the state airlines by private carriers could lead to a more varied structure of fares and a reduction in their cost, as has occurred on the North Atlantic routes.

Help for Industry and the Regions

The present recession has caused a number of member governments, including Britain's last Labour government, to try to protect jobs in ailing industries by means of massive financial subsidies. These impose huge burdens on the taxpayers and are a serious threat to fair competition within the Community.

We accept that there are occasions when it may be sensible for governments to provide financial help for a limited time for a specific industrial sector or company. But we strongly favour the more robust enforcement by the Commission of those provisions of the Treaty that restrict the extent to which national aids may encroach upon competition between Member States. There is simply no point in Britain or any other Member State trying to export its unemployment to its partners by means of subsidies, since the inevitable result will be retaliation in kind.

The enforcement of the Community's rules concerning national aids can save taxpayers' money by preventing the Member States from outbidding each other in a self-defeating attempt to attract foreign investment.

Where individual countries cannot themselves act effectively, regional assistance should be funded on a Community basis. So within the limits of our general policies on public spending Conservatives will continue to support the Community's Regional Fund. The emphasis should be on encouraging regions to help themselves and on promoting schemes with a long-term future, including investment in the infrastructure.

Improving the Environment

Industrial pollution, whether in the atmosphere or in rivers, pays no respect to frontiers. The Community can do much to overcome pollution by coordinating national efforts and jointly funding expensive research. Where legislation is necessary we prefer the establishment of quality objectives rather than the prescription of strict emission standards. The costs that arise from its implementation should be imposed on firms in the same way throughout the Community, so that those in one country do not face disproportionate expense. The attempt to establish common standards at Community level in matters such as lorry weights should be flexible, taking into account the different circumstances and priorities of Member States. It should also be worked out with the fullest regard to costs.

The Budget

In the Community, as at home, Conservatives are strongly opposed to excessive public expenditure. Our policies to reform the CAP, which accounts for over 70 per cent. of the Community budget, would reduce the burden which the CAP places on the taxpayer. We shall also strive to cut out waste in other Community spending programmes.

As for the development of other funds and policies from which Britain could benefit, where the Community's institutions can discharge a necessary task more effectively than national governments, there is clearly a strong case for responsibility to be borne at Community level. In most cases it should be a genuine exchange in which an increase in Community spending is accompanied by a saving in likely costs at national level.

Moreover, the budget should strike a fair balance of mutual advantage for every member, both in contributions and in expenditure. Labour's mismanagement of our economy ensured that in contrast to most of our partners Britain achieved virtually no economic growth in the last five years. But although Mr Callaghan claimed in 1975 to have negotiated an effective "corrective mechanism", our contribution to the Community budget has not been adjusted satisfactorily.

On the contrary, last year Britain, which is now officially classified as one of the Community's "less prosperous countries", was the Community's largest net contributor on one system of calculation. This is obviously unfair. We shall give the highest possible priority to ensuring that the system of payments into the budget is more closely related to ability to pay, and that Britain receives greater benefit from budgetary spending.

This applies even more strongly if there is to be any increase in the financial resources of the Community.

The European Parliament and the people

Extending Democracy

The directly elected Parliament has three main tasks: to subject Community business and expenditure to proper democratic scrutiny; to play a full part in the legislative procedure; and to give individual people a greater say in European affairs.

Both the heads of government in the European Council and the representatives of the national governments in the Council of Ministers (the principal decision-making body in the Community) must remain responsible to their national Parliaments. However, the European Parliament should be given sufficient information to be able to offer them constructive advice, urge a course of action upon them and, if necessary, condemn a particular agreement. In the course of this work, it should be able to question the Presiding Minister of the Council about the implications of its decisions for the Community as a whole.

The Parliament must make the Commission more accountable, and more sensitive to national differences, by systematically calling upon it to justify its proposals, decisions and actions. It must check that the Commission's powers are exercised efficiently in the interests of the *people* of the Community.

The Parliament must give close examination to Community legislation and make the Commission justify the necessity for each proposal and indicate the benefits it will bring – especially where taxpayers' money is involved. In the past its objectives have often seemed obscure or over-ambitious, and the means of achieving them complex and unnecessarily heavy-handed.

Powers for the Job

If the Parliament uses its existing powers effectively they are fully equal to the tasks before it, especially as the directly elected members will have more time to devote to European matters. We fully endorse the section in the Treaty that prevents the Parliament from adding to its powers unilaterally and we have no plans for their extension. The Parliament should be complementary to the national Parliaments, improving not usurping their existing democratic control of government and bureaucracy.

In the light of experience we shall consider machinery for providing a formal link between the European Parliament and Westminster. Even after direct elections, the United Kingdom Parliament will still have a major role in considering proposed European legislation and in examining delegated legislation. There is a need for a reconsideration of the procedures available to the House of Commons for this task.

A Community for the people

We do not believe there should be a Community programme for every aspect of daily life, but direct elections to the Parliament should be the occasion to make the Community work for ordinary people, not just governments and industry. In the Parliament we shall examine every proposal carefully for its implications for the family and the consumer as well as industry and commerce. In addition, we shall continue to speak up for the rights of the individual by pressing for a Community Ombudsman and considering the need for a European Bill of Rights.

Excessive formalities and bureaucracy for travellers should be swept away. For example, we want to examine whether it is feasible to allow people to go anywhere in the Community without a passport. Arrangements for reciprocal medical treatment and social security in Member States should be simplified, and extended to cover the self-employed.

A certain amount has been achieved to facilitate the free establishment of the professions. However, if our young people are to take advantage of the wider horizons which the Community offers, further progress must be made – particularly in relation to the mutual recognition of basic qualifications.

Conservatives in the Community

The development of the European Community in the next 20 years will affect every man, woman and child in Britain. It is important that the people elected to represent us in the new European Parliament should be fully committed to the Community, so that they can made a constructive contribution to shaping its future.

The Labour Party is at best half-hearted about membership and at worst opposed to the whole concept of the European Community. Instead of working within the existing institutions to change policies so that they reflected Britain's needs more closely, Labour resorted to empty and ineffectual posturing. It could have little hope of influencing our partners when they feared that every criticism of a policy was a criticism of the principle of membership, and every proposal for reform an attempt to undermine the Community from within.

In contrast, the Conservative Party believes that the best hope for Britain's future peace and prosperity lies in continued and successful membership of the European Community. We know that changes are needed; but we are more likely to achieve them if we seek allies within the Community rather than making enemies. We shall not attempt to convince our partners of our case by the strength of our threats but by the force of our arguments. A strong Conservative group in Europe will cooperate closely with the new Conservative Government at home to implement our policies and to ensure that our views are heard in all the institutions of the Community.

More than that, it is in Britain's own interest that the Left should not be in a majority in Europe. A Socialist Parliament will press for more intervention, more subsidies, more centralised direction, more public expenditure, more protectionism and less competition.

We believe in less government interference, less centralisation, less wasteful expenditure, more freedom of choice, more competition and in leaving people free to take their own decisions.

The approach we have put forward in this manifesto provides the basis on which Conservatives in the European Parliament will try to strengthen Britain's contribution to Europe. In the past, together with our Danish allies, we have co-operated closely with the Christian Democrats and others. In the new Parliament, we shall seek to establish a working relationship with other like-minded parties from all countries so that together we can create a Community that will seek to *serve* the people of Europe not dominate them.

Where Labour sought to make the worst of membership, we shall seek to make the best; where Labour sought to make a failure of negotiations, we shall seek to make a success; where Labour sought to frustrate the Community, we shall seek to build a better Community.

In this approach our Conservative Government, backed by a large Conservative group in the European Parliament, will have far greater weight because it carries with it the hopes and aspirations of friends of the Community from all parties.

EEC Socialists

Need to pursue humane and cooperative goals

The Confederation of the Socialist Parties of the European Community did not issue a manifesto as such principally because the British Labour Party could not and would not agree to a Community-wide manifesto for the Socialist Group of the European Parliament. However, the Confederation did issue the following political declaration which was a compromise. Members of the British Labour Party took part in its drafting which emerged after a party leaders' conference in Brussels in June 1978. This declaration is the one document on which all members of the Socialist Group stood. It stated:

We, the Socialist parties of the European Community are committed to the pursuit of the common goals of freedom, social justice, equality and harmonious economic development.

Our parties have inherited different experiences down the years. They operate in countries where the level of economic development, the intensity of social struggle, cultural traditions, awareness of social problems and the interplay of internal political alliances profoundly differ, yet we share a common goal of a more human and egalitarian Europe for all our citizens, as part of a new international order based on democratic socialist principles.

Our drawing more closely together in Europe is quite compatible with respect for each other's individuality.

Throughout Europe, it is the Socialists who, in the cause of human welfare, are battling to eradicate injustice and inequality, and to ensure a harmonious development of society.

In the European Community, the most important objective for Socialists is the liberation of the individual from every form of dependence, exploitation and need and the giving of more power and rights to each individual.

To achieve this objective we must change the economic and social structures in our countries. We realise that whilst each country can by itself do much towards this end, joint action between us in some fields can accelerate our progress.

After twenty years of existence, the Community must now advance to a new phase in which the emphasis – in policy and in action – will be changed from the dictates of commercial interest to the pursuit of humane and cooperative goals. The first phase of the life of the Community has ended with only free trade achieved but with little regional and social balance.

We note with concern:

— the inability of our present social structure to solve the grave problem of unemployment;
— a trend towards less equality and solidarity as seen in the ever-widening gulf between the rich and the poor throughout the world and within the European Community;
— that uncontrolled growth in production and consumption, especially in the wealthier regions of the world, is being achieved at the cost of exhausting and polluting the environment, and of declining living and working conditions for millions of workers – something which Socialists cannot permit.

We accept that our duty to posterity, and to the millions of people living in dire poverty, compels us to accept restrictions in the use we make of the world's natural resources and to work for a better distribution of wealth, both within the Community and between the Community and the Third World.

Our fight for a society in which available resources are distributed fairly demands that we shape and guide social and economic development. The conventional economic policy instruments have proved inadequate; an active employment policy and the planning of the economy will be necessary to reduce unemployment. We also seek a fairer distribution of available work, with an important place being given to a shorter working span, a shorter working week, and a systematic policy of vocational training and retraining. Here we must take particular account of those groups which face the greatest difficulties on the labour market; young people, women, older workers and foreign workers.

We believe that the best way to achieve these conditions is through a common policy agreed between the main industrial nations. This common policy can be achieved only in close cooperation with all Trade Union organisations, particularly the ETUC. Our parties emphasise the growing role that the ETUC has to play in defending the personal and material interests of the working people of Europe and in achieving social progress and democratisation of the economy.

The ETUC must be more involved in the preparation of, and the procedure for, making decisions. Our parties also intend to work out their own proposals in close collaboration with the Trade Union movement and to encourage every possible step towards greater freedom for the workers of Europe.

In addition to reducing unemployment, an improvement in working conditions is urgently required. The third industrial revolution has been accompanied by great technological progress, but also by an increase in the scale and concentration of economic power, producing massive and impersonal production units which make individual workers and consumers feel insignificant and powerless. Increasing mechanisation and mass production mean that work is rarely geared to the aptitudes and wishes of the individual worker. Inhuman working conditions lead to alienation, increasing absenteeism and inefficiency. The traditional small and medium-sized undertakings are often unable to keep up with the large undertakings and are threatened with extinction.

We oppose this trend. Therefore we shall campaign for:

increased responsibility for workers within the enterprise. Democracy within industry and the economy as a whole should be developed in forms appropriate to each country and in cooperation with trade unions;

democratic control of major industrial concentrations and multinational concerns: respect for competition rules, checking transfers of profits, greater control of the movement of capital and the allocation of investment;

active encouragement of small and medium sized enterprises, and development of workers-cooperatives, and similar social instruments.

The Socialist parties therefore undertake to strive for an economic policy aimed at establishing:

Full employment
Stability
A fairer distribution of income and wealth
An effective and democratic economic structure
Economic democracy
Improved social security
Better living and working conditions
Improved educational opportunities.

The right to work is and will remain one of the basic aims of Socialism. It is a fundamental human right for men and women. The principal tasks of the European Community and its member countries must therefore be to combat unemployment and to ensure full employment. In this connection Socialists place greatest emphasis not only on a policy of full employment but also on a policy aimed at creating better working conditions.

Socialists therefore advocate humane and harmonious growth, which means that innovation, investment and the creation and location of jobs will take account of the need for a balanced society, particularly with regard to the environment.

We Socialists will continue to strive for a more equitable distribution of income and wealth. We note with particular concern that efforts to assist the development of the Community's less-favoured regions have made little headway.

We therefore demand a clear and vigorous regional policy designed to reduce differences in living standards between the various regions in the Community. At the same time we demand an effective social policy capable of removing the many inequalities between groups of citizens in our countries.

Democratic Socialism stands for an equitable educational system which offers equal opportunities and maximum possibilities of development for all. In Europe we want a social expenditure policy which will ensure that everyone, irrespective of social background, sex or age, can avail himself of opportunities for continuing education throughout his life.

The exhaustion of raw materials and the dangers of environmental pollution are most alarming. Only a worldwide effort can enable the nations to implement a policy designed to maintain the ecological balance and save raw materials; Europe should give a lead in this direction.

Of great importance here will be a Community energy conservation programme, together with a Community effort to develop alternative energy sources. We recognise that the further development and use of nuclear energy can be considered only if there is public ownership and control to ensure adequate safeguards against security and environmental hazards.

We welcome the reestablishment of democracy in Greece, Spain and Portugal; we strongly support the accession of these countries to the Community. Moreover we believe that democratic Europe has an urgent responsibility to contribute to the strengthening of democracy in these countries and must demonstrate its solidarity with the working people of the countries concerned.

We know that the economic and social structures of these countries and the particular products concerned make it necessary to have certain arrangements for adaptation and an appropriate timetable of transitional periods, in order to respect the legitimate interests of all people – both in the Community and in Greece, Portugal and Spain.

The enlargement of the Community must become a source of new strength and dynamism for Europe.

Europe should see itself as a force for peace. In our view, social progress based on freedom and a sense of responsibility within and outside the Community are possible only if we remain at peace. We wish to contribute towards this end and therefore support the policy of détente between East and West. Our aim is to work towards a situation in which European peace becomes a reality.

Europe has failed to achieve an organised peace – for the mere absence of war does not constitute a secure peace. We therefore support a policy consciously aimed at preventing war. We want to see a policy of détente between the power blocs.

The Socialist parties in Europe are the best guarantee that in future, the renunciation of the use of force, stability, cooperation and non proliferation of nuclear weapons will remain the basic principles of international politics.

We spare no effort to achieve the renunciation of violence at regional and world level. Freedom, justice and solidarity are not only principles ruling the way of life of our countries but also a reliable guide for the international order that we are striving for.

With regard to the present military balance in the world and developments in the field of armaments technology, negotiations on arms control are becoming more and more important. The arms race must be stopped, as it swallows up huge resources and could endanger strategic stability through the increasing development of new weapons technology. The policy of limiting and reducing arms must be so conceived as to make it possible to stop the arms race spiral.

As regards our relations with Eastern Europe, we favour a policy of détente and cooperation as set out in the Final Act of the Helsinki Agreement. The first effort at cooperation between East and West in Europe since the Second World War includes practical plans for cooperation in the economic field as well as in science and human relations. These plans can become a reality only if the true spirit of the Helsinki agreement, including the area of human rights, is supported by all signatories.

Only a Europe which declares itself in solidarity with the world's poor can make a genuine contribution to peace. In the medium and long term the prosperous countries will have to accept a slower increase in their material affluence in order to overcome the North-South conflict.

This is why we would also intensify European cooperation with the developing countries. The success achieved so far – in particular through the Lomé agreement – shows that we are on the right path towards further progress. The basic principles of this cooperation are the following:

commitment of the Community to the overall advancement of the developing countries;

full recognition of the independence of the developing countries and their right to freedom from intervention, whether politically or commercially motivated;

greater benefit to the developing countries through trade relations;

scientific and technical cooperation designed to benefit everyone;

the conclusion of an agreement on joint action with a view to imposing at world level, effective and equitable rules for the monetary system and economic transactions.

We attach the highest importance to the preservation and protection of human rights and civil liberties within the Community. In particular, we abhor and will strongly oppose any discrimination on grounds of sex, colour, ethnic origin or religious belief. The Community countries must implement fully the provisions of the European Convention of Human Rights. At the same time, the Community should be in the forefront of the struggle for human rights throughout the world and, wherever possible, should use its influence to support this struggle.

We want a democratic Europe. Because we are convinced that the conditions in which we live and which we can expect in the future require increasing responsibility on the part of government, we consider it absolutely essential that government bodies should be openly and publicly accountable to the people. Responsibilities should be devolved to smaller administrative units. We are against the uncontrolled and uncontrollable exercise of power. This applies also to the business world.

In the direct elections to the European Parliament to be held in 1979, the citizens of Europe must make their choice for or against a policy which is consistently geared to the equitable distribution of income, knowledge and power.

The directly elected European Parliament must initially develop within the framework of the existing treaties. We recognise that any further transfer of powers from national governments to the Community institutions or from national parliaments to the European Parliament can take place only with the clear and direct assent of the national governments and parliaments.

The year of the first European elections has dawned. The progressive policies of the Socialist Parties are now more relevant than ever to the need of Europe's people since it is manifest that capitalism cannot solve the problems which exist. Work for the solution of today's problems must proceed at both national and Community level and can be facilitated by actions based on closer European cooperation.

For successful action in the interests of all the people the voice of the Socialist Movement must be strong, in the directly elected European Parliament and in the Parliaments of the Member States.

We want to build a Europe in which every individual can live in peace and in freedom. Democracy and Socialism are for the citizens of Europe, the guarantee of peace and freedom.

The Labour Party

Policies for fundamental reform of EEC

In this manifesto, we set out Labour's policies for the fundamental reform of the EEC. This is not a programme of government – for the European Assembly does not have, and must not have, the right to override our own Parliament and decide matters of government policy. But Labour members of the European Assembly – elected with your support *will* be able to help all of us in our campaign to bring greater justice and commonsense to the way the EEC operates.

Britain has now been in the Common Market for just over six years, and there can be no doubt that the British people have been deeply disillusioned by the experience of EEC membership. In particular, the promises and the forecasts of the benefits that joining the EEC would bring have been shown to be false. Unlike the Tories and Liberals who made those promises so freely, the Labour Party warned the British people in 1975 of the dangers of Common Market membership. Today, we stand by everything we said because it has been proved correct. The Common Agricultural Policy is an expensive farce, forcing us to accept, at one and the same time, high food prices and vast food mountains. Our contribution to the EEC budget is monstrously unfair – with Britain having to pay, during next year alone, nearly £900 million more into the budget than we will get back. And, through the EEC take-over of important powers to make laws and levy taxes, our right to democratic self-government has been gravely weakened.

Labour is determined to change all this. But it will mean tough negotiations and hard bargaining with our EEC partners. It will also mean a major revision of the Treaty of Rome. This is why it is so important for Labour to be strongly represented in the EEC Assembly: not only to give as much support as possible to British Ministers in these negotiations, but also to articulate and publicise our case throughout the Community – and to help persuade the other eight Parliaments and peoples of the EEC of the pressing need for fundamental reform.

Indeed, we believe that the changes we seek are in the interests not only of the British people, but of working people in all of the member states. For the objectives of the Labour Party are surely shared by ordinary people everywhere: the elimination of exploitation and injustice, the fight against all forms of inequality, the right to a job and to decent housing, the extension of health and welfare facilities and better education for all. Above all, we see our task as the elimination of the poverty and need which still afflicts large sections of society, throughout the EEC, and especially amongst the aged, the young, the sick and the deprived.

We insist that the EEC must become an instrument of social justice rather than of private profit-seeking. The Labour Party heartily welcomes and will work for the enlargement of the Community, including, in the first instance, Spain, Portugal and Greece. We hope their accession will strengthen democracy in all three countries. Enlargement, in our view, will mean that the Community simply cannot avoid the need to change.

The Labour Party thus approaches these European elections in a spirit which is critical yet constructive. Our objective is to work towards the creation of a wider but much looser grouping of European states – one in which each country is able to realise its own economic and social objectives, under the sovereignty of its own Parliament and people.

The Role of the Assembly

The EEC Assembly is not a real Parliament. True, it does have certain limited powers. In the main, however, it is largely a consultative body. We believe it should remain so.

Its most substantial powers lie in its partial control over the Community budget. It has the final say over what is known as "non-compulsory expenditure", which, in effect, means the 25 per cent. or so of the budget which is not eaten up by the Common Agricultural Policy. This includes spending on the Regional and Social Funds. The

Assembly has the right to be consulted by the Commission, and to request that body to ammend proposals which it proposes to submit to the Council of Ministers. It also has various rights of supervision over the activities of the Commission, as well as the sledgehammer power – virtually unuseable in practice – of dismissing the Commission as a whole.

The Labour Party is firmly opposed to any extension of these powers. In our view, the European Assembly cannot constitute a proper instrument of democratic control – unless, that is, we are prepared to see the EEC develop into a new federal "superstate", complete with a powerful European-level government. Such a European government would, it is true, be directly accountable to the Assembly: but such a government would also have the power to override at will the wishes of both governments and parliaments of each of the member states.

Such a development would take power and decision-making even further away from ordinary people instead of making it more responsible and more accountable to them. We do not believe this would be in the interests of the British people, or in the interests of the people of the other member states. Thus, we will vigorously oppose *any* moves in this direction. The basis of democratic control, we believe, must continue to be vested firmly in the right of the European peoples to govern themselves, as far as possible, through their own national Parliaments able to determine, for themselves, their own laws, their own policies and their own priorities. This is not because we are nationalist or anti-Europe but because in our view this is the way to strengthen democracy in Europe as a whole.

Our concern is to strengthen parliamentary democracy in each of the member states. For Britain, certainly, membership of the EEC has seriously weakened the role and functions of the House of Commons. The European Court is accepted as a supreme Court, able to override certain decisions of our own Parliament. Community legislation is either directly applicable in the law of member countries or imposes an obligation on member countries to legislate. It is essential that this situation be remedied. The powers of the House of Commons to amend or repeal European legislation which applies to the UK must be established if the rights of the electorate to decide policy are to be preserved. Labour will:

- give back to the House of Commons the powers to reject, change or repeal EEC legislation; amend the 1972 European Communities Act so as to restore to the House of Commons the power to decide whether or not any European Economic Community regulation, directive or decisions should be applicable to the United Kingdom;
- subsequently seek appropriate changes in the Treaty of Rome to give EEC recognition to such an amendment. Enlargement of the Community will provide the opportunity for this to be achieved, but failure to gain Community approval for this fundamental change will not deter us in any way from passing the necessary legislation at Westminster;
- make British ministers directly accountable to the House of Commons on European matters.

Democratic Control of the Economy

Labour's priorities in economic policy are clearly established. We aim to restore full employment, reduce inflation, promote rising living standards and faster economic growth. These are the goals of socialists throughout the Community. But they can only be secured if the economies of the EEC are under the clear control of democratically elected government – not left to the mercy of market forces. Moreover, our economic and industrial objectives can, we believe, be met only if there are radical changes in the Treaty of Rome.

The role of the trade unions, both nationally and internationally is also of vital importance in the struggle to attain our goals. We will therefore be seeking the active cooperation of the trade union movement, in all of the member states, in both the formulation and the implementation of our policies. And we shall give a particular emphasis in our policies to the extension of industrial democracy throughout the EEC. To assist in the reduction of unemployment the party stands in favour of the introduction of a 35 hour week with a corresponding reduction in overtime working.

Full employment, a thriving economy and an end to poverty – how, then, can all these be achieved? We believe that the long-term solution lies in the British Government having the freedom to apply Labour's industrial policies:

- the taking into public ownership of firms occupying key positions within our economy, under secure democratic control;
- the negotiation and conclusion of planning agreements with strategically placed

companies to ensure their public accountability and to ensure that our planning effort is effective;

- the taking of additional statutory powers – over prices, investment and job location, for example – to support these negotiations;
- the selective and creative use of state aids, to safeguard jobs, and to support the operation of planning agreements;
- the use, wherever necessary, of import penetration ceilings and orderly marketing arrangements to enable our economy to expand and create jobs without endangering our balance of payments.

All these instruments of economic planning and democratic control must be at our disposal if we are to achieve a return to full employment and economic expansion. However, the Treaty of Rome, which is based on the concept of free market economy throughout the EEC, places considerable restraints on their use. The EEC Commission has the power, for example, to block the granting of various forms of state aids if they threaten to interfere with the free play of the market. The Treaty also prevents member states, for all practical purposes, from taking direct action on imports.

The Labour Party has always rejected the view that market forces should determine our economic priorities. In this we stand full square with democratic socialists and trade unionists throughout the Community. For we believe that any socialist government – whether in France, Italy, the UK or elsewhere – will need to take measures similar to those outlined above in order to plan their economies and to work towards full employment. Socialists and trade unionists within the EEC share our concern, furthermore, with the growing power of multinational corporations and financial institutions.

Our intention is to work with our socialist and trade union partners to ensure that each member state is able to pursue socialist industrial policies – the only policies which can succeed in overcoming unemployment. And we will seek specific derogations (i.e. exemptions) from Community requirements on industrial and regional policies. We will also press for alterations in the Treaty of Rome to ensure that the Commission cannot stand in our way, or in the path of our socialist colleagues. We aim to develop a Europe which is democratic and socialist and where the interests of the people are placed above the interests of national and international capitalist groups.

Similarly, we believe that the EEC Treaty commitment to the free movement of capital represents a serious threat to the jobs and interests of working people within the EEC – and especially for those in the less strong economies. The easing of exchange controls also intensifies the vulnerability of Britain and others to speculative flows of funds. Given the increasingly disorderly character of international currency markets, we especially support the retention of powers to impose strict controls on capital movements – and we respect the right of our partners to take the actions they deem necessary to protect their economies from policies of recession and unemployment.

The exchange rate, too, represents an essential instrument of economic policy. We believe that each member state should be free to determine, as far as it is able to do so, the value of its own currency; and we will thus continue to resist British membership of the Economic and Monetary System. The EMS, we believe, would limit the degree to which member states can alter their exchange rates and encourage, or even enforce, recourse to deflationary policies (and hence increased unemployment and economic stagnation) to overcome the balance of payments difficulties. Similarly, the Labour Party will maintain its opposition to Economic and Monetary Union, the introduction of which would have serious consequences for the level of employment throughout the Community. Instead, we will seek the maximum co-operation of our European partners – and particularly of our trade union and socialist colleagues – in working for a return to full employment through a programme of concerted action on growth.

We will also seek to gain the cooperation of our socialist partners in rejecting any upward harmonisation of VAT or any reduction in the existing range of zero-rated VAT items in Britain. To do otherwise would impose an unacceptable tax burden on everyday necessities. The same goes for any moves to harmonise corporation tax where this results in profits distributed to shareholders being treated more leniently than at present.

The Community Budget

The Labour Party believes that the Community budget should promote a fairer distribution of resources within the EEC and the convergence of the economic performance of member states. We also feel that justice and equity demands that contributions and receipts should be related in some way to each country's wealth.

However, at the moment, the way the Community raises and spends its money disregards all of these principles. Two of the wealthiest Common Market countries, Denmark and Holland, are numbered amongst the major net beneficiaries. In contrast, the UK pays into the budget considerably more than it receives. In 1977, Britain was the second largest net contributor, although seventh out of nine in terms of GDP per capita. By 1980, if the present system continues, we shall head the list of net contributors.

In 1977, we paid into the budget some £737 million and received back £368 million – a net contribution of £369 million. But by 1980, our *net* contributions, for that year alone, will have risen to no less than £895 million – a total, over the four years from 1977 amounting to nearly £2,800 million.

We shall press for radical changes in the Community budget – both in the way it is collected and in the way it is spent. For the present arrangements simply cannot be in the long-term interests of the Community.

Britain is unfairly penalised because of the predominance of agriculture in the budget. We import large quantities of agricultural produce, the taxes on which form a large portion of the budget. And, because of the relative efficiency of our agriculture and the small percentage of our population that works on the land, we gain little from the way in which the budget is spent.

We will therefore be insisting on a radical reform of the CAP and a shift in emphasis in Community expenditure from agriculture and towards regional and social policies. At the same time we are seeking a more equitable collection of community funds so that it is closely related to the GDP per head of member states. What is more, however, we shall be looking for a sharp reduction over the years, in real terms, in the absolute size of the budget itself.

Agriculture

The need for fundamental reform of the CAP is now widely accepted throughout the Community. The three main issues of concern are:

- under-consumption and inappropriate production caused by inflated producer prices and technological advance;
- a growing conflict between consumers and the producer-oriented CAP;
- the incompatibility of common prices and diverging currencies.

The CAP has created serious problems for British agriculture, distorting the balance of production, decreasing consumption, and hindering the rational expansion of the industry. In seeking a reform of the CAP we are seeking to establish a more rational European agricultural industry – one in which production takes place in the area of least cost; in which prices are not fixed so high that consumers cannot afford to purchase what the farmer produces; and in which farmers produce for the market and not for the intervention store.

We recognise that the CAP was intended, among other things, as a method of support for the poorer peasant farmers of the EEC, and that with enlargement of the Community their number will increase. But we cannot accept that this method of agricultural support is either the most effective or the most equitable. We believe that where a social case for the need for agricultural support in certain areas is proven then the support should come either from the European social funds or from national exchequers. We do not believe that European consumers – and inevitably the less well off consumers – should subsidise backward agriculture through inflated food prices.

Our proposals for reforming the CAP are well known and have been explained in detail in a number of statements by the party's National Executive Committee, including *Labour's Programme*, 1976. They include:

- a sharp reduction in support prices and an end to the scandal of food surpluses – which cost £1,000 million a year for storage alone;
- more scope within the CAP for national support arrangements such as the variable beef premiums to suit the different needs of member states;
- open access for imported foods such as New Zealand butter and lamb, Canadian wheat and cheese, and Australian beef, coupled with deficiency payments;
- a change in emphasis from price support to structural and social reform – with national governments taking an increasing responsibility;
- better use of surpluses by a reduction in prices.

We shall continue to use the green pound as a mechanism to alleviate some of the worst excesses of the CAP. We will not devalue the green pound – which would increase our food prices – by any more than the devaluation in the market rate of the pound sterling. We believe such action is in the interest of the Community as a whole. For if we were to devalue the green pound any further the massive rise in UK food prices would cut consumption and leave even larger stocks of surplus food. Furthermore, we believe that the Community's so-called common prices are calculated in such a way as to throw the burden of adjustment on the weaker currencies while shielding the gross undervaluation of the green currencies of the stronger economies. We insist therefore that the "common prices" be linked to a basket of EEC currencies and not, as at present, to the currencies of the "snake". We will also strongly resist any move to phase out Monetary Compensatory Amounts unless this is done in the context of a fundamental reform of the CAP and a general reduction in common price levels.

We believe that our case for reform of the CAP is so strong that it will receive support from working people throughout the Community. We will certainly do our utmost to gain the cooperation of all our EEC partners. If, however, despite our efforts to gain the cooperation of our partners, such major reforms are refused, we shall withdraw from the operations of the CAP as a whole. As a first step we give notice that we intend to refuse to accept any further increases in support prices in the absence of fundamental reform.

Fishing

Urgent and drastic action to preserve the future of both the Community fishing industries and the future supplies of our already vastly depleted fish stocks is also needed. With Britain contributing the major portion of the Community's fish stocks, we realise that there is little commonground for the formulation of an acceptable Common Fisheries Policy. The present CFP – cobbled together shortly before British entry – is wholly inadequate. But the measures the Labour Government has proposed to the Community – with their dual aim of conserving fish stocks and protecting the livelihood of all those who depend on fish – will benefit not only British fishermen and those employed in the ancillary industries, but also all those in the Community dependent on fish.

Energy

We believe in the closest cooperation and harmonisation of energy policy especially in the field of research and development and conservation. However we are entirely opposed to the transfer of any power to control energy or energy policy from member states to the Commission, the Council of Ministers or the Court. We will ensure that the benefits of this country's indigenous fuels are retained for the British people.

We believe it is in the interests of all member states to be able to pursue a planned and integrated energy policy, responsive to social needs and broad national requirements. A rigid common energy policy would work against such interests.

The EEC and the Third World

The Labour Party believes that the EEC should do far more to improve the plight of the countless millions of deprived people in the Third World. We welcome the Lomé Convention as a small step forward. But we want certain fundamental changes in EEC aid and development policy. First the policy should encompass *all* the needy areas of the world; in particular much more aid should be given to the Indian sub-continent.

Second, the policy on food aid must cease being an activity devised to dispose of the unwanted surpluses of the CAP and the dumping of surplus food on world markets. The EEC must end the absurd practice of subsidising European sugar beet producers through the CAP whilst West Indian cane workers live in poverty, partly due to lack of demand for their produce.

But aid is not enough. The root cause of continuing poverty and underdevelopment in the Third World lies in the unequal trade relations with the industrialised countries. The developing countries must be guaranteed access to Western markets for their manufacturing industries. We recognise that this may, in the short term, cause problems. But this merely underlines the relevance of socialist policies. We must have a *planned* growth of trade rather than allow it to be subject to the vagaries of the world market and speculative commodity deals. Moreover, if in Western Europe we return to full employment and faster economic growth, this will itself provide bigger markets for third world exporters, and make a contribution to speedier economic development throughout the world.

Conclusion

The Community we are seeking is one which is more just, more equal and better adapted to the needs of a rapidly changing Europe. As at present constituted, it helps maintain a capitalist system which rewards the rich and powerful at the expense of the poor and weak. It makes more difficult the realisation of traditional socialist goals – jobs for all, an end to poverty, help to the needy, rising living standards and the abolition of privilege.

The policies contained in this manifesto represent the foundation of our approach to the problems of EEC membership, and Labour members of the EEC Assembly will work towards these goals in close cooperation with the Labour Party at Westminster, and will argue the case for the reform of the Community, in accordance with Labour Party policy. The policies we advocate are relevant, not only to Britain but to socialists in all the EEC member states, and we are therefore sure that they will be taken up by the socialist parties throughout the Community. We believe, however, that taking these policies to the EEC Assembly is only part of an all-out effort by the Labour Party to reform fundamentally the Common Market.

We readily admit that the role of Labour members of the EEC Assembly will be limited in the pursuit of these reforms, for the EEC Assembly does not and should not have the power to implement them (this is a task for national parliaments). But Labour members of the Assembly will act as representatives of the dissatisfaction with EEC membership that exists in Britain today – they will support and fight for the policies that we have outlined in this manifesto. In short, we believe that the views of the British people towards the EEC must be faithfully represented in the Assembly, and there is no doubt that the Labour Party is best suited to this responsibility.

We recognise and reaffirm that Britain's membership of the EEC depends on the continuing assent of Parliament. We declare that if the fundamental reforms contained in this manifesto are not achieved within a reasonable period of time, then the Labour Party would have to consider very seriously whether continued EEC membership was in the best interests of the British people.

We will, however, work closely with like-minded parties and with the trade unions towards a policy of joint action on all parts of our programme. We are not afraid to spell out our underlying aim: a fundamental and irreversible shift in the balance of wealth and power in favour of working people throughout the Community. Socialism cannot be contained within national boundaries. The Labour Party is convinced that it is in the interest of all socialists, and the Labour movement throughout Western Europe, to join us in demanding radical changes in the EEC.

European Liberals and Democrats

United Liberals for a United Europe

The Federation of Liberal and Democratic Parties of the EEC published its "Programme for Europe" from which has been summarised the main features of Liberal European policy. The preamble to the programme stated:

For us, European liberals and democrats, European unity means more than agreements between national governments in areas where their interests happen to coincide. To us it implies a redefinition of the role of the nation state in the light of present-day needs and constraints. It means a union of peoples as well as states. We recognise the fact that the nation state has become, in some cases, too small to solve many of the major political, economic, social and enviornmental problems that face us, in others too large to reflect and respond to the particular needs of their different regions. The kind of European union we wish to see will be endowed with institutions capable of taking joint European decisions in areas where national action can no longer be sufficient and will also allow the regions which make up so much of our cherished cultural diversity, to play an increasingly important role.

We have always been in the forefront of the battle for direct elections to the European Parliament. These have at last arrived and they add a much-needed European dimension to the political scene in our countries. Accustomed for generations to operating within the national frame of reference only, kindred political forces have now had to seek out each other across age-old frontiers with a view to establishing a common electoral platform with which to present themselves to 181 million European voters.

European liberals and democrats, never having forgotten their common roots, rapidly set up the machinery for common political action. Having established the Federation of Liberal and Democratic Parties in the European Community in 1976, we were the first to adopt, at a Congress representing all our member parties, our European electoral programme which is now presented to the public. In it we seek to apply our European liberal and democratic principles to the great issues of our time. We believe that by tackling major problems on a European scale we shall have a better chance of solving them.

The European dimension is an essential element in our vision of how these problems are to be solved. We demand the creation of a European economic and monetary union. In this new and wider context, which also takes into account the need to coordinate our economic progress with that of the developing world, our proposals deal with the use of energy resources, the provision of food supplies, the need for genuine employee participation in decision-taking at work, the laying of a greater emphasis on the human scale in business operations and the fair distribution of wealth.

We aim at an open society in which cooperation will supersede confrontation and division through full public debate of the issues and full accountability to democratic parliaments. Flexible and democratic planning in which all social and economic forces as well as government and parliament must play their part, can provide a framework of stability which will allow for the dynamic display of entrepreneurial forces to function within a social market economy for the benefit of all.

Role of the European Parliament

We believe in parliamentary democracy as the system best suited to serve the interest of the people. Therefore we attach great importance to the European Parliament. Once it has been directly elected, it must seek to play the vital parliamentary role of exercising control over the Community's executive and bureaucratic machine. It must strive for the reshaping of our European institutions in order to make them more effective and to provide for more open government. It will also have to be vigilant in defence of individual and collective rights and liberties against possible dangers from government on a large, European scale. And finally, it must become the true centre of European political debate and action.

To this end, it should make itself the natural focal point for the development of popular forces organised at European level so that these are no longer established on a solely national scene. Only then will there be a basis for political union and will Europe become a political reality to its citizens. European liberals and democrats will promote the creation of such forces. In particular, they want to see the mass media develop a European dimension. Parliament is an essentially liberal and democratic institution. It is through parliament that our modern democracies have come into being. It is in parliament that the interest of the people as a whole can prevail over the interests and prejudices of groups and classes – that majorities can govern and minority groups provide the necessary counterbalance.

The new European Parliament, elected by universal and direct suffrage, must bring these vital parliamentary traditions to bear on the problems of our Community. It must acquire sufficient moral and political strength to become an effective force. It must propose measures which will make the Community evolve towards a true European union. Our aim is a Union able to speak with one voice in world affairs whilst respecting and protecting the particular characteristics of our nations and regions. Our aim is unity in diversity.

The Liberal Programme for Europe included the following major points:

The Rule of Law

Liberals rest their entire policy on respect for the Rule of Law, including the protection of human rights and fundamental freedoms in accordance with existing Declarations.

They believe that the directly-elected European Parliament should, as one of its first acts, draw up a European Union Declaration on Basic Human and Civil Rights of an advanced character, embodying *inter alia* the abolition of the death penalty and the right of asylum for victims of political persecution.

Citizens of all Member States should likewise be enabled to appeal to the European Court in Luxembourg against actions by the Community Institutions held to violate human rights. They should likewise have immediately the right to vote in local elections wherever they may be residing in the Community at the time.

European Institutions

The Institutions must be given enough authority to allow them to carry out their Community tasks successfully. They must be democratic, so that future developments will take place according to the will of the people. The present Institutions (Council, Commission, Parliament, Court and Economic and Social Committee) are a good starting point for further development, but the areas now coming outside their competence should gradually come within it by action taken in accordance with the Treaties.

The present distribution of powers within the Institutions is unbalanced, the Council having become too dominant. The Treaties should therefore be correctly interpreted in accordance with the spirit of their authors. In particular, the majority voting principle should increasingly be applied to votes in the Council wherever the Treaties so indicate, and the powers both of the Commission and of the Parliament should be similarly strengthened.

The greater weight which the Parliament will acquire as the result of direct elections should enable it to exert considerable influence even if it is not accorded any increase in its formal powers which, however, already comprise some control over the Community budget.

It will in any case have as soon as possible to agree on a common electoral procedure for use in the second election and this will of course have to be based on some form of proportional representation.

And it will also have eventually to produce and submit to the Ministers a scheme for a Union of a novel type, based on a development of existing Institutions, which will have to be ratified by all the Nine Parliaments before it can come into operation.

Social Matters

Liberals believe that the first duty of all the Nine Governments is to relieve the present unemployment of young people and that collective measures should be taken to this end including suitable training schemes. But young people should be told that they may have to change their jobs more than once and be prepared to learn new skills at intervals during their lives.

Women should obtain complete equality with men in all jobs in which they are not disadvantaged thus eventually bringing about a redistribution of roles between women and men.

Liberals will defend the individual against excessive powers of Trades Unions, or indeed any social or economic group seeking to suppress the individual's freedom.

Whilst a reasonable income for the unemployed, the sick or the elderly must be guaranteed, Liberals are against the creation of top-heavy and expensive social systems which endanger these very goals. Individual participation and responsibility in the financing of the social systems must be encouraged and any further extension of them should be related to economic growth.

Liberals also stand for the right of employees to share in the responsibility for the running, stability and development of the concerns where they work and to acquire some financial interest in them. They have detailed schemes to advance in this connection.

Education

All should be able to develop themselves in accordance with their abilities, and education should be a permanent process. Educational policy should remain the preserve of national or regional authorities, but there should also be a European educational policy designed above all to promote, more especially at University level, an understanding of the various European cultures.

All qualified students should have the right to attend any University in any country of the Community and the equivalence of degrees and certificates of education should gradually be recognised.

The Environment

There must be certain common standards in combating pollution, more particularly trans-frontier pollutions. The European Parliament and national Parliaments must cooperate with the Council of Europe among other things to protect fish stocks and to reduce the pollution of major waterways, the Channel, the Baltic and the Mediterranean. Despite the economic cost, the principle should be accepted that "the polluter should pay".

"Growth" must not be an end in itself. Technology, too, must be a means and not an end. Economic decisions must be appraised in the light of their environmental effect. Rapid and irrational economic growth, together with massive centralisation, must be rejected.

Nuclear fission energy must be accepted, but only when there is no alternative. In addition to strict economy in the use of energy, priority should thus be given to the more efficient use of existing and new types of "conventional" energy and research into the development of nuclear fusion.

The Community should take the lead in proposing an environmental code taking full account of the needs of developing countries.

The Regions

Regions are so many and varied that it is dangerous to generalise, but decentralisation of political power is a fundamental principle of Liberal policy.

The diversity of Europe is also its strength. Regional feeling should not be suppressed but rather encouraged within existing national states. Should such feeling be pushed as far as separation, the fact that it would be within a larger union should make it more acceptable.

Peripheral regions are often the poorest, but integration, combined with an adequate Regional Fund with real powers, should spread benefits throughout the Community.

National Governments should not be allowed to reduce their own aid to regions because of EEC aid. All administrative restrictions and frontier formalities on the internal frontiers of the Community should be abolished.

Economic Policy

The objective should be steady and balanced growth with full employment. Existing difficulties in the way of this endanger all open and "pluralistic" societies.

To counter them we must rely on the dynamism of private enterprise together with the democratic management of the economy through flexible planning by Government, managements and the Unions based on prices and incomes "guidelines", thus rejecting the two other means of achieving stability, namely savage deflation and mass unemployment, or some rigid plan imposed on the people by political means. Liberals are in any case opposed to class policies whether of the Left or of the Right. Change in industry, necessitated by technological advance, requires a concerted Community approach. There may have to be selective public intervention but, if so, the effect should be to create viable and competitive enterprises. Provision of funds for "dead ducks" must be avoided.

Economic and Monetary Union

Only with EMU, and a common currency, can the members of the EEC jointly overcome the economic and social problems that confront them all. But to arrive at it, and hence at a genuine common market, there must be parallel economic development and gradual integration of the various economies.

Since under the Treaty, the Community budget will increasingly depend on receipts from VAT this tax must have a uniform basis of assessment thus also eliminating all customs control.

As a first step towards EMU, Liberals welcome the European Monetary System and notably:

(a) The maintenance of flexible exchange rates pending the introduction of a standard European currency – not possible until full integration is achieved;
(b) An increase in the powers of the European Monetary Fund and in reciprocal credits conditional on greater cooperation;
(c) A European currency in parallel with national currencies.

Energy

Liberals accept that existing nuclear installations will have to make a contribution towards filling Europe's likely deficiency in energy, but we are concerned by possible environmental dangers and doubts regarding the future supply of fissionable material. Liberals therefore stress the need to develop other sources of energy.

It is, however, an illusion to think that the Community can ever be self-sufficient in energy, its oil and gas reserves being limited and coal, even if its production is stimulated, only providing a useful supplementary supply.

It will therefore be essential to conserve energy. Our future needs can only be satisfied by a combination of alternative supplies, conservation (including improved insulation and a war on waste) and greater efficiency in production and usage.

Because of the risk-capital required, private industry should play an important part in securing future supplies of energy.

Joint Community action is essential. There should be a European investment policy to finance new sources of energy.

Small and Medium-sized Businesses

These undertakings play a vital part in the economy of the Member States. Owing to their quick reactions they are often the best able to develop new activities and to counter unemployment. Beyond a certain point, industrial concentrations can be counter-productive – a fact recognised by some large holding companies that have central finance but allow production to operate in smaller units. In a word, the latter are an essential element in the free market economy which Liberals essentially stand for.

A coordinated Community policy of aid to such undertakings should therefore include *inter alia*:

A monetary system avoiding the harm done by currency fluctuations
Harmonised and simplified taxation
Credits to assist finance
Encouragement of joint research programmes
Harmonisation of the relevant company laws
Promotion of exports, and ability to tender for contracts.

Transport

Since varying methods of financing transport limit the advantages of a common market, measures regulating competition should be applied by the Community with the general object of creating a free market in this respect.

The Ministers should consider carrying out the proposals for a common transport policy already put forward by the European Parliament in September 1974.

Agriculture

European agricultural policy cannot in practice be divorced from social environmental and regional considerations.

Its general object must be to ensure at least a basic supply of food at reasonable prices from the farmers on terms enabling them to enjoy a tolerable standard of living.

But no integrated Common Agricultural Policy can function properly in the absence of economic and monetary stability, and one of the main objects of Liberal policy will, after the necessary phasing out of monetary compensation payments, be to prevent the accumulation of surpluses by measures aimed at relating supply to demand and by initiating short term price changes, the present system of market intervention becoming more flexible. Some scheme for buffer stocks would be acceptable if suitably administered and new storage provided.

On fishing, European Liberals place the emphasis on conservation which in their view can only be assured by a common European policy. If the agreed policy should result in hardship for any individual fishing community, special measures of assistance should also be accepted.

The Third World

There must be a common EEC policy for the development of the Third World with the chief emphasis being placed on the elimination of extreme poverty.

It is in the Community's interest that this should be done, for many raw materials essential to its existence may not otherwise be available.

Liberals support the proposal that the EEC members should together provide official aid amounting to at least 0.7 per cent. of their GNP by 1983.

But such aid should be very carefully administered and no aid should be granted to régimes which grossly and persistently violate Human Rights. Neither should the benefits of aid accrue to any privileged group trying to reserve them for itself.

Recognition of the principle of a social market economy does not exclude guarantees of a minimum income for producers of raw materials and collective efforts to avoid violent fluctuations in their price.

Private investments should be encouraged subject to proper safeguards for both investors and recipients; so should the spread in the Third World of intermediate technology and small private enterprise.

The activities of the multi-national corporation should be governed by an agreed Code of Conduct.

Foreign Policy, Security and Defence

These are closely linked and cannot be profitably considered in isolation.

A divided Europe can only be an object of world politics, and the whole purpose of creating a European Union is consequently to transform it into a positive and beneficent force whose influence, notably in the organisation of peace and human rights, can be generally exerted. To this end the present cooperation of the Foreign Ministers should be extended and some joint external representation of the Community gradually achieved.

The North Atlantic Alliance must remain the basis of European security, but the Community cannot neglect its own defences (N.B. from 1973 onwards the Liberal Group in the European Parliament urged the regular consideration of defence problems by the Community Ministers of Defence and the creation of some body for the production in common of purely defensive modern conventional weapons. A Resolution to this effect was passed by the European Parliament at the end of 1975).

At the same time, the Community should further all constructive proposals for disarmament and arms limitation, and, in particular seek some real relaxation of East/West tension by success in the negotiations for Mutual and Balanced Force Reductions now in progress at Vienna.

The United Nations is invaluable as an international forum in which such matters as the creation of a new economic and legal order can most profitably be discussed. But the European Community should assist it to function better in its role as a guardian of peace and defender of human rights.

There is a case for the appointment of a UN High Commissioner for Human Rights.

Liberals welcome the prospective enlargement of the Community, but it must not jeopardise the development of European Union which remains one of the chief objects of Liberal policy.

Conclusion

European liberals and democrats want the present European Community to develop into a true Union of states and peoples. This Union must be democratic and lend new vitality to many of the traditions of which we Europeans are justly proud. It must enable us to develop our economic and social environment according to the principles of a social market economy, a fair distribution of wealth and real equality of opportunity for all men and women. It must enable Europe to make its full contribution towards solving major world problems. Finally, it must be open to all European countries who wish to join, bear their part of its obligations and share its ideals and aspirations.

In our programme which was democratically adopted at our Congress of November, 1977, we have set out how this great task should be carried out. As first European party formation we have proposed a number of policies that must be pursued in order to achieve these aims.

The coming elections to the European Parliament mark an important milestone in our turbulent history. For the first time the voters of Belgium, Denmark, France, the Federal Republic of Germany, Ireland, Italy, Luxembourg, the Netherlands and the United Kingdom are asked to exercise their political rights as European citizens. This constitutes both a historic occasion and a great opportunity for the future. It is of the highest importance that this opportunity be seized.

The coming elections are only a beginning. Beyond them, we look to the future and to the many tasks that lie ahead. A new, uniform electoral system will have to be worked out which will ensure fair representation of all European political forces at the European level. The present European Community must be developed into a true Union, capable of serving the interests of its citizens and of acting on their behalf for the benefit of all.

By a massive turnout at the polls, European citizens will demonstrate that they are determined to use their newly acquired rights to the full. By voting for a candidate standing for one of the member parties of the Federation of European Liberal and Democratic Parties they will add to the strength of those who want to build our common, European future on the sure foundations of freedom, justice and humanity.

Member parties of the Federation of Liberal and Democratic Parties of the European Community are:

Bélgium – Partij voor Vrijheid en Vooruitgang; Parti des Réformes et de la Liberté to Wallonie; Parti Libéral Bruxellois. **Denmark** – Venstre, Danmarks Liberale Parti. **Federal Republic of Germany** – Freie Demokratische Partei. **France** – Parti Républicain; Parti Radical Socialiste; Mouvement des Radicaux de Gauche. **Italy** – Partito Repubblicano Italiano; Partito Liberal Italiano. **Luxembourg** – Parti Démocratique; **Netherland** – Volkspartij voor Vrijheid en Democratic. **United Kingdom** – Liberal Party. Secretariat: Boulevard de l'Empereur 3, B 1000 Brussels – Tel: 511 04 28/513 40 70.

Only Liberals have Eurovision

The UK Liberal Party also issued the following addition to the Euro-Liberal group manifesto:

Thirty-four years ago the last major European war ended. In the years to come the second weekend of June 1979 will be as significant a turning point as VE Day was in 1945. Civil war among the peoples of Western Europe has given way to peaceful resolution of differences through the ballot box. This is the real achievement of European integration.

The UK Liberal Party is fighting the first direct election to the European Parliament on a platform which consolidates our achievements and builds on them. We are the only UK political party which is united and fully committed to the ideal of European unity. The real choice at these elections lies between ourselves and those candidates fighting to turn the clock back to the days of trade wars and the risk of armed warfare.

The Liberal vision of a united Europe is not a centralised super-state. Our Europe is one in which local, regional and national diversity flourishes, and in which all regions get a fair share of the common prosperity. That is the context in which we, alone of the parties, are fighting in *all 79* UK constituencies; we believe that Northern Ireland's troubles are best solved in the context of a Europe of the Regions.

A Liberal and democratic Europe

European integration has made most progress in the economic field: a customs union and a common agricultural policy. It has also developed outside the framework of the Common Market. Decisions affecting employment prospects or wage levels in Yorkshire or Scotland are now often taken in Dusseldorf or Brussels. Large scale business is often multi-national, and will be more so in the future. We must build a political counterpart to economic integration, so that the people of the European Community can reestablish political control over the matters that are increasingly unmanageable by national governments.

Europe must become a democratic Europe of the people, acting as a counterweight to the growing Europe of Big Business. The present institutions of the European Communities have unfortunately been allowed to become too bureaucratic and dependent on national governments. Far too many people in Britain accept this and some want to take it further. Those who cling to the myth of Westminster control over Community decisions are, for all their protestations, the enemies of democracy. The myth now simply serves as a smokescreen behind which power is exercised secretly by the Council of Ministers and the Committee of Permanent Representatives.

A Representative and Effective European Parliament

The directly elected European Parliament must seize the initiative:

it must insist that the second parliament, to be elected in 1984, be *truly representative*

it must become an *effective check* on what goes on in Brussels;

it must bring the *benefits of integration* closer to the people, and it must *protect individual rights.*

The European Parliament will only be fully effective if the political forces in it work together across national lines. Liberals practice what they preach. Our partner parties are active in government in six of the nine EEC members. Liberal parties in eight Community countries form a *single, united grouping* for this election – European Liberal Democrats (ELD).

In contrast the Conservatives, the Scottish and Welsh Nationalists and the Northern Irish parties have no equal partners in Europe, whilst the British Labour party is at odds with the more internationally minded Socialist parties. For this reason, no other British party can make the same contribution in the European Parliament, as part of a powerful transnational force.

This message accompanies the common ELD election programme which has been fully and democratically debated with our European partners.

The programme has been accepted by all member parties who are fighting on a common manifesto.

The UK Liberal Party puts particular stress on reform of the common agricultural policy (whilst accepting its basic principles) and on a massive expansion in the Community's regional policy. Taken together these two reforms would help solve the present imbalance in the UK's contribution to the Community budget. More detailed proposals in these areas form part of the agreed common programme.

The Case for British Liberals in Europe

The rest of Western Europe is using a far more democratic electoral system for these elections and this will ensure a substantial Liberal group in the new European Parliament. There is a risk however that the British electoral system – imposed by a Conservative-Tribune group alliance led by Mrs Thatcher – could lead to an absurdly unrepresentative British delegation.

However, we believe that this will not happen for three reasons:

Firstly – we are electing a representative *European People's Parliament* not a government.

Secondly – there are a substantial number of British voters with Liberal sympathies who are prepared to vote Liberal when the choice is one of *representatives*, not a government.

Thirdly – we believe that people of this country will be best served by electing members who are committed to the European idea and can take a constructive part in the development of Community policies with their European partners.

This is why we believe that many more will vote Liberal for Europe than did in the recent General Election.

Europe and Britain

There is a direct link between the Liberal role in Europe and the policies of political and economic reform, and of cooperation rather than confrontation, on which we campaigned last month. A balanced and representative British contingent in the European Parliament would highlight further the defects in the Westminster system of politics and build up more pressure for necessary reforms at home.

The millions who responded to David Steel's message at the General Election, but felt they had to choose between a Callaghan and a Thatcher government, have it in their hands to transform British politics as well as to contribute to Europe's future. A massive Liberal vote on 7th June would send a large number of British Liberal MPs to the European Parliament, and ensure that the next five years in Britain will be less divisive and one-party dominated.

This is a totally new and different sort of election from any that we have previously experienced. It is an exciting and imaginative jump towards a better future. Only the Liberal Party in this country appreciates this. A Liberal vote is the best way to get to that future.

The Scottish National Party

A Voice for Scotland

On June 7 you have a chance to give Scotland a voice in Europe by voting for a Scottish National Party candidate in the European Parliament elections.

The SNP alone among the political parties in Scotland warned the Scottish voter in the 1975 referendum that Common Market membership would mean higher food prices, more unemployment, subsidies for butter mountains and wine lakes, and severe damage to Scottish fishing interests. Its record of opposition to the present form of the Common Market qualifies it uniquely to speak for Scotland in the European Parliament.

SNP members in the European Parliament will spell out to the Common Market that Scotland rejects a status that condemns her to only *eight* MPs, while Denmark, with the same population, has *sixteen.* They will insist in front of European opinion on Scotland's right to join the international community as a free and equal nation.

There are few aspects of European affairs which do not impinge on Scottish interests. But to the Scottish people Europe is a cultural and geographical entity which embraces all European countries, whether inside or outside the Common Market.

The SNP is firmly opposed to the emergence, by design or default, of a European "superstate". It believes that the benefits of trade and the free movement of peoples among European countries can be obtained within the framework of a politically decentralised Europe which reserves to the member nations the widest possible freedom of social and economic action. SNP members in the European Parliament will therefore oppose moves to transfer decision-taking from existing parliaments to the European Parliament, as to other Common Market institutions. At the same time, in the interests of democracy, they will support greater powers of scrutiny and control for the Parliament over the Brussels Commission and other Common Market bureaucracies.

Among the priorities of SNP Members will be:

Abolition of the Common Agricultural Policy – to put an end to the scandal of butter mountains and wine lakes, ensure fair prices for the consumer, a fair return for the farmer and incentives to maintain and increase food production in Scotland to levels which achieve trading self-sufficiency.

Abolition of the Common Fisheries Policy – to give Scotland's fishermen, processors and consumers, the security of a 100 mile exclusive limit and a flexible licensing policy to safeguard the interests of local fishing communities, while insisting on Scotland's right to a 200 mile exclusive economic zone.

Opposition to a Common Energy Policy – involving an excessive rate of depletion of Scotland's oil reserves and the dumping in Scotland of dangerous waste material from nuclear power stations outwith Scotland.

Protection of Consumer Interests – to make the European Parliament a voice of the "man and woman in the street" against the powerful interests which dominate the EEC, and to stop bureaucratic meddling by the Brussels Commission in the day-to-day lives of individuals.

Reform of the Regional Fund – to secure for Scotland adequate financial compensation for the disadvantages of her present status as a remote "province" of London and Brussels and as a net contributor to the Common Market budget.

Opposition to a European Currency System – tying Scotland to monetary and economic policies tailored to the needs of the "Golden Triangle" of the Common Market.

Ensuring respect for Scots Law

(a) to ensure that at the crucial formative stages of Common Market policies adequate consideration is given to their implications for the Law of Scotland, and that regular consultation takes place with the Scottish interests concerned.

(b) to seek the European Parliament's acknowledgement that a Scots judge should sit in the Community Court of Justice in Luxembourg as of *right* and not just by "grace and favour" of Westminster.

Cooperation with the Third World – SNP members will seek to change the protectionist and discriminatory policies of the Common Market which harm the interests of poorer countries.

Scotland is at present denied any effective representation in the real Community power centres of the Council of Ministers and the Brussels Commission. The only way that a whole-hearted Scottish point of view can be presented to the Common Market is by the election to the European Parliament of SNP members pledged to put Scotland first.

SNP members of the Westminster Parliament have shown that they can force concessions from London. Over the last four years SNP's sole representative in the European Parliament, Winnie Ewing, has vigorously defended Scottish interests and gained the respect of her European colleagues for herself and for her country.

An enlarged SNP group in the European Parliament will stress that the Scottish people should have the democratic opportunity to decide for themselves in a referendum whether Scotland should seek to be a full member of the Common Market, like Belgium, Ireland and the Netherlands or a free-trade partner like Norway, Sweden and Switzerland.

President and Members of Commission

Mr Roy Jenkins
President

M François –
Xavier Ortoli

Herr Wilhelm
Haferkamp

Mr Finn Gundelach

Sgr Lorenzo Natali

Mr Henk Vredeling

M Claude Cheysson

Herr Guido Brunner

Mr Raymond Vouel

Sgr Antonio Giolitti

Mr Richard Burke

Viscount Etienne
Davignon

Mr Christopher
Tugendhat

Mr Roy Jenkins, President of the EEC Commission since January 1977, with responsibilities for the Secretariat-General, legal service, information and the Spokesman's Group. Nominated by United Kingdom.

Mr Jenkins was Home Secretary, 1974–76. He had been re-elected to Labour's shadow cabinet in 1973, having resigned as Deputy Leader of the Parliamentary Labour Party in April, 1972, in disagreement with Labour policy towards the EEC. Opposition spokesman on home affairs, 1973–74; Chancellor of the Exchequer, 1967–70; Home Secretary, 1965–67; Minister of Aviation, 1964–65. Economist, author and journalist. MP for Birmingham, Stechford, 1950–76, and for Southwark, 1948–50; contested Solihull, 1945. B November, 1920; ed Abersychan Grammar School; Balliol College, Oxford (secretary and librarian, Oxford Union). Chairman, Fabian Society, 1957–58; member, committee of management, Society of Authors, 1959–60. Promoted Obscene Publications Act, 1959. Director of financial operations, John Lewis Partnership, 1962–64. President, United Kingdom Council of European Movement and of Labour Committee for Europe. President, Britain in Europe referendum campaign, 1975.

M François-Xavier Ortoli, Vice-President of the Commission with responsibilities for economics and finance, credits and investment, Statistical Office. Nominated by France.

M Ortoli was the previous President of the Commission, from January 1973; Minister of Industrial and Scientific Development, 1969–72; Minister of Economic Affairs and Finance, 1968–69. B February, 1925; ed Lycée Albert-Sarrout in Hanoi; Law Faculty in Indo-China; Ecole nationale d'administration. Rose to become, in 1955, Assistant Director in the Private Office of the Minister of Economic Affairs. Secretary-General, Inter-Ministerial Committee for European Economic Cooperation, 1961; Technical Adviser to the Private Office of the Prime Minister, then Director of the Private Office of the PM, 1962; Minister of Supply and Housing, 1967–68; Minister of Education, 1968.

Herr Wilhelm Haferkamp, Vice-President of the Commission with responsibilities for external relations. Nominated by Germany.

Herr Haferkamp has been a member of the Commission since 1967 and a Vice-President since 1970. B July 1923; primary and secondary education and studied economic and social sciences at Cologne University. President of the Regional Centre of the Confederation of German trade unions in Nordrhein-Westfalen, 1957–63, previously being a member of its administration executive and head of the social policy department. Member, consultative Committee of the ECSC high authority, 1963–65; member, federal executive, Confederation of German trade unions and head of economic policy department, 1962–67.

Mr Finn Gundelach, Vice-President of the Commission with responsibilities for agriculture and fisheries. Nominated by Denmark.

Mr Gundelach was, from 1962–67, Deputy Director-General of Gatt (Kennedy Round) and from 1967–72, as Ambassador and Head of the Danish mission to the EEC, was involved in accession negotiations. Member of the Commission since 1972. B April 1925; ed Aarhus University. At Ministry of Foreign Affairs, 1951–55; Permanent Representative to UN in Geneva, 1955–59; Director of Gatt, responsible for commercial policy in Geneva, 1959–61; Sub-Director-General of Gatt, 1961.

Signor Lorenzo Natali, Vice-President of the Commission with responsibilities for enlargement, protection of the environment, nuclear safety, contacts with member governments and public opinion in preparation for direct election. Nominated by Italy

Signor Natali was for seven consecutive terms of office returned to the Italian Parliament as representative for the Abruzzi constituency. Became Under Secretary to the Prime Minister and Under Secretary at the Ministry of Finance and the Treasury; Minister for the Merchant Navy, Minister for Tourism and Entertainment, Minister for Public Works and Minister for Agriculture. Former member, central leadership, Christian Democrat Party. B October 1922. Lawyer.

Mr Henk Vredeling, Vice-President of the Commission with responsibilities for employment and social affairs, Tripartite Conference. Nominated by the Netherlands.

Mr Vredeling is a former member of the European Parliament. Vice-President of the Commission since 1977. Member of second chamber (Partij van de Arbeid: Labour Party) 1956–76. Adviser to the Algemeen Nederlandse Agrarische Bedrijfsbond (General Agricultural Association). B November, 1924; ed secondary modern; agricultural college at Wageningen.

M Claude Cheysson, Commissioner with responsibilities for development. Nominated by France.

M Cheysson has been a member of the Commission since 1972. Was Ambassador to Indonesia, 1966–70, when he became chairman of the board of *Enterprise minière et chimique*. Began career as administrator in the Ministry of Foreign Affairs in 1948. Secretary-General, Commission for Technical Cooperation in Africa, 1957–62; Director-General, Technical Organisation for the Exploitation of Sahara Minerals, 1962–65; Director-General, Industrial Cooperation Organisation and Minister plenipotentiary (Grade 1) 1966.

Herr Guido Brunner, Commissioner with responsibilities for energy, research, science and education. Nominated by Germany.

Herr Brunner has been a member of the Commission since 1974. Joined Ministry of Foreign Affairs in Bonn, 1955; held office of State Secretary, 1958–60; at UN in New York, 1960–67; various posts at Ministry of Foreign Affairs, 1968–72; leader of delegation at multilateral preparations for the CSCE in Helsinki, 1972–73; leader of German delegation at second stage of Geneva conference, 1973. B May 1930; studied law at universities of Munich, Heidelberg and Madrid.

Mr Raymond Vouel, Commissioner with responsibilities for competition. Nominated by Luxembourg.

Mr Vouel, member of the Commission since July 1976, joined the Government of Luxembourg in 1964 holding the posts of State Secretary for Public Health, for Employment, for Social Security and for the Mining Industry. Re-elected as an MP in 1969, he was chairman, Parliamentary Socialist Group, 1970–74; general secretary, Luxembourg Socialist Workers' Party, 1970. Re-elected as MP in 1974, he served in the Government as Vice-President and Minister for Finance and Land Development. B 1923.

Signor Antonio Giolitti, Commissioner with responsibilities for coordination of Community funds, and regional policy. Nominated by Italy.

Signor Giolitti, member of the Commission since 1977, was elected as a PCI (Communist Party) member of the Assemblea Costituente. Under Secretary at the Ministry of Foreign Affairs in the first Republican Government. Left the PCI in 1957; became active member of PSI (Socialist Party), being on the party's central committee and party leadership. Minister for the Budget and Economic Planning in the 1964, 1970–72 and 1973–74 Centre-Left Governments. Represented Italian Government at IVth special session of UN General Assembly, 1974; President of the OECD Council of Ministers, 1974. B February 1915; graduate in law.

Mr Richard Burke, Commissioner with responsibilities for taxation, consumer affairs, transport, and relations with European Parliament. Nominated by Republic of Ireland.

Mr Burke, on the Commission since 1977, was elected to Dáil Eireann in 1969 and 1973 for South County Dublin. Fine Gael chief whip, 1969–72, and spokesman on Posts and Telegraphs, 1972–73; Minister for Education, 1973–76. B March, 1932; ed Upperchurch (Nova Scotia), Christian Brothers, Thurles and Dublin, and University College, Dublin. Secondary teacher. Read law at King's Inns, Dublin. Barrister (1973).

Viscount Etienne Davignon, Commissioner with responsibilities for internal market and industrial affairs. Nominated by Belgium.

Viscount Davignon became chairman of the governing body of the International Energy Agency in November 1974 and joined the EEC Commission in 1977. Doctor of Law. Cabinet Attaché, 1961; Deputy Chef de Cabinet, 1963; Chef de Cabinet to M Spaak and then to M Harmel, 1964; Director General for Policy from 1969. B October, 1932.

Mr Christopher Tugendhat, Commissioner with responsibilities for budget and financial control, financial institutions and taxation, personnel and administration. Nominated by United Kingdom.

Mr Tugendhat joined the EEC Commission in 1977. Conservative MP for the City of London and Westminster, South, 1974–76, and for Cities of London and Westminster, 1970–74. An Opposition spokesman on employment, 1974–75, and on foreign and Commonwealth affairs, 1975–76, Director, Sunningdale Oils Ltd, 1971–76: Phillips Petroleum International (UK) Ltd, 1972–76. Author and journalist. *Financial Times* leader and feature writer, 1960–70. B February, 1937; ed Ampleforth College, Gonville and Caius College, Cambridge (President of the Union, 1960).

The present Commission under Mr Roy Jenkins held its inaugural meeting in Brussels on January 6, 1977. The next Commission appointments will run from January, 1981.